POLITICAL INSTITUTIONS IN
THE FEDERAL REPUBLIC OF GERMANY

POLITICAL INSTITUTIONS IN THE FEDERAL REPUBLIC OF GERMANY

Manfred G. Schmidt

OXFORD
UNIVERSITY PRESS

OXFORD
UNIVERSITY PRESS

Great Clarendon Street, Oxford OX2 6DP

Oxford University Press is a department of the University of Oxford.
It furthers the University's objective of excellence in research, scholarship,
and education by publishing worldwide in

Oxford New York

Auckland Bangkok Buenos Aires Cape Town Chennai
Dar es Salaam Delhi Hong Kong Istanbul Karachi Kolkata
Kuala Lumpur Madrid Melbourne Mexico City Mumbai Nairobi
São Paulo Shanghai Taipei Tokyo Toronto

Oxford is a registered trade mark of Oxford University Press
in the UK and in certain other countries

Published in the United States
by Oxford University Press Inc., New York

British Library Cataloguing in Publication Data
Data available

Library of Congress Cataloging in Publication Data
Data available

ISBN 13: 978–0–19–878259–9
ISBN 10: 0–19–878259–4

5 7 9 10 8 6 4

Typeset in Minion and Congress Sans
by RefineCatch Limited, Bungay, Suffolk
Printed in Great Britain by
Biddles Ltd., King's Lynn, Norfolk

CONTENTS

LIST OF TABLES

INTRODUCTION

This book deals with the major political institutions in the Federal Republic of Germany from its birth in 1949 until the aftermath of the national election in September 2002. The text offers a comprehensive overview of both the tradition and the transformation in the political institutions of the Federal Republic of Germany before and after the unification of West and East Germany in 1990. The structure, the functions, and the logic of Germany's political institutions will be highlighted in seven chapters. The topics covered include (1) the constitutional foundations of the Federal Republic; (2) the executive at the federal level and in the states of Germany; (3) parliament and the interaction between parliament and the Bundesrat, and the representation of the sixteen state governments; (4) the judiciary or the supremacy of the law; (5) the political leadership, the electoral system, the party system, and pluralist and corporatist state–interest group relations; and (6) continuity and discontinuity in the institutions, the political process, and public policy before and after 1990.

This book focuses on a country with a political history of remarkable discontinuity. Few nations experienced such numerous radical regime changes in the nineteenth and twentieth centuries as Germany. In little more than 130 years Germany has been governed by seven different regimes: a constitutional monarchy (1871–1918), an unstable democracy in the period of the Weimar Republic (1919–1933), national socialist totalitarianism (1933–45), military occupation (1945–49), two separate German states in the post-1945 period, a liberal democratic order in West Germany and a Soviet-style communist regime in the Eastern part of the country, and since 1990 a unified German state on Western democratic principles, which, like its predecessor before 1990, transfers a substantial part of its sovereignty to the European Union and international organizations.

The study of political institutions in the federal republic of Germany

Most observers in the early post-Second World War period were utterly pessimistic about the viability of Germany's democracy (Neumann 1950; Litchfield 1953). Too numerous and too powerful seemed to be the legacies of the authoritarian past, and too heavy the political and economic load the country had to shoulder through military defeat. War caused destruction, occupation, and the influx of more than 11 million refugees and expellees from the Eastern parts of Germany and adjacent areas during the Second World War and the post-war period. Post-1945 Germany had also inherited millions of supporters of Hitler's National-Socialist Workers' Party. According to estimates, six and a half million were members of the NSDAP. They and their family members accounted for about 25 per cent of the total population at the end of the Second World War (Kielmansegg 1989: 15). Would it be possible to develop a democratic state with a heritage like this? 'The choice is to kill them or win their support!'[1] According to Eugen Kogon, the author of a famous report on concentration camps in National-Socialist Germany (Kogon 1978), this was, in theory, the choice in post-war Germany. In reality, however, that choice did not exist—unless mass murder on a scale even beyond the holocaust was regarded as acceptable. The only way out of the predicament was to mobilize the support for the new political order in West Germany not only among the younger age groups, but also among the followers of Hitler, the Chancellor and 'Führer' in the 1933–45 period.

That this way out was ultimately feasible depended upon a wide variety of favourable circumstances, the most important being a long period of unprecedented economic growth and rapidly rising standards of living for the many in the 1950s and 1960s. And to the surprise of many observers Germany's transition to democracy after 1948/9 ultimately turned out to be a 'success story' (Dalton 1993: 4).

This is not the only puzzle which post-1949 Germany poses to the observer. Another lies in the relation between wealth and foreign policy. The Federal Republic of Germany is a big and wealthy country, measured by the total number of the population and indicators of economic strength. It is the most populous nation in Western Europe. And according to estimates of the economic product per capita Germany counts among the twelve richest countries in the world (Maddison 2001: 276–79). But despite the large population and the high level of economic productivity Germany's foreign policy stance differs markedly from a power politics approach. In contrast to pre-1945 Germany the Federal Republic of Germany has opted for a 'trading state' approach as opposed to a 'big power' policy, to quote Rosecrance's useful distinction of two routes to wealth and international reputation (Rosecrance 1986). Furthermore, integration into international and transnational organizations, such as the European Union (EU) and NATO, has characterized the foreign policy stance adopted in the Federal Republic of Germany, regardless of whether the country was ruled by a Christian Democratic prime minister or a Social Democratic chancellor. The single reliable indicator of the non-existence of a power politics approach in present-day Germany is the exclusion of the country from the club of nuclear power states and the acceptance of that exclusion among German political leaders and the mass public.

Germany also deserves that close attention should be paid to its political institutions. In contrast to all other member states of the European Union, except Austria, Germany is a federalist country. Germany is thus marked by a constitutional structure which observers from unitary states such as Britain or the Nordic countries often find difficult to comprehend. It is not a country with one government, it is rather 'a single country with 17 governments':[2] one in the capital, Berlin, and one in each of the sixteen regional states (Länder). Decentralization and power sharing rather than concentration of power characterize the Federal Republic. Most notably, power is shared between central government (Bundesregierung, or federal government) and the government of each of the Länder. Power sharing also concerns parliament, the lower house (Bundestag), whose legislation often needs the consent of the upper house, the Bundesrat, the representative of the state governments or upper house, to quote a common English phrase (although the Bundesrat is strictly speaking not a parliamentary institution). That may practically speaking mean co-governance of the opposition party, if the opposition party controls the majority of the seats in the Bundesrat. Moreover, federalism is only one part of the complex interplay between a wide variety of government and co-governing actors in modern Germany. The wide variety of co-governing actors or 'veto players' (Tsebelis 1995, 2002) makes politics and policy making in Germany a difficult and often frustrating enterprise. A wide variety of co-governing forces and veto players can result in time-consuming processes of consensus formation and conflict resolution. The multitude of co-governing forces, such as coalition parties in federal government, the powerful state governments, the autonomous central bank, a powerful Constitutional Court and self-administration bodies in local government, social insurance and higher education, may even generate a highly fragmented and slowly working decision-making process. In the worst case a blockade of the decision-making process cannot be precluded.

But numerous co-governing forces or veto players do not only impair governance; they can also be part of good governance—through guaranteeing stability and predictability, through fragmenting and dispersing rather than concentrating power resources as well as through the supremacy of the law over politics which the co-governance of the Federal Constitutional Court normally implies. Moreover, the complex and complicated structure of Germany's democracy, a mix of majoritarian and consociational democracy together with a high level of constitutionalization of politics, may impair speedy policy reactions and impede bold short-term policy changes. But the potential disadvantage of these circumstances must be counter-balanced with their benefits. The foremost-mentioned are the high capacity for integration; the absence of tyranny of the few or tyranny of the many; the integration of the opposition in the process of will formation and decision making; and the greater degree of certainty to implement what has been decided after lengthy bargaining (in contrast to a more uncertain implementation process in majoritarian and centralized decision making).

Following the format of all other publications in the Oxford University Press series on Political Institutions, structures and changes in political institutions are at the heart of this book, while public policy topics are not discussed in detail. But at least some of the idiosyncrasies of Germany's public policy which have been shaped by the political institutions of the country deserve to be mentioned here. For example, Germany's economic policy makers have placed a major emphasis on price stability on the one hand and competition law on the other. Thus, they emphasized policies which are typical of market-oriented governments and are compatible with institutions like a market economy and an autonomous central bank. But Germany is by no means a purely market-driven society. Rather, it is famous for its social market economy based on private ownership, competition law, and comprehensive social transfers and services (*Soziale Marktwirtschaft*) (see Grosser et al. 1988) and it has also become notorious for big government, including an advanced welfare state and ambitious employment protection. Germany's policy outputs and outcomes indicate a distinctive public policy profile, namely a 'policy of the middle way' (Schmidt 1987, 1989, 2001*a*), that is, a route between the extreme poles marked by US-style market-driven capitalism on the one hand and social democratized welfare capitalism of Swedish origin on the other. The 'policy of the middle way' is deeply anchored in the political institutions of the country and in a party system dominated by two major pro-welfare state parties, the Christian Democratic parties—CDU and CSU—and the Social Democratic Party (SPD).

Regarding conceptual lenses and theoretical perspectives, it should be pointed out that this book has been deeply impregnated by an augmented political-institutionalist approach. The major components of that approach comprise historical institutionalism, parties-do-matter theory, the school of the socio-economic determination of public policy, work on power resources as well as hypotheses on the interplay of international and transnational factors, and nation state politics.[3]

The plan of the book

The structure and functions of Germany's political institutions will be highlighted in seven chapters. Chapter 1 focuses attention on the constitutional foundations of the Federal Republic. This chapter shows that an anti-totalitarian spirit pervades both the constitution and the real world politics in the country. The first chapter further points out that Germany's constitution, the Basic Law, provides for a republican form of government; a human-rights-based democracy; a federation; commitment to a strong social policy stance; integration of the country into the European Union; and the powerful role of political parties. Germany's post-1949 constitution thus completely differs from the 'Behemoth' of the National-Socialist period in 1933–45, to quote from Franz Neumann's insightful study (Neumann 1944); and it differs no less dramatically from Thomas Hobbes's 'Leviathan', the absolutist sovereign, which has been authorized to do anything except order a subject to kill himself.

Chapter 2 explores the structure, the role, and the institutional context of the executive in Germany's political system. In a process of learning from political catastrophes in the Weimar Republic (1919–33) and the era of national socialism (1933–45), the architects of the post-1949 republic have provided for a strong Chancellor and a weak President. According to a widely shared view a 'Chancellor Democracy' has emerged from these structures—in contradistinction to the 'Chancellor Dictatorship' of von Bismarck in the German Empire of 1871. However, the Chancellor Democracy is constrained by the constitution, the law, and a large number of co-governing forces and veto players. Decentralization and coordinated federalism play an important role in this context. A major role is also played by the political parties. It is their dominance, the theory goes, which has created a party state (*Parteienstaat*) in Germany, that is, a state in which most major political decisions are shaped by political parties. In contrast to this and in further contrast to the powerful role of the President in the Weimar Republic of 1919–33, the role of the Federal President in Germany after 1949 is normally confined to ceremonial functions and other dignified parts of the constitution.

Chapter 3 focuses attention on the legislature, one of the classical public powers besides the executive and the judiciary. The structures and political functions of the legislature, above all the national parliament, and its role in articulating and aggregating preferences will be highlighted in this chapter. But due to the complicated federalist structure of Germany, the study of the role of parliament also requires a closer analysis of the role played by the states and the national representation of the states, the Bundesrat. Like Chapter 2, Chapter 3 again focuses the reader's attention on the fact that the majority which governs today's Germany does not govern alone. It is rather power sharing between the Bundestag, the lower house, and the Bundesrat, the upper house, as well as power sharing between the federal government and the state governments which structures a large part of the political process in Germany.

The organization of the judiciary, the role of the Federal Constitutional Court, and the pros and cons of the supremacy of the law in Germany's Second Republic are the central topics of the fourth chapter. This chapter focuses attention on the degree to which conflict resolution in the Federal Republic of Germany takes place within the context of the unusually powerful role of the judiciary and the law.

Linking people and political institutions is the central topic of Chapter 5. In this part of the book attention will mainly be centred on the electoral system, voting behaviour, parties and the party system, organized interest groups, networks between the state and the interest associations, and on the political elites both prior to and after unification. Moreover, this section explores the extent to which representative democracy and direct democracy coexist and interact with each other in the Federal Republic.

The policy consequences of the political institutions and the policy choices of the major political actors are the topics of Chapter 6. This chapter discusses the constraints on public policy in Germany and highlights some of the possibilities to circumvent at least some of the numerous veto players. Moreover, this part of the book examines the extent to which public policy in Germany has been shaped by the trend towards increasing European integration. The sixth chapter also addresses a major question of politics and policy making in Germany from a cross-national and a historical perspective. It does so by focusing on the distinctiveness of the public policy profile of pre- and post-unification Germany. The key words in this context are the policy of the middle way and the trading state approach in foreign policy instead of a big power approach. Furthermore the sixth chapter explores in more detail the extent to which both continuity and discontinuity have marked Germany's political institutions and policies in the pre- and post-1990 periods.

The final chapter draws some conclusions. It points out that the wide variety of co-governing forces and veto players in the domestic political arenas can turn politics and policy making in the Federal Republic of Germany into a very difficult enterprise. But major political changes in the decades before and after unification in 1992 underline the validity of a general view of the Federal Republic's political institutions: it is the view that a moderate to high level of elasticity and adaptability characterizes the policy-making process in Germany despite the indisputable existence of numerous veto players and co-governing tendencies. Furthermore, the emphasis on the trading state approach (and the reluctance of the leaders of the Federal Republic of Germany to opt for major military policy moves in out-of-area missions) contradicts the view that Germany is on the way towards a power state approach or even to a 'Fourth Reich'. Finally, the data and the studies on Germany's politics and society unequivocally testify to the view that this country has left its authoritarian and totalitarian past behind and has become a full member of the club of established constitutional democracies. This is not to belittle the deficiencies which plague policy makers in Germany. But overall, the political performance of the Federal Republic has been satisfactory or good and occasionally exceptional.

This book's intended audience

The present book was written for a wide audience. It is of course literature for students and scholars in political science. But it is also written for students and scholars in adjacent faculties, above all history, economics, business administration, and law. Furthermore, the book is written in a style which makes it accessible also for readers with a more general interest in politics in Germany. The book will enable students to understand the nature of Germany's political institutions; evaluate the strength and the weakness of the institutional structure of the country; explore the relationships between institutions and the political process; understand the impact of political institutions on Germany's public policy profile, and locate the idiosyncrasies, such as federalism and the mixing of majoritarian democracy and negotiation democracy, as well as the commonalities of Germany's polity and other modern democracies.

....

NOTES

1 'Man kann sie nur töten oder gewinnen' (Kogon 1947, cited in Kielmansegg 1989: 16).

2 'Model Vision: A Survey of Germany', *The Economist*, 21 May 1994: 29.

3 For earlier applications of this approach see Schmidt (1989, 1993, 1998, 2001*a*, 2001*b*, 2002*a*, 2002*c*).

1

Against 'Leviathan' and 'Behemoth': The Anti-Totalitarian Constitution of the Federal Republic of Germany

It is impossible to understand the political institutions and political process in the Federal Republic of Germany without considering the impact of the constitution and the important part played by the judiciary. In contrast to the National-Socialist state (Kershaw 1998, 2000) and East Germany's socialism from 1949 to 1990 (Fulbrook 1995), the law and the judiciary are omnipresent in the Federal Republic of Germany (Batt 2001). The importance of the law and the judiciary is reflected by a high level of legal security, the presence of a 'law- and court-minded people' (Conradt 2001: 228), and the claim that the law is supreme (see Chapter 4). Even if that may underestimate the role of the political process, governing the Federal Republic undoubtedly means to a large extent 'governing with judges' (Stone Sweet 2000). It is for these reasons that it is particularly appropriate to begin an introduction to Germany's political institutions with an overview of the institutional design provided by the constitution of the country. This overview will show that an anti-totalitarian spirit pervades the constitution, constitutional policy, and the political process in Germany and that the anti-totalitarian spirit was deliberately adopted. It will further point out that Germany's constitution, the Basic Law, provides for the rule of law; a republican form of government; a human-rights-based democracy together with an important role for political parties; federalism; commitment to ambitious social policy; and integration of the country into the European Union. Finally, this chapter shows that real world politics in Germany are broadly consistent with what the constitutional design prescribes. But the chapter also focuses on the coexistence of comparative institutional advantage and institutional disadvantage in Germany's constitutional structures.

A state with a written constitution

In contrast to the United Kingdom of Great Britain and Northern Ireland, the Federal Republic of Germany is a state with a written constitution. And in contradistinction to the United States of America, the constitution of the Federal Republic was designed not only to serve 'as a system of governance but also to foster a secure and preferred way of life' (Kommers 1997*b*: 39). The 'Basic Law' (*Grundgesetz*) is the generic term for the constitution created for the West German part of the divided country in 1949. The founders of the constitution chose that label rather than the more dignified term 'constitution' in order to emphasize the provisional and transitional character of the West German state. The formation of a West German state under the rule of the Basic Law should allow for the unification of Germany at a future date. As a consequence of the Cold War, Germany was divided into a Western part (under American, British, and French rule) and an Eastern part under Soviet rule from 1945 until 1990.

Critics argue that the Basic Law was installed on top of the bayonets of the occupation powers. This is not wrong, but it represents an exaggerated view. The Western Allies undoubtedly dominated the process of democratizing West Germany. Without their consent West Germany's transition towards a democratic state would have been inconceivable. Furthermore, the initiative for the restoration of democracy in the Western part of the divided country came from the Western Allies. The Western Allied military governments ordered the West German states to call a constituent assembly by 1 September 1948, which was to be in charge of drafting a constitution for the three Western zones of the occupied country. The prime ministers of the West German states, fearing that a constituent assembly and the resultant constitution would solidify the division of Germany, hesitated to acquiesce and only reluctantly gave in to what the Western Allies demanded.

The Parliamentary Council was in charge of drafting the constitutional convention (Deutscher Bundestag and Bundesarchiv 1974–7). The Council comprised sixty-five delegates of the state parliaments, and five non-voting deputies from Berlin. The distribution of power between the political tendencies in the Parliamentary Council anticipated the distribution of power in post-1949 West Germany. Two of the largest parties in the Council, the

Christian Democrats and the Social Democrats, held twenty-seven seats each. Five seats each were taken by the liberal Free Democratic Party. The German Party, the Centre Party and the Communist Party controlled two seats each. West Berlin was represented by 3 SPD-deputies and one deputy each from the CDU and the FDP. In the face of the ideological distances between the political parties, the distribution of seats in the Parliamentary Council allowed for two types of absolute majority: first, a minimum winning coalition comprising Christian Democrats, Liberals, and the German Party as well as the Centre Party, and, secondly, a grand coalition between the Christian Democratic Parties and the Social Democratic Party. But in order to exceed a two-thirds majority threshold the formation of a grand coalition was imperative. The Parliamentary Council was thus marked by a constellation of political forces which has pervaded political life in the Federal Republic of Germany, namely the formation of a formal or informal grand coalition as a precondition of major legislative acts.

On 8 May 1949, the majority of the Parliamentary Council passed the Basic Law. Ratification of the Basic Law was up to the state parliaments, not to a popular referendum. All state parliaments accepted the Basic Law with the required two-thirds majority with the exception of the Bavarian parliament, which nevertheless confirmed the membership of Bavaria to the Federal Republic of Germany, as two-thirds of the state parliaments voted in favour of the new constitution. The Western Allied occupation forces also consented—subject to certain reservations specified in the Occupation Statute concerning mainly the status of Berlin and the organization of the federation. The route towards the foundation of a separate West German state was now open. The promulgation of the Basic Law took place on 23 May 1948. One day later the constitution, the Basic Law, came into force. Initially, the Basic Law was valid only for the Western states and for Berlin, but the latter stipulation was suspended by the Allied powers. In 1957 the Saarland joined the Federal Republic of Germany. And since 3 October 1990, the day when the German Democratic Republic acceded to the Federal Republic of Germany, the Basic Law has been the constitution of both West and East Germany.

Restrictions on sovereignty

From the start, West Germany was a semi-sovereign democratic country both in political-geographic and in constitutional terms: West Germany never had all the elements of international sovereignty, owing to external control. Furthermore, the state of the Federal Republic of Germany has been tarried by an extraordinarily wide variety of checks and balances. West Germany was a country shorn of its eastern flank, with an enclave, West Berlin, deep in the territory of the communist East German state. And even after the Basic Law came into force in 1949, West Germany remained for a longer period a penetrated political system. The sovereignty accorded to the Federal Republic state was restricted both regarding foreign policy and domestic policy (Litchfield 1953; Hanrieder 1995: 4–8). Just as the Soviet Union was the occupying power in East Germany, so supreme authority in West Germany lay with the Allied occupying powers, America, Britain, and France. The legal basis of the supreme authority of the Western Allies resided in the Occupation Statute issued in May 1949. Under this Statute, the Western Allies retained several powers, such as questions of disarmament, reparations, decartelization, foreign affairs, foreign trade, and exchange. Moreover, at the outset 'any amendment to the Basic Law required sanction from the Allies, who also retained powers of emergency—in effect, the authority to suspend the constitution if necessary' (Smith 1986: 45). These powers were indeed 'sufficiently numerous to make the Basic Law appear a subordinate document' (Smith 1986: 47). At this time West Germany clearly 'was not a sovereign state'.[1] Government in Germany in those days rather resembled government of the occupation forces and by the occupation forces,[2] although with a gradually increasing role for the democratically elected government.

The status of a penetrated political system formally ended ten years after the end of the Second World War with the coming into force of the Germany Treaty between the Western Allies and the Federal Republic of Germany on 5 May 1955. In the Germany Treaty, the Federal Republic gained most of its sovereignty. But the former Allies, the United States, the United Kingdom, France, and Soviet Russia, continued to reserve certain powers, mainly with regard to the status of West Berlin, the reunification of Germany, and a future peace treaty between Germany and the Allied Powers of the Second World War. The reserved powers of the Allies only ceased to exist as a consequence of the Two-plus-Four-Treaty of 1990 between the two German states and the four Allied Powers of the Second World War.

The spirit of liberal-democratic constitutional theory

The Basic Law defines the 'constitutional structures' (Huber, Ragin, and Stephens 1993) of the Federal Republic of Germany broadly in accordance with liberal-democratic constitutional theory (Kommers 1997a, 1997b). Five of the most important constitutional structures are set out in Article 20 of the Basic Law. These are a human rights-based democracy under-pinned by the doctrine of the separation of powers and the party state, republicanism, the rule of law, federalism, and the commitment to social policy. Added to these principles was the provision according to which the federation may, by legislation, transfer sovereign powers to international organizations.[3] Neither Hobbes's 'Leviathan' nor the National-Socialist 'Behemoth' (Neumann 1977) has been the blueprint for the constitution and for political life in the Federal Republic of Germany rather, but a constitutional democratic theory mainly of American and European tradi-tions, including numerous veto players, a high degree of power sharing, a competitive party system, a state with ambitious social policy goals, and the openness of the constitution to the delegation of sovereignty to inter-national and transnational organizations.

Democracy

Democracy rather than an autocracy was the first major constitutional structure prescribed by the Basic Law. In contrast to US-style presidential-ism or a semi-presidential order such as in France or Finland, the Basic Law opted for a parliamentary form of government. Within a parlia-mentary government, the executive is accountable to parliament and dependent upon the support of the majority of the deputies, and govern-ment can be recalled by a parliamentary majority. In contrast to a direct democracy, the architects of Germany's constitutions have chosen a pre-dominantly representative democracy. The only exception to representa-tive democracy at the federal level is a referendum in the case of a new delimitation of the federal territory.[4] But direct participation of the people plays a more important role in the states and in local government. More-over, in contrast to all preceding constitutions in Germany, the Basic Law explicitly allocates to political parties the task 'to take part in forming the political will of the people'[5] and to represent the people in the legislature. Furthermore, in contrast to any other constitution, the Basic Law circumscribes the role and the structure of the political parties in more detail. Parties must be freely elected; their internal organization must conform to democratic standards; and the parties must publicly account for the sources of their funds—a requirement which was circumvented in various party finance scandals, with the refusal of Helmut Kohl, Federal Chancellor in 1982–98, to name the donors of funds secretly given to the CDU as a spectacular case.

'The party state', 'militant democracy', republicanism, and the rule of law

Article 21 of the Basic Law is the constitutional basis of Germany's controversially debated 'party state' (*Parteienstaat*). A party state may be conceived of as a state and largely also a society in which party competition is pervasive and where all major political decisions are shaped by political parties and their representatives (von Beyme 1993; Smith 1986: 66–9). In contrast to the Weimar Republic, however, the constitutional foundation of democracy in the Basic Law comprises also the notion of a 'well-fortified democracy' or 'militant democracy' (Kommers 1997b: 34, 37–8). A well-fortified democracy is a concept which contrasts sharply with the utter tolerance towards extremist parties in the Weimar Republic. The notion of a 'well-fortified democracy' is anchored in the belief that intolerance of declared opponents or enemies of a democratic order is legitimate. It also states that a democratic state is entitled to 'defend its fundamental democratic values against anti-democratic forces and prevent these powers from abusing the democratic order by abolishing it once they became the majority' (Michalowski and Woods 1999: 23). The major instruments of the 'militant democracy' include banning unconstitutional political parties, prohibition of anti-system associations, and forfeiture of basic rights for anyone who abuses his freedoms in order to undermine the democratic order. All these measures must be determined by the Federal Constitutional Court in order to minimize political abuse of the institutions of militant democracy.

A further constitutional structure defined in the Basic Law is republicanism. According to this principle Germany's post-Second World War order is a republic with the President as the head of the state, as opposed to a monarchy such as in Imperial Germany in the period from 1871 to 1918.

Governance of the rule of law is the third constitutional arrangement provided by the Basic Law, as opposed to governance of an unconstrained authoritarian state, such as Hobbes's 'Leviathan' and the National-Socialist 'Behemoth' (Neumann 1977) in the period from 1933 to 1945.[6] Within the context of the German constitution, the rule of law has been associated with four more specific principles. The first is that legislation shall be subject to the constitutional order, and that the executive and the judiciary shall be bound by law and justice.[7] Separation of powers is the second principle—in contradistinction to the concentration of the state powers, such as in National-Socialist Germany in 1933–45 and in East Germany's socialist state in the period between 1945 and 1989–90. The major function of the separation of powers in the Federal Republic is to create a system of 'extensive checks and balances' (Dalton 2000: 281) or mutual control, restraint, and moderation of the public powers, in order to prevent each of the powers—executive, legislature, and judiciary—from becoming unconstrained. Judicial review is the third element in this context. It is the right of all citizens to have all acts of a public authority reviewed judicially by independent competent judges, not by lay judges elected from political assemblies as in Ancient Greece. Finally, the ban on retroactive laws provides the fourth element. According to this ban no one can be prosecuted on the basis of a law that was not in force at the time of the act in question.

Federalism

Germany's constitution comprises federalism as a fourth element of the constitutional structures, as opposed to a centralized unitary state. It thus provides for vertical dispersal of power between the federation and the states (*Länder*). Since unification in 1990, German federalism consists of sixteen states—in contrast to ten states and West Berlin before unification. Before 1990 the gap between richer and poorer states was relatively small. But due to the disparities between East and West Germany, post-1990 federalism has been marked by widely diverging levels of economic wealth, divergent vote shares of the various political parties, and different cultural traditions. At the same time, Germany's federalism emphasizes the goal of equal living conditions in the federal territory and the preservation of legal and economic unity throughout the federation. Thus, the Federal Republic has been marked by the unique profile of a 'unitarian federalism' (Hesse 1962). Furthermore, Germany's federalism is characterized by extensive cooperation and interlocked politics between the federal government and the state governments, as well as by no less extensive horizontal coordination between the states.[8] The other side of that coin consists of a low degree of autonomy of the states, but that has been compensated for by increasing codetermination of the states in public affairs at the level of the federation. The consequences of these institutional arrangements for the political process are non-trivial: the autonomous room for manoeuvre available to federal government and each of the state governments is narrowly circumscribed. And in order to get things done, the federal government and the political parties in parliament upon which it is based must cooperate in most policy areas with the states or at least with the majority of the votes in the Bundesrat.

The welfare state

According to the Basic Law, a strong commitment to social policy is imperative. This is the constitutional background of Germany's advanced welfare state, or 'social state'[9] (*Sozialstaat*), as the welfare state is typically called in Germany's political discourse. The constitution uses a less accessible technical vocabulary. The Basic Law does not explicitly mention the welfare state, but it refers to a 'social federal state'[10] and 'social government'.[11] The essential point is this: both concepts mark a major step beyond the purely liberal version of the rule of law.[12] While liberal rule of law abstains from intervening in private property rights, the 'social government' approach supports ambitious social regulation of the economy and the society.[13] The principle of a 'social government' stands for social justice and obligates the authorities, in the words of the Federal Constitutional Court, to provide 'the basic conditions for a humane existence of each of its citizens'.[14] It must be added that neither the constitution nor the federal constitutional court have defined the details of social policy making. Provision of a commitment to social policy is a broadly defined, diffuse mandate addressed to the legislator, which does not specify the type or the amount of social benefits.[15] Germany's policy makers are therefore free to choose, for example, between a liberal social policy approach, a social democratic type of Swedish origin, or a centrist-conservative arrangement along the lines of a social-insurance based welfare state, as long as each of these welfare state regimes provides the basic needs for all citizens.

The delegation of sovereignty

A sixth constitutional structure in Germany concerns the delegation of sovereignty to international or transnational organizations. The Federal Republic of Germany may by legislation and with the consent of the Bundesrat transfer sovereign powers to international or transnational organizations. The constitution thus provides for an open state principle. This reflects Germany's entrance ticket for reintegration into the world of the Western democracies after 1945: membership in the military alliance of the Western nations and in the European Community presupposed the delegation of sovereignty rights. In an amendment to the Basic Law in 1992, the open state principle was applied specifically to the situation in the newly introduced European Union.[16] The reformulated Article 23 of the Basic Law provided explicitly the openness of the German constitution to the process of European integration—as long as the European Community is committed to the rule of law, democracy, social and federal principles, as well as to the principle of subsidiarity, and as long as the European Community also protects the fundamental rights of the citizens to a degree comparable to that afforded by the Basic Law.

Learning from catastrophes

Germany's constitutional structures are products of 'learning from catastrophes' in the history of the country (Schmidt 1989). The experience of National Socialism initiated a process of learning after 1945 which resulted in a pervasive anti-totalitarian spirit in political life in the western part of Germany. The anti-communist sentiment produced by the creation of an authoritarian socialist state in East Germany further strengthened the search for, or restoration of, liberal constitutional safeguards against unconstrained state authority. These safeguards include, above all, the rule of law, a powerful role for the judiciary, federalism as a further brake on excessive state authority, a representative democracy, and a wide variety of constitutionally guaranteed civil liberties which were meant to protect the citizens against violations of their rights.[17]

Germany's constitutional structures are also attributable to learning from the institutional pathology of the Weimar Republic (Fromme 1962). Among these, a powerful role for the President, plebiscitary elements, and a weakness of the Chancellor vis-à-vis parliament and President must be counted foremost. The architects of the Basic Law aimed to avoid the political-institutional pathologies of the Weimar Republic, including the vulnerability of the Weimar constitution to the pseudo-legal seizure of power on the part of the National-Socialist German Workers' Party. Several institutional arrangements were introduced to achieve these ends. These include checks and balances against potential misuse of powers, a clear-cut division of labour between the Federal President and the Federal Chancellor in favour of the latter, emphasis on representative democracy rather than direct democracy, high consensus requirements for major legislation, priority for stable government at the cost of powerful roles for parliament, and a constructive vote of no confidence. According to the vote of no confidence parliament can express its lack of confidence in the Federal Chancellor only by electing a successor with the majority of its members. This institution is meant to ensure that a negative coalition in parliament against an incumbent Chancellor, such as was the case in the constitution of the Weimar Republic, is not sufficient. The vote of no confidence rather requires that the opposition against the incumbent also has a majority in favour of a new Chancellor.

Idiosyncratic traditions have influenced the process of institution building since 1945 in the western part of Germany. The emphasis placed on 'social government' in the constitution, for example, followed the long-standing tradition of a relatively advanced welfare state in Germany. Moreover, the federal structure of the state restored an institution which had long played a major role in pre-1933 Germany.

Constraints on majoritarian rule

In contrast to the Weimar Republic, powerful institutional constraints on the majority in the legislature and the executive are a further characteristic of the constitutional structures in post-Second World War Germany. The basic rights for example legally protect citizens from unconstrained state authority and potential tyranny of the majority. Constitutional guarantees for the basic rights and the constitutional structures of the state discussed above, including a guarantee for federalism, are a second and a third example. That legislative change of the constitution requires two-thirds majorities of the lower and the upper houses is a further constraint on majority rule. Practically speaking, two-thirds majorities in parliament and in the Bundesrat presuppose the formation of a formal or informal grand coalition between the major parties as well as a coalition between the federal government and the majority of the votes in the Bundesrat. A similar effect is generated by legislative acts which require the consent of the Bundesrat (which is the case for most important or very important policy making processes). In the case of a divided majority in the Bundesrat and the Bundestag, a not untypical situation, the required consent of the Bundesrat turns the opposition party into a veto player, if not a co-governing actor, provided that the opposition party can count on the majority of the votes in the Bundesrat.

Implementation

To what extent were the constitutional structures prescribed by the Basic Law implemented? The following chapters answer this question in more detail. But a brief overview is useful at this stage (see Table 1). That the rule of law is of major relevance in Germany and that the basic rights as stipulated in its constitution are widely respected can hardly be doubted in the light of a wide variety of sources. Cross-national comparisons of civil liberties, for example, have consistently classified the Federal Republic of Germany together with other advanced constitutional democracies in Europe, North America, Japan, Australia, and New Zealand into the highest categories (Freedom House 2001). Comparative measures of democracy support this result: the Federal Republic of Germany can pride itself on being one of the well-established democracies (Lijphart 1999). Undoubtedly Germany is also a federalist state, although the distinctive characteristics of her federalism reside in limited autonomy of the states, a high degree of cooperation between the states and the federal government, as well as a 'unitarian federalism' (Hesse 1962), that is, a high level of legal and economic unity similar to that of a unitary centralized state, such as France.

Moreover, Germany belongs to the club of advanced welfare states. Thus, federalism also meets the constitutional prescription of a 'social federal state'. Finally, Germany is firmly integrated in the European Union and contributes actively to the process of European integration.

Comparative institutional advantage and disadvantage

By and large, the constitutional prescriptions for Germany's political institutions have been successfully implemented (Isensee and Kirchhof 1987–2000). Successful implementation, however, can be associated with

TABLE 1 Constitutional structures of the Federal Republic of Germany

Constitutional design	Constitutional design: demarcation	Implementation of constitutional design	Type	Major comparative advantage	Major comparative disadvantage
1. Rule of law	authoritarian state, totalitarianism ('Leviathan', 'Behemoth'); purely liberal rule of law	largely successful	'social rule of law' supremacy of the law	high degree of law and order, reliable and predictable legal institutions	jurisdictional overregulation, juridification, dominance of governing with judges, trend towards governing like judges
2. Republic	monarchy	successful	federal republic	no conflicts between potentially contradictory constitutional structures (republicanism vs. monarchy)	deficit in ceremonial institutions
3. Human-rights based democracy	authoritarian state, totalitarianism	largely successful	hybrid (majoritarian and consensus-democratic forms together with plebiscitary elements at state level and in local government)	significant constitutionalization of democracy, high political productivity	typical deficiencies of democracies, such as short-termism, externalization of costs to third parties, potential tyranny of the majority, if unconstrained; strong 'party state'

4. Federalism	unitary state	high degree of unitarian federalism with high level of interlocking politics	successful	Sharing of power, dispersion of power resources, co-governance of opposition possible	tends towards deficient problem-solving capacity, frequency of elections: perennial electoral campaign
5. Active Social Policy	a state which imposes a minimum of duties on the citizens, purely liberal rule of law	advanced centrist welfare state with social insurance-based pillars, implicit basic income, and partly autonomous, partly legally circumscribed social partnership-based industrial relations	successful	effective protection against pauperization; relatively high level of social security, ambitious employment protection; significant reduction of social inequality	strong equality–efficiency trade-offs and strong employment–social security trade-offs; suppression effects on other fiscally costly policy sectors
6. Cooperation in building a United Europe	nationalistic solo runs	foundation in an untransparent multilevel system of governance	largely successful	participation in benefits of European integration (such as peaceful conflict resolution and transnational problem-solving of transnational problems)	untransparent, bureaucratization, structural democratic deficit of the European Union

Sources: Entries are mainly based upon von Beyme 1999; Freedom House 2001; Hancock 1995; Hancock et al. 2002; Hesse and Ellwein 1992; Kaase et al. 1996; Kaase and Schmid 1999; Kommers 1997b; Lijphart 1999; Rudzio 2000; Scharpf 1994, 1999; Schmidt 1992a, 1998; 2002c; Schwarz 2001; Wachendorfer-Schmidt 1999, 2000, 2001; 2003; Zacher 2001.

comparative institutional advantage, but it may also result in comparative disadvantage. Germany's constitutional structures are no exception to this rule.[18] For example, Germany can rightly pride itself on a high degree of law and order as well as reliable and predictable legal institutions. But the price to be paid includes jurisdictional overregulation, juridification, the dominance of governing with judges, and a certain trend towards governing like judges (see, for example, Stone Sweet 2000).

In a similar vein, the major merits of Germany's democracy are a significant constitutionalization of democracy and high political productivity. These, in turn, guarantee political participation for the adult population, the election of leaders and voting leaders out of office, as well as a high degree of responsiveness by political leaders vis-à-vis the demands of the voters. However, the typical deficiencies of democracies, such as short-termism, externalization of costs to third parties, and potential tyranny of the majority, if unconstrained, have also plagued the Federal Republic of Germany. The deficiencies also include a strong 'party state', as party-based patronage and party-centred processes of will formation and decision making suggest.

Furthermore, the advanced welfare state which emerged in the Federal Republic deserves to be praised. It has created effective protection against pauperization; a relatively high level of social security; ambitious employment protection; and significant reduction of social inequality. But the price to be paid for these achievements should not be belittled: these include equality–efficiency trade-offs, employment–social security trade-offs, and massive suppression effects of financing the welfare state on other fiscally costly policy sectors.

Finally, collaboration in the construction of a deeper and wider European Union may be a heroic enterprise with massive benefits such as transnational problem solving of transnational policy problems and peaceful conflict resolution between members who had long been enemies. But at the same time the European Community is also a technocratic enterprise with a huge democratic deficit and often untransparent processes (Abromeit 1998; Bach 1999).

The grand coalition state

From the constitutional structures as stipulated in the Basic Law and the rhythm of the democratic political process emerged a type of democracy in which majoritarian and non-majoritarian structures coexist (Abromeit 1993). It is also a democracy in which constitutional law and inviolable constitutional values narrowly constrain the scope for political decisions. Furthermore, the political process in the Federal Republic requires extended cooperation. Cooperation requirements challenge not only the federal government and state governments, but also the incumbent parties and the major opposition party, if a blocked decision-making process is to be avoided. In these circumstances, solo runs of a government are the exception rather than the rule. And effective governing presupposes in most cases the prior formation of a formal or tacit grand coalition of the major established parties and a coalition between the federal government and state governments. The Federal Republic of Germany can therefore be regarded as the embodiment of a 'grand coalition state' (Schmidt 2002*b*).

··

KEY TERMS

- anti-totalitarian constitution
- Basic Law
- 'Behemoth'
- democracy
- federalism
- 'governing with judges'
- grand coalition state

- human-rights-based democracy
- 'Leviathan'
- party state
- rule of law
- semi-sovereignty
- social federal state

··

QUESTIONS FOR CHAPTER 1

1 What are the major constitutional structures prescribed in the constitution of the Federal Republic of Germany?

2 To what extent and in what forms have these constitutional structures been implemented?

3 What are the causes of the totalitarian spirit of the Federal Republic's constitution?

4 To what extent is the constitution of the Federal Republic a product of learning from the deficiencies of the Weimar Republic?

5 To what extent do the constitutional structures of the Federal Republic of Germany differ from those of the United States of America and Great Britain?

....

NOTES

1 'The Berlin Republic. A Survey of Germany', in *The Economist*, 6 Feb, 1999: 3.

2 See for example the title of the SPD's brochure of a speech delivered by Kurt Schumacher, the Chairman of the SPD, on 11 June 1952: 'Die Staatsgewalt geht von den Besatzungsmächten aus' (cited in Hanrieder 1995: 458, footnote 9).

3 Article 24 Basic Law.

4 Article 29 Basic Law.

5 Article 21 Basic Law.

6 'Rule of law' is one of several varieties of translating the notion of the *Rechtsstaat* which includes also the tradition of 'a state governed by the law of reason' (Kommers 1997*b*: 36). Alternative translations include 'law state' and 'a state governed by law'.

7 Article 20 III Basic Law.

8 The authoritative account of interlocked politics (*Politikverflechtung*) is Scharpf, Reissert, and Schnabel 1976. For post-unification federalism see Wachendorfer-Schmidt 2003.

9 Currie 1997: ix–x; Michalowski and Woods 1999: 30. An alternative translation is 'social welfare state' (Kommers 1997*b*: 34–6).

10 Article 20 I Basic Law.

11 The German term is *soziale Rechtsstaat* (Article 28 I Basic Law: 'The constitutional order in the States must conform to the principles of the republican, democratic, and social state under the rule, within the meaning of this constitution.')

12 The German equivalent is the notion of *liberale Rechtsstaat.*

13 See Zacher 2001.

14 Bundesverfassungsgericht—Entscheidungen (BverfGE) 82, 60: 79–80 (1990) cited in Michalowski and Woods 1999: 31; see also Kommers 1997*b*: 35–6.

15 See Article 20 I, Basic Law I: 'The Federal Republic of Germany is a democratic and social federal state.'

16 'Gesetz zur Änderung des Grundgesetzes vom 21.12.1992', in *Bundesgesetzblatt* I: 2086.

17 According to the Basic Law all state authority is constrained by the basic rights stipulated in the constitution.

18 See Table 1, columns 5 and 6.

GUIDE TO FURTHER READING

Freedom House (2001), *Freedom in the World: 2000–2001. The Annual Survey of Political Rights & Civil Liberties* (New York: Freedom House). Comparative survey of political rights and civil liberties in democracies and autocracies.

FROMME, F. K. (1962), *Von der Weimarer Verfassung zum Bonner Grundgesetz: Die verfassungspolitischen Folgerungen des Parlamentarischen Rates aus Weimarer Republik und nationalsozialistischer Diktatur*, 2nd edn. (Tübingen: Mohr (Siebeck) †). Important study on the commonalities and differences of the constitution of the Weimar Republic and the Basic Law for the Federal Republic of Germany.

GOETZ, K. H., and CULLEN, P. J. (eds.) (1994), *Constitutional Policy in Unified Germany, German Politics*, 3/3 (London: Frank Cass). Studies in continuity and discontinuity in constitutional policy in pre- and post-1990 Germany.

Grundgesetz für die Bundesrepublik Deutschland (2002) (Munich: C. H. Beck). The constitution of the Federal Republic of Germany.

ISENSEE, J., and KIRCHHOF, P. (eds.) (1987–2000), *Handbuch des Staatsrechts der Bundesrepublik Deutschland*, 10 vols. (Heidelberg: C. F. Müller). Important handbook on the constitutional law in the Federal Republic of Germany.

KOMMERS, D. P. (1997), *The Constitutional Jurisprudence of the Federal Republic of Germany*, 2nd edn. (Durham NC: Duke University Press). The most comprehensive study on constitutional jurisprudence in post-war Germany in English.

MICHALOWSKI, S., and WOODS, L. (1999), *German Constitutional Law: The Protection of Civil Liberties* (Aldershot: Ashgate Dartmouth). Useful introduction to German constitutional law.

STONE SWEET, A. (2000), *Governing with Judges: Constitutional Politics in Europe* (Oxford: Oxford University Press). Excellent study on constitutional politics in the Federal Republic of Germany and other European states.

2

Governing a Semi-sovereign State: Germany's Executive and its Institutional Context

Overview

This chapter explores the structure and the role of the executive in the political system of the Federal Republic. It also places Germany's executive in the context of the 'party state', and analyses the numerous veto players in the political process, the powerful role of the states in Germany's federalism, and the extensive delegation of public policy functions to civil society. Chapter 2 thus aims to introduce some of the most central idiosyncrasies in Germany's political institutions to the reader.

Introduction

The architects of the post-1949 republic learnt from the political catastrophes in the Weimar Republic and the National-Socialist era 1933–45, and created a system with a strong Federal Chancellor and a weak Federal President. It has been argued that a 'Chancellor Democracy' has emerged from these structures. Indeed the Federal Chancellor does have control of a wide variety of resources. But he is also massively constrained by the constitution, statute law, and a large number of co-governing forces and veto players. Among these, Germany's federalism has played a particularly important role. A relevant part is also played by the political parties. It is their dominance, the theory goes, which has created a *Parteienstaat* ('party state') in Germany, that is, a state in which most major political decisions are shaped by political parties.

In contrast to Britain and to many other unitary states, modern Germany is a single country with a federal government (*Bundesregierung*) and sixteen state governments. These states, the *Länder*, are powerful entities—both within their own jurisdiction and at the federal level. At the federal level, the power of the states is institutionalized in the Bundesrat, the council of the representatives of the sixteen state governments, and in numerous partly formal, partly informal modes of cooperation. The importance of the Bundesrat is particularly visible in legislation—and in this area the Bundesrat is often as important as the Bundestag, or national parliament. For constitutional reasons, legislation in Germany often calls for the formation of unusually broad coalitions made up of the incumbent parties and the major opposition party, and the majority in the lower and upper houses of parliament. This results in non-majoritarian constitutional structures which differ markedly from British-style majoritarian democracy. Among these the—formal or informal—'grand coalition state' (Schmidt 2002b: 89–90) deserves to receive attention first.

2.1 A 'Chancellor Democracy'?

The founders of the constitution of the Federal Republic of Germany opted for a parliamentary government as opposed to US-style pres-identialism or semi-presidentialism of the French variety. In a parliamentary government, the executive is accountable to the lower house and thus depends upon the support of the majority in the national assembly.

Parliamentary form of government

As regards parliamentary government, the Federal Republic of Germany resembles the British form of government. But in contrast to Britain, the architects of the German constitution chose a republican parliamentary government rather than a monarchy. In contrast to the unified top of the executive in a presidential system, as in the United States of America, the top of the executive of the Federal Republic of Germany is double-headed. It consists of the Federal Chancellor and the Federal President.[1] The architects of the German constitution after 1945 also opted for a federalist state, and therefore a dispersal of political power and a de-concentration rather than concentration of power. Moreover, the founders of the constitution of the Second German Republic provided for a strong Chancellor and a weak President—in marked contrast to Germany's First Republic, the Weimar

Republic 1919–33, in which a weak Chancellor and a strong President coexisted, but also in contrast with the chief executives in semi-presidential countries such as France or Finland (King 1994; Helms 1996b). The post-1949 parliamentary system in Germany is thus marked by a vertical fragmentation of power above all between the federation and the states on the one hand and a powerful position of the Federal Chancellor vis-à-vis parliament and the Federal President on the other.

Power resources of the Federal Chancellor

The Federal Chancellor is at the centre of the political decision-making process. According to the constitution, he determines and is responsible for the general policy guidelines in domestic politics and in foreign affairs. These guidelines are binding for the departments, but it must be added that two other provisions restrict the guidelines' competence. These are the right of each minister to conduct his department independently and under his own responsibility (departmental principle or principle of ministerial autonomy), and the obligation of the cabinet as a whole to decide upon differences of opinion between ministers (cabinet principle). Within these constraints, the Federal Chancellor is head of government and controls a wider variety of major power resources (Helms 2001). The power of organization underlines the dominant position of the Chancellor. The power of organization leaves the Chancellor largely unconstrained in defining the total number, scope, and jurisdiction of the various departments of federal government except for the ministries for defence, justice, and finance which are mandatory (Schroeder 1987). In the second Schröder government starting in 2002, for example, the federal government comprised the Chancellor's Office, the Press and Information Office of the federal government, and thirteen ministries, of which ten were allocated to the Social Democratic Party, and three to the Green Party. Almost all of Schröder's predecessors had opted for a larger cabinet size, except for the first Adenauer government in 1949 with thirteen ministries. In all other legislative periods the total number of federal ministries exceeded the Adenauer and the Schröder governments. Nineteen ministries were institutionalized in the fourth Adenauer government (1961–3), twenty in the second Erhard government (1963–5), again nineteen in the grand coalition period (1966–9), sixteen in the second Brandt government (1972–4), between sixteen and seventeen in the Schmidt governments (1974–82), between sixteen and eighteen in the Kohl government of 1990–94, and sixteen in the period from 1994 to 1998.[2]

The Chancellor is also responsible for selecting and dismissing the federal ministers. But that power resource is also not unconstrained. Both formal appointment and dismissal of a federal minister require the approval of the Federal President. A similar condition marks the power of the Chancellor to nominate the Vice-Chancellor.[3] *De jure* he is largely unconstrained in that nomination. In practice, however, the role of the Vice-Chancellor, the Chancellor's deputy, is normally taken by the leading politician of the junior coalition partner. In the case of the Schröder government this was Joschka Fischer, the Minister for Foreign Affairs, a leading politician of the Green Party.

A further power resource of the Chancellor resides in his right to veto together with the Federal Minister of Public Finances those parliamentary resolutions which would raise public expenditure beyond the level stipulated in the federal budget or decrease the revenue volume defined in the budget.[4]

Moreover, in a state of defence of the nation against attack by armed forces the power of command of the army lies in the hands of the Chancellor, not in those of the President, as in the Weimar Republic. If further proof of the dominant position given to the Federal Chancellor is called for, one could point to the high unlikelihood of the dismissal of the Chancellor between two national elections. Dismissal of the head of government is permissible only via a constructive vote of no confidence in parliament. According to the constructive vote of no confidence, dismissal of the Chancellor is possible only through electing a successor with the majority of the members of parliament and by requesting the President to dismiss the Chancellor. In order to topple the Chancellor, the parliamentary opposition thus needs a majority of the votes in Parliament in favour of a new candidate. This is an institutional safeguard against destructive majorities, as in the Weimar Republic, when parliament was able to topple the Chancellor without a majority for a new candidate. Up to the time of writing, the vote of no confidence, however, has been motioned only twice in the political history of the Federal Republic of Germany—in 1972 unsuccessfully against Chancellor Brandt,[5] and on 1 October 1982 successfully, when Helmut Kohl (CDU) won the vote of no confidence against Helmut Schmidt (SPD).

Last but not least, the Federal Chancellor can count on the Chancellor's Office, the German equivalent of the Prime Minister's Office with a staff of about 500 (Helms 1996; Niclauss 2000: 67–9). The main task of the Chancellor's Office is to coordinate and supervise the activities of the federal ministries. The policy unit of the Chancellor's Office is in charge of this function and implements its task by so-called 'mirror-units', that is, policy units which mirror the jurisdiction of a single ministry, and 'cross-sectional units', or policy units whose responsibilities cut across several ministries. Furthermore it is up to the Chancellor's Office to prepare the government's policy guidelines and to supervise implementation of the directives.

The architects of Germany's constitution gave an influential position to the Federal Chancellor in order to place priority on a stable government at the cost of powerful competences of parliament. Most of the Chancellors in the Federal Republic of Germany have used the strong position which the constitution has given them, most notably Konrad Adenauer (in office from 1949 to 1963), Helmut Schmidt (Chancellor from 1974 to 82), Helmut Kohl (1982–98), Gerhard Schröder (in office since 1998), and Willy Brandt (1969–74), though to a lesser extent after his re-election in 1972. In contrast to this, Ludwig Erhard (1963–6) and Kurt Georg Kiesinger (in office from 1966 to 1969) are commonly regarded as Chancellors who did not fully exploit the potential of the office of the chief executive. There were various reasons for this, among them grand coalition requirements in the case of Kiesinger, and Erhard's weak position in the Christian Democratic parties. Konrad Adenauer, however, the first Chancellor of the Federal Republic, maintained the mightiest position of all chief executives in the Federal Republic of Germany. It was above all his method of semi-autocratic governing which resulted in a Chancellor-dominated government or 'Chancellor Democracy' (Niclauss 1988)—a method which successors of Adenauer employed with differing degrees of success. 'Chancellor Democracy' means that the Federal Chancellor is at the centre of the formal and the informal decision-making process and that he plays a central role both in domestic politics and foreign affairs. It further involves an adversarial approach which emphasizes the contrast between government and opposition. Moreover, the concept of Chancellor Democracy focuses on the plebiscitary component which a powerful Chancellor adds to political leadership.

Constraints on Chancellor Democracy

'Chancellor Democracy' points to a powerful chief executive. This supports the often cited view of Wilhelm Hennis, a famous German political scientist, that the powers of the Federal Chancellor 'leave nothing to be desired. At the moment of his election his stallion is bridled and saddled . . .' (Hennis 1964: 27). But Hennis rightly added: 'he only needs to be able to ride it' (ibid. 27). Chancellor Democracy is not to be equated with unconstrained rule. And whether the Chancellor uses the powers of his office and, if so, to what degree and with what consequences, is contigent upon a wide variety of determinants (Smith 1991). Notwithstanding the Chancellor's substantial powers, the constraints on his choices are not trivial. Constitutional rules and statute law constrain the policy and the range of options available to the Chancellor to a large degree. Moreover, governing a Chancellor Democracy is not confined to hierarchical steering, but resides also in coordination and bargaining. It thus comprises components of a 'co-ordination democracy' (Jäger 1988). In contrast to von Bismarck's 'Chancellor Dictatorship', the constraints on Chancellor Democracy result also from the need for close cooperation between the head of government on the one hand and the coalition partners, as well as the leaders of the Chancellor's party on the other.

Moreover, the patronage potential of the Federal Chancellor may exceed that of a prime minister who does not have the power of organization, but it is smaller than the patronage power of the British Prime Minister or the French President (Helms 1996a, 1996b, 2002). In the latter cases, the chief executive can appoint top positions in public administration. But that option hardly exists for the German Federal Chancellor because public administration is largely within the discretion of the states and thus beyond the reach of federal government. Furthermore, the power of the Federal Chancellor does not fully match the power of the British Prime Minister. The right to dissolve parliament is not at the disposal of the Federal Chancellor, in contrast to Britain's chief executive. As a consequence Germany's Chancellor cannot decide upon the timing of the next election. He can only indirectly work his way towards dissolution of parliament. But that presupposes, first, that parliament rejects a vote of confidence for the Chancellor and, second, that the Federal President upon the Chancellor's proposal opts for dissolution of parliament.[6]

Party politics and coalition requirements also constrain the degrees of freedom for the Federal Chancellor. The degree to which the head of government can exploit the competence to define the policy guidelines thus depends not only upon constitutional rules and regulations in the standing orders of the federal government. That degree is also contingent upon political circumstances, such as the power of the Federal Chancellor in relation to the federal ministers and the political parties in his government (Helms 2002). Of major importance is the extent to which the Federal Chancellor is able to mobilize the support of leading politicians in the coalition he presides over (Jones 1991). Of major relevance is, of course, also the composition of government, regardless of whether a single party is governing, which is rare in Germany, or a coalition, the most typical form of government in this country. When the political-ideological positions of the coalition parties differ widely and when these parties are cohesive, the room to move for the Federal Chancellor is significantly smaller. He has greater leeway for action in a government with more homogeneous policy positions and less cohesive parties, such as the CDU-CSU-led governments of the 1950s in contrast to the second half of the period of the SPD-FDP coalition from 1969 to 1982. Furthermore, the structure of a coalition makes a difference. In a surplus majority coalition, that is a coalition with a very large majority, the Chancellor's room for manoeuvre tends to be significantly smaller than in a minimum winning coalition or a minimal winning coalition (Laver and Schofield 1992). There are many other influential factors, such as the degree to which the various ministers emphasize their relative autonomy within the departments of the government and the reputation of the ministers in their parties and in the coalition as a whole. Last but not least, the organizational capacities of the Chancellor and the Chancellor's Office play a major role. And so do the leadership qualities of the head of that Office.

Whether or not the Federal Chancellor takes the cabinet as a forum and as a centre of decision making does not necessarily determine his room for manoeuvre. Helmut Schmidt, the Federal Chancellor from 1974 to 1982, for example, gave high status to the cabinet. In contrast to this, Helmut Kohl, in office from 1982 to 1998, and Gerhard Schröder, the Chancellor of the red-Green coalition which came into power in 1998, relied more upon interest aggregation, bargaining, and decision making in extra-parliamentary and extra-governmental institutions, such as coalition committees, coalition working groups, and other forms of informal deliberation and decision making, such as the Alliance for Jobs, an informal corporatist institution comprising the Federal Chancellor, ministers from federal government, trade union representatives, and spokesmen of the entrepreneurs. Finally, the personality of the Chancellor makes a difference. Strong characters like Konrad Adenauer were fully able to exploit the potential room for manoeuvre available to them. To a significant degree this pertains to Helmut Schmidt and to Helmut Kohl most notably in the process of German unification. The position held by Ludwig Erhard (in office in 1963–6) and Kurt Georg Kiesinger, the Federal Chancellor of the grand coalition between the CDU, the CSU, and the SPD in the 1966–9 period, represents the opposite pole, as typified by a famous bon mot of Kiesinger's government spokesman. Kiesinger, he argued, found himself in the role of 'a walking intermediate committee' between the two coalition parties.[7]

Rules for electing the Federal Chancellor

The rules for electing the Federal Chancellor are laid down in the constitution. According to Article 63 of the Basic Law the Federal Chancellor shall be elected without debate by the lower house of parliament upon the proposal of the Federal President. Furthermore, the candidate who obtains the votes of the majority of the members of parliament, the so-called chancellor majority, shall be elected. The person elected must be appointed by the Federal President. This has been common practice in the Federal Republic. All Federal Chancellors passed the threshold of the chancellor majority in the first ballot, regardless of whether the election of the Chancellor followed a national election, or a change in power during a legislature, a not uncommon case, as the changes in 1963, 1966, and 1982 demonstrate (see Table 2).

Article 63 defines the ' "positive" investiture requirements of the constitution' (Saalfeld 1998: 148). To rule out governments without sufficient parliamentary support is its major function. The constitution thus makes the election of the Chancellor contingent upon sufficient support of the majority in parliament. Solo runs of the Federal President against the political will of the parliamentary majority would be in vain. The Federal President rather finds himself once again restrained to a subordinate position vis-à-vis parliament.

A more complicated situation arises if the candidate proposed by the

TABLE 2	Federal Chancellors and opposition candidates, 1949–2002

Federal Chancellor and party affiliation of the Chancellor	Year of birth	Year of election	Cause of election	Opposition candidate	Vote for the Chancellor (% members of Parliament)
Konrad Adenauer (CDU)	1876	1949	Parliamentary election	Kurt Schumacher (SPD)	50.2
Konrad Adenauer (CDU)		1953	Parliamentary election	Erich Ollenhauer (SPD)	62.4
Konrad Adenauer (CDU)		1957	Parliamentary election	Erich Ollenhauer (SPD)	55.1
Konrad Adenauer (CDU)		1961	Parliamentary election	Willy Brandt (SPD)	51.7
Ludwig Erhard (CDU)	1897	1963	Adenauer's resignation	Willy Brandt (SPD)	55.9
Ludwig Erhard (CDU)		1965	Parliamentary election	Willy Brandt (SPD)	54.8
Kurt Georg Kiesinger (CDU)	1904	1966	Disintegration of the CDU/ CSU/ FDP coalition	Willy Brandt (SPD)	68.5
Willy Brandt (SPD)	1913	1969	Parliamentary election	Kurt Georg Kiesinger (CDU)	50.6
Willy Brandt (SPD)		1972	Parliamentary election	Rainer Barzel (CDU)	54.2
Helmut Schmidt (SPD)	1918	1974	Brandt's resignation	Helmut Kohl (CDU)	53.8
Helmut Schmidt (SPD)		1976	Parliamentary election	Helmut Kohl (CDU)	50.4
Helmut Schmidt (SPD)		1980	Parliamentary election	Franz-Josef Strauß (CSU)	53.6
Helmut Kohl (CDU)	1930	1982	Constructive vote of no confidence	Helmut Schmidt (SPD)	51.5
Helmut Kohl (CDU)		1983	Dissolution of Parliament	Hans-Jochen Vogel (SPD)	54.4
Helmut Kohl (CDU)		1987	Parliamentary election	Johannes Rau (SPD)	50.9
Helmut Kohl (CDU)		1990	Parliamentary election	Oskar Lafontaine (SPD)	57.1
Helmut Kohl (CDU)		1994	Parliamentary election	Rudolf Scharping (SPD)	50.3
Gerhard Schröder (SPD)	1944	1998	Parliamentary election	Helmut Kohl (CDU)	52.7
Gerhard Schröder (SPD)		2002	Parliamentary election	Edmund Stoiber (CSU)	50.6

Sources: Schindler 1999: i. 1025–7, 1117–21, iii. 4359; Frankfurter Allgemeine Zeitung, 24 Sept. 2002: 1–2, 23 Oct. 2002: 1–2.

President is not elected by the majority of the deputies to parliament. To date, this has never happened, but if it were to, the Federal President would turn into a crisis mediator. If the candidate proposed for the Chancellor's office is not elected, parliament has the choice to elect within fourteen days a Federal Chancellor with more than one-half of its members. If no candidate has been elected within this period, the constitution demands a new ballot without delay. In this ballot, however, the candidate obtaining the largest number of votes shall be elected. This ballot defines a lower threshold than the normal procedure which requires a majority of the members of the Bundestag. The further procedure depends upon the nature of the majority. If the candidate elected has obtained the votes of the chancellor majority, the Federal President must appoint him within seven days of the election. However, if the person elected does not obtain the chancellor majority, the Federal President has a choice to either appoint the person elected or dissolve parliament within seven days. This case most visibly manifests the Federal President's role as a reserve crisis manager.

The process of recruiting and selecting the head of federal government is of course influenced not only by constitutional rules. The election of the Chancellor in parliament takes place long after the candidates have been chosen in the political parties. Moreover, the selection of the candidate in the lower house depends ultimately upon the election outcome, most notably on the distribution of power between adversarial coalitions of parties. Depending upon the strength and composition of these coalitions, the candidate proposed by the Federal President is not necessarily a representative of the largest party in parliament. For example, the elections to the Bundestag in 1969, 1976 and 1980 resulted in the formation of an SPD-led government, although the SPD's share of the popular vote was smaller than the vote for the Christian Democrats. The major determinant of the selection of the Chancellor is the distribution of parliamentary seats between the parties or coalition of parties competing for office. The most likely candidate is the one who is expected to win a majority of deputies, regardless of whether he is a member from the second strongest party, such as Brandt in 1969 and Schmidt in 1976 and 1980, or a member of the strongest party, such as Adenauer (CDU) in 1949, 1953, 1957, and 1961, Erhard (CDU) in 1965, Kiesinger (CDU) in 1966, Brandt (SPD) in 1972, Kohl in the elections between 1983 and 1994, and Schröder in 1998 and 2002.

2.2 Two roles of the Federal President: guardian of ceremonial functions and potential crisis mediator

In contrast to the head of government in a presidential or semi-presidential system (the USA or France, for example), the Federal Chancellor finds no partner of equal rank in the Federal President. The President's role in post-1949 Germany has been subordinate to the Federal Chancellor and parliament both formally and informally. The constitutional restrictions imposed on the President were designed to keep the excesses of the Weimar Republic at bay (Helms 1998). In the Weimar Republic the popularly elected President was also the commander-in-chief of the armed forces and the person authorized to appoint and dismiss the Chancellor as well as dissolve parliament. This system played a fatal role in transferring power to the National Socialists when President von Hindenburg appointed Adolf Hitler as Chancellor of the Empire (*Reichskanzler*) and when the Hitler government enacted the Reichstag Fire Emergency Decree of 28 February 1933 which invalidated numerous basic rights. In contrast to the Weimar Republic, the founding fathers of the Federal Republic of Germany prevented a renewed institutionalized conflict between the head of state and the federal government by a wide variety of constitutional arrangements, including—at least in normal periods—a mainly representative and ceremonial role for the President.

This is not to belittle the importance of the Federal President. The President is the representative of the republic both at home and abroad. He is also the ceremonial head of the state. Moreover, he has a role to play in the process of government formation. He formally proposes the Federal Chancellor and the federal ministers to parliament (see section 2.1). Furthermore, he signs legislative acts. It is thus also up to the President whether a law comes into force—a hotly debated issue in Germany in 2002 when the Federal President decided on the highly controversial immigration law in favour of the red-Green coalition. In addition, it is incumbent on him to examine, and where appropriate to certify, that the legislative acts were passed in the constitutionally prescribed manner. Furthermore, the President has the right of pardon in the federation. Within his discretion is also—upon the proposal of the Federal Chancellor or other institutions—the appointment and dismissal of federal ministers, federal judges, top-level civil servants of the federation, and military officers. Moreover, in a parliamentary crisis, the Federal President adopts the role of crisis mediator and conciliator. And when the executive and the legislator are malfunctioning, such as in a state of prolonged blockade of the decision-making process, the Federal President can declare a state of legislative emergency that would enable the government to rule by decree together with the Bundesrat, the upper house.[8]

Overall, however, the founders of Germany's constitution have reserved a relatively weak role for the Federal President. The President of the Federal Republic of Germany has almost none of the competences of the President of the Weimar Republic, the *Reichspräsident*, not to mention the powers of the president of the United States of America or Russia's president. The Federal President in Germany is not the commander-in-chief. He does not play any significant role in foreign policy. There is nothing which would even faintly resemble the French President's *domain reservé* in foreign policy. In contrast to the Weimar Republic, the Federal President in post-1949 Germany neither possesses dictatorial powers nor does he have the right to govern by emergency decree. In further contrast to the Weimar Republic, his role in appointing the Chancellor is subordinate to that of the parliament. Following Walter Bagehot's famous distinction between 'efficient parts' and 'dignified parts' of the constitution (Bagehot 1963), that is, institutions which matter in the policy making process versus those which may be publicly attractive without being relevant for policy making, it can be argued that the Federal Chancellor belongs to the efficient parts. The Federal President however embodies mainly the dignified parts of the constitution. But due to insufficient power resources and a lack of tradition-based legitimacy the Federal President personifies the dignified parts of the constitution with less ceremonial appeal than a monarch. These deficits tempted a former Federal President to recommend the upgrading of the presidency through popular election and codetermination rights in the selection of federal judges and judges of the Federal Constitutional Court (von Weizsäcker 2001).

In contrast to the President of the Weimar Republic, the Federal President is not directly elected. He is elected by the Federal Convention (Bundesversammlung). The Federal Convention consists of the members of the national parliament, that is, the representatives of the federation's demos, and an equal number of members delegated from the state parliaments, representing the people of the various regional states of the federation. The term of office for the President is five years. He may be re-elected only once. The five-year limit and the rule that re-election is possible only once are supposed to ensure that the President does not accumulate too much power. Moreover, the indirect election of the President aims to avoid the rise of a new charismatic leader. Furthermore, the election in the Federal Convention emphasizes the federalist character of Germany's republic and the aspiration of the states to have equal rights. This is part of the counter-weight to partisan politics which the Federal President is supposed to represent.

In reality, however, the party state has also pervaded both the recruitment process and the election of the Federal President (Helms 1998). This pertains above all to the political status of the candidates as well as to partisan majorities and coalition politics. With the exception of two candidates nominated by the Green Party, Luise Rinser in 1984 and Jens Reich in 1994, all contestants for the presidency were affiliated to a political party. Most of them had served in major political positions before they were nominated for the presidency. In most of the presidential elections in the Federal Republic of Germany a candidate of the CDU-CSU or the Liberal Party triumphed over the Social Democratic Party (see Table 3). The first President of the Federal Republic, Theodor Heuss, was a member of the Free Democratic Party. Heuss was followed by Heinrich Lübke (CDU), who stayed in office from 1959 to 1969. Gustav Heinemann, in office from 1969 to 1974, was the first Federal President from the Social Democratic Party. Walter Scheel, a member of the liberal coalition partner of the SPD, followed Heinemann in the 1974–9 period. Karl Carstens (CDU), Heinemann's successor from 1979 until 1984, was the first of three presidents from the Christian Democratic parties. He was followed by Richard von Weizsäcker (CDU) (1984–94) and Roman Herzog (CDU), a former President of the Federal Constitutional Court (1994–9). In 1999 Johannes Rau (SPD) was elected the eighth Federal President and the second Social Democrat to hold the post.

In most of the presidential elections, the party affiliation of the elected President converged with the partisan complexion of federal government. There were only three exceptions. Two of them indicated a change in power in the near future. The election of Gustav Heinemann (SPD) in 1969 with the support of the Free Democratic Party, the opposition party at that time, underlined the intention of the liberals to consider an alliance with

TABLE 3	Presidential elections, 1949–1999

Year	Candidates	1st ballot	2nd ballot	3rd ballot	% vote in final ballot
1949	Theodor Heuss (FDP)	377	416		52.0
	Kurt Schumacher (SPD)	311	312		
	Rudolph Amelunxen (Zentrum)	37	0		
	Others	9	0		
	Abstentions	76	37		
	Invalid votes	2	3		
1954	Theodor Heuss (FDP)	871			88.2
	Others	18			
	Abstentions	95			
	Invalid votes	3			
1959	Heinrich Lübke (CDU)	517	526		50.9
	Carlo Schmid (SPD)	385	386		
	Max Becker (FDP)	104	99		
	Abstentions	25	22		
	Invalid Votes	0	0		
1964	Heinrich Lübke (CDU)	710			69.3
	Ewald Bucher (SPD)	123			
	Abstentions	187			
	Invalid votes	4			
1969	Gustav Heinemann (SPD)	514	511	512	50.0
	Gerhard Schröder (CDU)	501	507	506	
	Abstentions	5	5	5	
	Invalid votes	3	0	0	
1974	Walter Scheel (FDP)	530			51.3
	Richard von Weizsäcker (CDU)	498			
	Abstentions	5			
	Invalid votes	0			
1979	Karl Carstens (CDU)	528			51.2
	Annemarie Renger (SPD)	431			
	Abstentions	72			
	Invalid votes	1			
1984	Richard von Weizsäcker (CDU)	832			80.9
	Luise Rinser	68			
	Abstentions	117			
	Invalid votes	11			

TABLE 3	*Continued*				
Year	Candidates	1st ballot	2nd ballot	3rd ballot	% vote in final ballot
1989	Richard von Weizsäcker (CDU)	881			86.2
	Negative vote	108			
	Abstentions	30			
	Invalid votes	3			
1994	Roman Herzog (CDU)	604	622	696	52.7
	Johannes Rau (SPD)	505	559	605	
	Hildegard Hamm-Brücher (FDP)	132	126	0	
	Jens Reich	62	0	0	
	Hans Hirzel (Republikaner)	12	11	11	
	Abstentions	2	0	7	
	Invalid votes	2	1	1	
1999	Johannes Rau (SPD)	657	690		51.8
	Dagmar Schipanski (CDU)	588	572		
	Uta Ranke-Heinemann (PDS)	69	62		
	Abstentions	17	8		
	Invalid votes	2	1		

Source: Schindler, 1999: 3186–9; www.Bundestag.de/gremien/146/1549a.html 26 Feb. 2002.

the Social Democrats who were at that time the coalition partner of the Christian Democratic parties. That Karl Carstens was elected Federal President in 1979, that is, in the period of the social-liberal coalition of the SPD and the FDP, reflected the increasing power of the CDU-CSU, the Bundestag's opposition party in that period, in the Bundesrat and proved to be an early indicator of a future change in the post of the Chancellor, which materialized in the election of Helmut Kohl on 1 October 1982.

2.3 The power resources of the federal government and the veto players

The Federal Chancellor and the Federal Ministries are at the centre of executive authority in the German federation. But because the federal government is dependent upon the support of the majority in the Bundestag, the parliamentary groups of the incumbent parties are so closely linked to the government that they may also be regarded not only as a part of the legislature but also as an important element of the executive.

Which power resources are at the disposal of the federal government and the party groups in parliament upon which the government rests? And which constraints, co-governing forces, and veto players confront the federal government? The federal government controls a wide variety of instruments and assets. Privileged constitutional powers deserve to receive attention first. The federal government is the major part of the executive of the whole Federation, the *Bund*. It is to that extent more important than the executive of the semi-autonomous states (*Länder*), although these are governed by influential minister-presidents, and far more important than local government and the various parapublic institutions.

Exclusive and concurrent legislation

Measured by legislative powers, the Federation (*Bund*) has the power of exclusive legislation and concurrent legislation. The power of exclusive legislation includes overall authority of the federation over foreign policy, defence, civil and criminal law, regulation of citizenship, and other regulatory functions of domestic policy, broadly similar to those of the British Home Office or the American Department of the Interior. Moreover the Federation has extended powers of legislation in a state of defence.[9]

Considerable powers of the Federation are also associated with concurrent legislation. In this field, the Federation has the power to legislate over all matters deemed in need of uniform rules across the country. The precondition is that the intervention of the Federation is necessitated by the establishment of equal living conditions or the preservation of legal and economic unity.[10] These clauses have been the entrance door for the federal government to intervene in a wide variety of policy areas. These include civil law, commercial law, atomic energy, labour law, housing, air pollution, and social policy arrangements such as social insurance for the aged, health insurance, and unemployment insurance.[11] The Federation has fully used the possibility to extend its regulation via concurrent legislation. It has thus become deeply involved in policy areas which were initially mainly under the rule of the states. The outcome has been increasing centralization and reduced autonomy of the states, because the states have concurrent legislative power only as long as and to the extent that the Federation does not exercise its right to legislate by statute. However, the loss of the autonomy of the states due to transfer of sovereignty to the Federation has at least partially been compensated by extended codetermination of the state executives in the institutions of cooperative federalism and the potential to review, amend, or block any federal legislation that is deemed to affect the interests of the states.

Complementary power resources of federal government

The power resources of the federal government include indirect control of a privileged position in parliament, the centre of legislative decision making (von Beyme 1997), as long as the parliamentary groups of the incumbent parties support the government. But that has been standard in the political history of the Federal Republic of Germany. The major links are the two roles which the parliamentary groups of the incumbent parties can adopt in the lower house: first, the role of the legislative agenda-setter, that is, an actor who largely decides which issues will be put on or excluded from the political agenda and, second, the role of the legislative veto player, whose consent is required for legislative change.

The impact on recruitment and selection of candidates to top-level positions in the judiciary and the executive is also part of the power resources of the federal government and the parliamentary groups of the governing parties. For example, half of the members of the Federal Constitutional Court are elected by the Bundestag, and half by the Bundesrat.[12] The federation also has an important voice in the nomination of judges of the highest courts at the level of the federation.[13] Another major resource of the federal government consists of proposals for the appointment of the president, vice-president, and other members of the board of directors of the German Central Bank. Formal appointment falls to the Federal President, but the proposal of the candidates, commonly regarded as the decisive move, is up to the federal government.

The constitution authorizes the federal government to appeal to the Federal Constitutional Court. This involves a further power resource of the government. The appeal to the Federal Constitutional Court may be direct or indirect. The indirect appeal requires the cooperation of the parliamentary groups of the governing parties and demands a formal appeal to the Constitutional Court from the parliament. A direct appeal to the

Federal Constitutional Court is permissible for the federal government in four different cases: (1) in a so-called abstract judicial review of the constitutionality of an act, (2) in a concrete review of the constitutionality of a specific act, (3) in the case of litigation between organs of the state (Article 93 I, Basic Law) and disputes between the federation and the states according to Articles 93 I and 84 IV of the Basic Law. (4) The federal government can also put in a claim for a ban on an unconstitutional political party (see Chapter 4).

The power resources of the federal government include the delivery of a wide variety of goods and services. These comprise patronage, for example appointment of party members to posts in administration, financial aid for specific target groups, and legislation in favour of the social constituencies of the government.

The federal government can also use the power of moral suasion to get things done. Bilateral or multilateral relations with strategically positioned interest groups may be one form of exerting governmental influence. Examples include bilateral deals between the government and single interest groups as well as corporatist arrangements between representatives of the government, labour, and entrepreneurs, such as the Alliance for Jobs in the Schröder government.

Tax revenue and public expenditure

Last but not least the federal government controls a proportion of the total tax revenue and the public budget. In both respects, however, the role for the federal government is limited. Taxation is mainly organized as a highly interdependent mix of state government and federal government policy. Moreover, the total share of the fiscal resources at the federal government's disposal is relatively moderate: the total expenditure of the federal government amounts to less than 30 per cent of the total outlay of general government[14] or broadly 13 per cent of gross domestic product.[15] Both proportions are small by international comparison. Both point to massive restrictions on the manoeuvrability of the federal government—for economic demand management and for all other activities with impacts on taxation and spending (Scharpf 1988). The German federal government is in terms of budgets, thus, rather a poor cousin, than a rich uncle.

However, three caveats must be added. First, the volume of the fiscal resources of federal government is not marginal. At stake is a substantial amount of money—265 billion euros in 2000, for example.[16] Secondly, the federal budget supports vital functions such as defence, transport, spending on research and development, and broadly a quarter of the total social budget. Thirdly, the reach of the federal government is not confined to the federal budget. Decisions of the federal government also impact directly or indirectly on the taxation and spending of state governments, local government, and social insurance funds. It can even be argued that the relatively small budget of the federal government creates a strong incentive to shift as much of the cost of federal legislation as possible to the states (which control the major part of public administration), the social insurance funds (in charge of a major part of social security), and local government (which is in charge of social assistance, the bottom social safety net, and thus plays the part of a deficiency guarantee for federal government).

Constraints and veto players

How important are the power resources of the federal government in Germany? The answers to this question differ. One school of thought sees an impressive accumulation of political power in the federal government, above all in those political parties which control the government. Others regard the power resources of the federal executive in Germany as moderate at the most. Proponents of this view emphasize the fragmentation of power resulting from federalism. Support for this view comes also from scholars who regard politics in the Federal Republic of Germany as subordinate to the judiciary. Proponents of a fourth view emphasize the economic constraints on policy makers, most notably the momentum of a market economy and the impact of globalization, and point to the limits of national policy solutions imposed by transnational organization, such as the European Union. Others argue that one needs to balance the power resources of the federal government against the resources of the many 'co-governing actors' and 'veto players' in Germany's polity. In this view, the German federal government is at best 'semi-sovereign'. Historical and international comparisons indeed reveal a 'semisovereign state' (Katzenstein 1987). In that state the government's room for manoeuvre has been narrowly circumscribed. Cross-national comparison also shows that the Federal Republic is a state full of co-governors[17] and veto players.[18] Compared with other constitutional democracies, an unusually large number of veto players and co-governing institutions constrain the steering capacity of the federal government in Germany (Schmidt 2000: table 7; Schmidt 2002c). These constraints include

- a parliamentary government as opposed to a presidential system and, hence, a higher vulnerability of the government to parliamentary veto players;
- coalition government as the most typical form as opposed to a single-party government and, hence, higher costs in consensus formation;
- high thresholds for changes of the constitution which provide 'veto points' (Immergut 1992: 27–8) to the opposition party and the upper house (as opposed to a system of government without opposition);
- extended judicial review including abstract review of the constitutionality of legislative acts (rather than a politicized pattern);
- advanced minority protection mainly through the constitutionally guaranteed basic rights (in contrast to unconstrained majority rule);
- delegation of public functions to expert institutions, such as an autonomous Central Bank and institutions for safeguarding a free and competitive market;
- delegation of public functions to interest associations and self-administrating communities, such as social insurance and autonomous collective bargaining between employers' and employees' associations on wages and working conditions;
- self-administration at the local level and in higher education, such as in the university system;
- constraints due to the transfer of sovereignty to international organizations, such as NATO and the World Trade Organization, as well as transnational organizations, for example the EU;
- power sharing between the federal government and the state governments;
- frequently divergent majorities in the lower and the upper house, largely due to non-synchronized trends in party support in lower house elections and in the parliamentary election in the states;
- and last but not least the quasi-permanent electoral campaign in

Germany which results from the high frequency of national elections and state-level elections of national importance.

The implication of the large number of potentially co-governing actors and veto players in Germany is twofold. First, it strengthens the hybrid character of the Federal Republic which fuses majoritarian and non-majoritarian elements. The non-majoritarian component resides in the numerous co-governing forces and veto points and in the unanimity or near-unanimity required to overcome a veto. Secondly, governing within this context is particularly cumbersome and time-consuming. The leeway for action on the part of the government is relatively small, the cost involved in widening the room for manoeuvre is considerable, and the price to be paid for the consent of all veto players is high. It often includes reduced redistribution, considerable time-lags, and highly fragmented problem solving. Moreover, the window of opportunity for large-scale reforms is often closed and difficult to open. These restrictions do not necessarily imply immobile policy making. But the cost involved in delivering major policy changes tends to be significantly higher than the cost of reform policy making in a state with few veto players and co-governing institutions, other things being equal.[19]

All co-governing forces and veto players mentioned above are major political actors in the Federal Republic of Germany. But two groups of veto players are particularly important. These are the political parties in a coalition and the key actors in Germany's federalism. Both the political parties and Germany's federalism will be discussed in more detail in the two following sections.

2.4 The rise of the 'party state' and the partisan composition of government

The government of the Federal Republic of Germany has been notorious not only for an influential Chancellor and the weak role of the President, but also for the important part played by the political parties.

Indicators of the importance of political parties
One indicator of the important role played by political parties is the

attention given to the parties in the constitutions and the statute law. In contrast to the pre-1949 regimes in Germany and in further contrast to most other modern democracies, the political rights and obligations of political parties are spelled out in the Federal Republic's constitution and statute law, most notably in the Law on Parties. The rights of the political parties include officially guaranteed participation 'in forming the political will of the people'.[20] A second indicator of the major part played by the parties is that they are entitled to receive sumptuous subsidies from public budgets of up to one-half of their total annual revenue. The other side of the coin consists of obligations of the parties. The precondition of full integration is that the parties are committed to the constitution and that their internal organization meets democratic norms. Moreover, the parties have to publicly account for the sources and use of their funds and for their assets. A third indicator of a powerful role for the parties can be derived from the weakness of plebiscitary institutions at the level of the federation, though not necessarily at the regional and local level (see section 5.6 below). But the weakness of direct democracy at the federal level enhances the importance of political parties in the policy process and tends to isolate their manoeuvrability from short-term responsiveness and short-circuited accountability to the preferences of the people. Fourthly, the political parties have largely exploited the scope for action made available to them. According to a widely shared view the outcome has been a party state (*Parteienstaat*), that is, a state dominated by political parties and marked by massive party-based patronage.[21]

The party-state view rightly emphasizes that political parties in Germany (as well as in other democratic nations) have been among the winners of the process of democratization. The party-state view also correctly argues that political parties have gained major importance in parliamentary democracies (Budge and Keman 1990), while their impact in presidential systems tends to be more muted. Experiences with political parties in the Federal Republic support this view: the political parties indeed monopolize recruitment and selection of parliamentary deputies and government officials in Germany. Furthermore, party-based patronage exists in the Federal Republic, although its magnitude is not comparable to the massive party patronage seen in Austria, particularly in the period of oversized coalitions between Austria's Socialists and the People's Party (1949–66 and 1987–2000). But there is ample evidence in support of the view that party-based patronage exists in Germany and that it clashes with the constitutional rule that 'every German is equally eligible for any public office according to his aptitude, qualifications, and professional achievements'.[22] In reality however, targeted appointment of party members for posts in public administration, the judiciary, and radio and TV corporations does occur. And the appointment of party members for posts in public or semi-public corporations such as public transport corporations and half-public, half-private savings banks at the state level and at the local level is not too rare (von Arnim 2001a, 2001b; Huber 1994).

The political parties are also commonly blamed for lack of responsiveness, for paternalistic-authoritarian treatment of the voters, overgenerous methods of public funding, and exploitation of a majority position for example by recruiting a large proportion of deputies to one of the numerous posts of Parliamentary Secretary of State in the Bundestag, a trend which tends to blur the borderline between the powers of the executive and the legislature (Huber 1994: 692).

Overall, political parties as well as their leading representatives and experts have gained influential positions in national and subnational political processes, elections, and recruitment of political leaders and administrative experts. Parties have also been important in laying down guidelines for policy making for incoming governments and in filling posts in government and administration. Party membership has also played a significant role in formally autonomous institutions such as the Federal Court of Justice and the German Central Bank (Wagschal 2001a).

Constraints on the party state

Proponents of the party-state view tend to exaggerate the influence of the political parties in the Federal Republic of Germany. They tend to neglect the wide variety of institutional restrictions on party behaviour in today's Germany. Examples include the important role, if not supremacy, of the law in the country, the existence of the Federal Constitutional Court as the guardian of the constitution, the momentum and selectivity inherent in intergovernmental relations between the federal government and the state executive authorities, the constraints stemming from the high level of integration of Germany in international and supranational organizations, such as the European Union, and the vulnerability to economic imperatives from global markets. In addition, the numerous veto players in Germany's political system of today play an important role. Moreover, studies in electoral behaviour point to partisan dealignment, a process which constrains the reach of the parties. Furthermore, the mass media have taken over many of the communication functions that parties once performed for themselves and the electorate. Another apparent threat to the role of political parties resides in the growth of interest groups and informal corporatist alliances between interest groups and government. In addition, decreasing proportions of party members as a percentage of the electorate speak against rather than for the party-state view.[23] And the negative image of most political parties among younger age groups cannot be regarded as supporting the party-state theory.

Furthermore, the influence of political parties on politics and society is not a constant. The partisan influence on politics and society rather varies from country to country, from one policy area to the other and from period to period. The Federal Constitutional Court in Germany for example, influenced by the theory of the party state advanced by Gerhard Leibholz (1951, 1966), a leading judge in the German Constitutional Court in the 1950s and 1960s, had long regarded political parties as privileged linkages between government and people and rewarded them accordingly through generous provision of public funds. Later the pendulum swung back to a more critical and restrictive view of the parties' role and their entitlement to receive public money.

Indicators such as the dominance or hegemony of political parties in recruiting and choosing political leaders, the control of government, and patronage suggest that party-state structures in the Federal Republic of Germany are strong. But in the light of these criteria and others, such as coalition building and party membership as a percentage of the population, the Federal Republic is not number one among the party states. Politicians in other countries have pushed the party state to a much higher level. This is the case in Austria and possibly Sweden, if collective membership of trade unions in parties is taken into account, and also in the former socialist countries in Central and Eastern Europe (Katz and Mair 1992).

The role played by parties also differs from one policy area to the other. In some of these areas the role of political parties is strong, for example in social policy, in others moderate or weak. Examples of the latter include chiefly policy domains governed by experts, such as monetary policy and competition policy. And despite the central roles of political parties in recruiting and selecting judges of the Federal Constitutional Court, the decisions and the non-decisions taken in the Court mostly follow the logic of juridical reasoning and constitutional rules rather than the tune of party competition (see Chapter 4 below).

Parties in government

The major parties in the Federal Republic of Germany before and after unification have been the Christian Democrats, the CDU and its Bavarian sister organization the CSU, and the Social Democrats (SPD). However, both parties have lacked the strength to position themselves as single governing parties at the national level. Both parties entered coalitions usually with smaller parties in order to gain the reins of power. At the time of writing—in October 2002—the Federal Republic of Germany is in the fourth year of a red-Green coalition made up of the Social Democratic Party and Alliance '90/The Greens. While Green parties have entered broad coalitions in Finland (1995), Italy (1996), France (1997), and Belgium (1999), a red-Green alliance in control of central government such as in Germany since 1998 is novel. But it must be added that red-Green experiments were not unfamiliar at the regional level before 1998, because the SPD and the Green Party entered coalitions in the states of Hesse, North Rhine-Westphalia, Berlin, Brandenburg, and Schleswig-Holstein, as well as in local government before that time (Lees 2000).

Participation in government at the national level however was until 1998 almost exclusively a privilege for established parties, most notably for the Christian Democrats, the Social Democrats, and the Liberals, with minor exceptions in the 1950s (see Table 4). Measured by the average share of the vote in national parliamentary elections between 1949 and December 2001, the Christian Democratic parties have been the most successful in elections of candidates to the Bundestag: 44.1 per cent of the popular vote went on average to the CDU and CSU, followed by the Social Democratic Party, which mobilized 37.5 per cent.[24] However, the Christian Democratic Party's control of the reins of power has been contingent upon parliamentary support from smaller coalition partners—with the exception of the national election in 1957, in which the CDU-CSU gained more than 50 per cent of the votes.

Among the smaller parties the Free Democratic Party has long been strategically positioned. Until unification in 1990 the FDP had been the king-maker, the needed pivotal party. In this period the FDP's coalitional strategy largely determined access to the reins of power. Coalitions with the FDP opened the road to power in federal government for the CDU-CSU in 1949–66 and 1982–98, while SPD-FDP coalitions have held on to the reins of power in 1969–82.

Indicators of the party make-up of national governments reflect the central position which the Liberals have held over an extended period. Although the smallest of the three established parties, the FDP has spent almost thirty-one years in government in the period from September 1949 to October 2002 (1949–56, 1961–6, and 1969–98, with a short interval in 1962 and in September 1982, the latter due to the dissolution of the SPD-FDP coalition). The SPD has had to content itself with twenty years in office (1966–82 and from 1998 until the time of writing). In contrast to this, the Christian Democratic parties, although of an electoral strength more than four times greater than the Liberals, have spent thirty-six years in office (1949–69 and 1982–98) and thus only six years more than the Liberals.

More sophisticated measures of the party composition of governments yield more valid data. The parties' share of cabinet seats is a particularly valid and reliable indicator. According to this measure, 52.4 per cent of the cabinet seats in the Federal Republic in 1950–2001 were held by the Christian Democratic parties, 25.7 per cent were taken by the SPD, 17.1 per cent went to the Liberals, and 5.6 per cent fell to other parties or non-party ministers.

Leftist parties in the federal government compared

Compared with other democracies in the post-Second World War period, centre-left or left-wing parties have participated in national government in Germany to a relatively small extent (Schmidt 1982a, 1982b, 2002c; Merkel 1993). But it must added that the most important centre-left party, the SPD, has played a more important role in the state governments, most notably in the north and the west of the country, and gained a strength in office equal to that of the Christian Democrats (Bauer 1998; Wagschal 2001b). At the federal level, however, the SPD's cabinet-seat share from 1950 to 2001—25.7 per cent—was lower than the cabinet-seat shares of the Social Democratic or Labour parties in Australia (30.7 per cent), Austria

TABLE 2 **The party political composition of the federal government, 1949–2002**

Legislative period	Date of formation of government	Chancellor (party affiliation)	Coalition type and coalition partners	Type of majority	Coalition type
1 (1949–1953)	15 Sept. 1949	Adenauer (CDU)	small coalition: CDU-CSU, FDP, DP	absolute majority	MW
2 (1953–1957)	9 Oct. 1953	Adenauer (CDU)	small coalition: CDU-CSU, FDP, DP, GB/BHE	two-thirds majority	SM
	23 July 1955	Adenauer (CDU)	small coalition: CDU-CSU, FDP, DP	absolute majority	SM
	21 March 1956	Adenauer (CDU)	small coalition: CDU-CSU, DP(FVP)	absolute majority	SM
3 (1957–1961)	22 Oct. 1957	Adenauer (CDU)	small coalition: CDU-CSU, DP	absolute majority	S
	20 Sept. 1960	Adenauer (CDU)	CDU-CSU coalition	absolute majority	S
4 (1961–1965)	17 Nov. 1961	Adenauer (CDU)	small coalition: CDU-CSU, FDP	absolute majority	SM
	19 Nov. 1962	Adenauer (CDU)	CDU-CSU	minority government	MIN S
	11 Dec. 1962	Adenauer (CDU)	small coalition: CDU-CSU, FDP	absolute majority	SM
	16 Oct. 1963	Erhard (CDU)	small coalition: CDU-CSU, FDP	absolute majority	SM
5 (1965–1969)	20 Oct. 1965	Erhard (CDU)	small coalition: CDU-CSU, FDP	absolute majority	SM
	28 Oct. 1966	Erhard (CDU)	CDU-CSU	minority government	MIN
	1 Dec. 1966	Kiesinger (CDU)	grand coalition: CDU-CSU, SPD	two-thirds majority	SM

Legislative period	Date	Chancellor	Party composition	Majority	Status
6 (1969–1972)	24 Oct. 1969	Brandt (SPD)	small coalition: SPD, FDP	absolute majority	MW, later MIN
7 (1972–1976)	14 Dec. 1972	Brandt (SPD)	small coalition: SPD, FDP	absolute majority	SM
	16 May 1974	Schmidt (SPD)	small coalition: SPD, FDP	absolute majority	SM
8 (1976–1980)	15 Dec. 1976	Schmidt (SPD)	small coalition: SPD, FDP	absolute majority	MW
9 (1980–1983)	5 Nov. 1980	Schmidt (SPD)	small coalition: SPD, FDP	absolute majority	MW
	17 Sept. 1982	Schmidt (SPD)	single party government: SPD	minority government	MIN
	1 Oct.	Kohl (CDU)	small coalition: CDU-CSU, FDP	absolute majority	SM
10 (1983–1987)	29 Mar. 1983	Kohl (CDU)	small coalition: CDU-CSU, FDP	absolute majority	SM
11 (1987–1990)	11 Mar. 1987	Kohl (CDU)	small coalition: CDU-CSU, FDP	absolute majority	MW
12 (1990–1994)	17 Jan. 1991	Kohl (CDU)	small coalition: CDU-CSU, FDP	absolute majority	SM
13 (1994–1998)	15 Nov. 1994	Kohl (CDU)	small coalition: CDU-CSU, FDP	absolute majority	SM
14 (1998–2002)	27 Oct. 1998	Schröder (SPD)	small coalition: SPD, Bündnis' 90/Die Grünen	absolute majority	SM
15 (2002–2006)	22 Nov. 2002	Schröder (SPD)	small coalition: SPD, Bündnis' 90/ Die Grünen	absolute majority	SM

Sources: Schindler 1999: i. 1141–9, iii. 4359–64.

Note: Column 1: Legislative period; column 2: date of formation of government (including date of election of the Federal Chancellor in the Bundestag); column 3: name of Federal Chancellor; column 4: party composition of federal government; column 5: type of majority or minority government; column 6: coalitional status (MIN = minority government or no majority, MW = minimal winning coalition, S = single party government, SM = surplus majority); for details of operationalization see Gallagher, Laver, and Mair 2001.

(54.5), Belgium (30.6), Denmark (54.9), Finland (30.2), Britain (33.3), Luxembourg (29.2), New Zealand (27.6), Norway (71.7), Sweden (77.3), Greece (34.7), and Spain (49.2 per cent in the 25 years since the onset of democracy).[25] Furthermore, and unlike single-party governments of a social democratic complexion, such as in Austria, Australia, Britain, or a Sweden, the German Social Democratic Party has shared power with other parties when participating in national government. These coalitions include a league with the CDU-CSU from 1966 to 1969, an alliance with the Liberals over a period of thirteen years, in 1969–82, and a partnership with the Green Party from 1998 until the time of writing. In contrast to the Swedish or Norwegian Social Democratic party and in further contrast to Labour parties in the Anglo-American democracies, the SPD has never been a hegemonic party in national government. Moreover, relative to the vote share gained in parliamentary elections, the Social Democratic Party has held the reins of power less frequently, while the degree of over-representation in office of the Liberals can hardly be overlooked (see Table 4).

Christian Democratic and Liberal parties in office

While the leftist parties in post-1949 Germany have participated in federal government to a moderate degree, the Christian Democratic parties, members of the family of centrist and centre-right parties, have gained a particularly powerful role in governing Germany at the national level.[26] Cross-national comparisons support this view. The high share of cabinet seats held by the CDU-CSU—51.4 per cent in 1950–2001—has been surpassed only by three other centrist parties. These are Italy's Democrazia Cristiana from 1950 to its dissolution in 1994, the Dutch Christen Demokratisch Appell, and the Canadian Liberal Party.[27]

The liberal Free Democratic Party has also played an important part in the cabinets of federal government in Germany. According to comparative data on cabinet seat shares of liberal parties in Western democracies since 1950, Germany is a member of a group of countries—composed of Belgium, Denmark, Finland, Iceland, Luxembourg, Netherlands, Portugal, and Switzerland—in which the liberal parties' participation in office (17.1 per cent in 1950–2001) exceeded the 10-percentage point mark.[28]

Last but not least, no secular-conservative party plays a role in Germany's party system and the political composition of the government both at the national and the regional level.[29] This is one of the most important political differences between the Federal Republic and countries in which secular conservatives have been the major incumbent party, such as in Japan (cabinet-seat share of secular conservative party 1950–2001 96.7 per cent) and the English-speaking family of nations, that is Australia (69.3 per cent), Great Britain (66.7 per cent), Ireland (67.7 per cent), New Zealand (71.5 per cent), and the United States of America (55.7 per cent), except Canada.[30]

Portfolios

Parties prefer specific portfolios and distance themselves from others, depending upon their political programme and the preferences of their social constituencies. The overall pattern of the distribution of federal ministries in Germany after 1949 has been as follows: the largest party in a coalition usually takes the Ministry of Finance, the Ministry of Labour and Social Affairs, the Ministry of Defence, frequently also the Ministry of the Interior as well as the more state-interventionist ministries, such as Transport, Post, and Telecommunications as well as Research and Technology. In centre-right-liberal coalitions and in coalitions between a centre-left party and the Liberals, the Free Democrats frequently gained control of the Ministry of Justice, the Ministry of Economics, and the Foreign Office. The ministries in the law-and-order domain, thus, have mainly been within the jurisdiction of centre-right or liberal tendencies with the exception of the red-Green governments since 1998. In contrast to this, the ministries at the heart of the welfare state have been allocated to the CDU-CSU or to the SPD, thereby restoring the centrist stance that characterized social policy in the Federal Republic of Germany and in the Weimar Republic until 1930. Furthermore, the Green Party, in power since 1998, has gained cabinet seats in foreign policy, regulation of atomic energy, health care, and, in 2001, in exchange for health care, consumer protection and agriculture. All other cabinet seats in the post-1998 period were allocated to the SPD, including the fusion of the former Ministry of Economics and two major divisions of the Ministry for Labour and Social Affairs in October 2002.

2.5 German federalism, or where the 'princes of the states' congregate

Germany is a federal republic. Like other federalist systems the architecture of Germany's political system is far more complex than the structure of a centralized unitary state, such as Britain prior to devolution, France, New Zealand, and the Netherlands. A polycentric multi-level system characterizes modern Germany. It is a country with seventeen governments: one in the guise of the federal government, located in the capital, Berlin, and one in each of the sixteen member states' polities (see Table 5). Membership in the European Union enhances this pattern by adding a further level to the complex multi-level system of governance.

A country with seventeen governments

A large number of collective actors and institutions participate in the political process and in policy making in Germany. Among these, the federation (*Bund*) with the federal government and the political parties on top, the sixteen semi-autonomous states (*Länder*), the Bundesrat, the council of the representatives of the sixteen state governments, a wide variety of cooperative institutions between the federation and the states, such as planning committees for the joint tasks of the federal government and the state executives, and numerous horizontal networks between the states deserve to be named first.

Each of the sixteen constituent states of Germany's federalism has the full outfit of government. Each state is headed by a minister-president, elected in the state parliament. Each state has its own constitution, co-government, legislation, and administration. Most of the states have a constitutional court of their own. Following the guidelines of the constitution (see Chapter 1), all German states have a parliamentary government responsible to an elected assembly, not a presidential system. In contrast to the pre-unification period, in which the Federal Republic comprised ten economically relatively homogeneous states and West Berlin, the post-1990 federalism has been marked by sharp economic disparities mainly between the poor states in the eastern part of the country, the area of the former socialist German Democratic Republic, and wealthier or rich states in the western part. The difference between the poorest and the richest state is twice the difference between the poorest and the wealthiest state in the USA.[31] Moreover, the accession of the former German Democratic Republic to the Federal Republic of Germany in 3 October 1990 has shifted the balance at least partly in favour of the northern and Protestant areas and also in favour of a majority of poor states in the east and less wealthy states in the west.

Although their powers may appear limited—their original powers are mainly police, education, cultural affairs, and local government—the states play a key role in politics and policy making in Germany (Jeffery 1999a, 1999b). It has even been argued that Germany is 'a republic of the states' princes'[32] (Steffani 1983: 199) with the minister-presidents as the republican version of the earlier princes of the states. This mirrors the important role of the states in federal legislation, their predominance in administration, and the national importance of most elections of state parliaments, but it also reflects the central role of the minister-presidents in Germany's federalism and in the political parties both at the *Land* and the federal level (Schneider 2001).

The Bundesrat

The power of the states is most visibly institutionalized in the Bundesrat, the collective representation of the states at the federal level. In contrast to the US Senate, which consists of elected representatives of the states, the Bundesrat is composed of members of the state governments which appoint and recall the deputies. The Bundesrat can thus be regarded as a delegated upper house, a 'conclave of states', and as a bureaucratic council following earlier precedents in German history closely (Lehmbruch 2000b, 2002). The present Bundesrat is the direct heir of older institutions. Among these, the Reichsrat, the upper house of the Weimar Republic, the Bundesrat of Imperial Germany, an ambassador's conference, and the institutional tradition dating back to the seventeenth century deserve particular mention. In further contrast to the Senate of the United States of America, the votes of the states in the German Bundesrat may be cast only as a block vote. If they do not meet that requirement, the dominant theory among experts in constitutional law goes, they will be counted as invalid.[33]

The votes of the states differ by size, but only moderately. This creates astounding differences in representation. The Basic Law allocates at least three votes to each state.[34] States with more than 2 million inhabitants have four, states with more than 6 million inhabitants five, and since 1990 states with more than 7 million inhabitants have six votes. The latter change served to provide the larger states, which pay for most of the fiscal redistribution from richer to poorer regions, with a blocking minority against the two-thirds majority that an amendment to the constitution requires in the Bundesrat. But despite this change in the constitution, the smaller states are still heavily over-represented in the Bundesrat. For example, Bremen with 660,000 inhabitants in 2001 has three votes, while 18 million North Rhine-Westphalians are represented in the Bundesrat with six votes only. It must be added, however, that over-representation of the small states in the Bundesrat is less extreme than over-representation in the US Senate and the Swiss Ständerat in which each state or, conversely, each *Kanton*, has two seats.

The Bundesrat plays a key role in the policy process. This largely reflects the central position of the upper house in federal legislation (see also sections 3.3 and 3.4 below), which turns Germany into a case of strong symmetrical bicameralism (Lijphart 1999: 214, 314; Vatter 2002). Legislative change of the constitution requires two-thirds majorities in the lower and upper houses. Thus, the majority of the votes in the Bundesrat can veto a change in the constitution desired by the federal government and the majority of the lower house. The Bundesrat also plays a powerful role in legislation below the level of constitutional change. Besides the case of exclusive legislation of the federation, such as in foreign policy and protection of the constitutional democracy, federal legislation which directly affects the interest of the states is liable to the consent of the Bundesrat. Five to six out of ten bills and, in practice, most legislation on major domestic issues, have since the late 1950s been subject to an affirmative vote of the Bundesrat.[35] The Bundesrat, thus, controls a veto point of greatest strategic importance. And even in legislation which does not require the consent of the Bundesrat, the upper house possesses a qualified veto. The Bundesrat can require a reconciliation procedure on controversial legislation regardless of whether its consent is formally required. When the reconciliation procedure has been exhausted, the Bundesrat may still raise an objection to a bill. This objection amounts to a qualified veto. If the veto is based on an absolute majority in the Bundesrat, it can be overcome by an absolute majority in the lower house of parliament, the Bundestag. If the objection is based on a two-thirds majority, the Bundestag can override the objection of the Bundesrat only with a two-thirds majority.

Dependence on the states in federal legislation constrains the steering capacity of the federal government to a large extent. The federal government, thus, often finds itself exposed to a situation in which it is not at all sovereign but rather dependent upon bargaining and consensus with the majority of the states in the Bundesrat. Even harsher are these constraints if rival majorities exist in the Bundestag and Bundesrat. This situation is not rare. Particularly dramatic are periods in which the opposition party in the lower house can count on the majority of the seats in the upper house. This was the case from June 1972 to March 1977 and from June 1978 to 1 October 1982 in the era of the SPD-FDP coalition (1969–82). The opposition party also controlled the majority in the Bundesrat in the period from June 1990 to November 1990 and from April 1996 to the end of the Kohl government in October 1998.[36] It is chiefly in these periods that 'party politicization' (Ismayr 2000: 23) overrides the Bundesrat's role of a counterweight to partisan politics (Lehmbruch 2000a).

The situation after the election in Saxony-Anhalt in April 2002 was even more complicated. The federal government, a red-Green coalition with a solid majority in the lower house of parliament, found itself confronted with a red-Green minority in the Bundesrat, a minority of SPD-led governments, a majority of CDU-led states, and two grand coalition states in Bremen and Brandenburg. A majority in the Bundesrat requires 35 out of a total of 69 votes. However, only 10 of the total 69 votes fell on red-Green coalitions in the states, namely North Rhine-Westphalia and Schleswig-Holstein. Although other SPD-led governments—among them the coalition of the SPD and the Party of Democratic Socialism (PDS) in Berlin—controlled 21 votes, the total number of votes for all SPD-led states amounted to 27 only (see Table 5).

In these circumstances, the federal government and the political parties on which it is based need not only the agreement of the majority of the states executives in order to pass legislation. They also need agreement from states governed or co-governed by the opposition party of the Bundestag. Thus, the governance of the Federal Republic through legislation often requires the formation of a grand coalition of the incumbent parties and the major opposition party as well as a coalition of the federal government and the majority of the state governments. Government in Germany thus often means government together with the opposition—unless the federal government finds ways and means to circumvent the power of

TABLE 5	The Bundesrat on 1 October 2002	
State	Parties in power	Votes in the Bundesrat
Baden-Württemberg	CDU + FDP	6
Bavaria	CSU	6
Berlin	SPD + PDS	4
Brandenburg	SPD + CDU	4
Bremen	SPD + CDU	3
Hamburg	CDU + FDP + Party of Rule of Law-Offensive	3
Hessen	CDU + FDP	5
Lower Saxony	SPD	6
Mecklenburg-West Pomerania	SPD + PDS	3
North Rhine-Westphalia	SPD + B90/Green Party	6
Rhineland-Palatinate	SPD + FDP	4
Saarland	CDU	3
Saxony	CDU	4
Saxony-Anhalt	CDU + FDP	4
Schleswig-Holstein	SPD + B90/Green Party	4
Thuringia	CDU	4
Total		69

Notes: Majority: 35 votes. CDU- and CSU-led governments (except grand coalitions between CDU and SPD): 35 votes, SPD-led governments (excluding grand coalitions): 27 votes, CDU/SPD-coalitions: 7 votes.
Party labels:
B90/Green Party = Bündnis '90/Die Grünen
CDU = Christian Democratic Union
CSU = Christian Social Union
FDP = Free Democratic Party
PDS = Party of Democratic Socialism
SPD = Social Democratic Party

the opposition party in the Bundesrat, for example by mobilizing support of one or two states governed or co-governed by the Christian Democratic Party.

Taxation: mainly a joint enterprise of federal government and states

The division of labour in taxation and administration strengthens the interdependence between federal government and states. Taxation is mainly a joint enterprise of the federation and the states. The revenues from the major taxes, mainly income tax, property tax and sales tax, are allocated to the federal government, the states, and local government according to rules specified mostly in the constitution. Changing these constitutional rules presupposes once again two-thirds majorities in the lower house and the Bundesrat. Thus, most policy changes in taxation presuppose compromise seeking and a high degree of consensus not only between the federal government and the state governments, but also between the incumbent parties and the major opposition parties. The room for manoeuvre for autonomous taxation policies is thus narrowly circumscribed for both the federal government and the states governments. Here, as in other areas of Germany's public policy, complex networks have emerged in which competition *and* cooperation, majority rule *and* bargaining, as well as competitive democracy *and* consociational practices prevail.

Administration: mainly a function of the states

A further key to Germany's federalism resides in administration and in the process of implementing federal legislation. Administration is mainly within the jurisdiction of the states. In most policy areas the states are the single responsible administrative agent for the federation. In contrast to the United States of America, the German federal government does not have an administrative infrastructure of its own at the regional or local level—with a few exceptions, mainly defence and foreign policy. Thus, most federal ministries do not possess the resources necessary to implement and monitor the policies enacted by the federal government.[37] This indicates a horizontal division of authority in Germany's federalism: while overall direction and legislative authority reside with the federation, with assured veto rights of the states, administration and implementation are largely a function of the states.

Administrative responsibilities involve a leverage for state administrations and state governments not only in implementation but also in legislation and increase their power resources. The administrative capacity of the states creates a strong pressure on the parliamentary majority and the federal government to harmonize legislation at an early stage with the expertise and the preferences of the states, unless they are willing to risk major implementation deficits.

Three types of public administration

The Federal Republic of Germany is not well understood by academic studies which interpret the administrative structure through the conceptual lenses of hierarchical and monocratic models of public administration, derived largely from the experience of French and Prussian absolutism. A more adequate perspective requires distinctions to be made between three types of public administration and administrative interest intermediation. The first is the French model of institutional isolation of a monocratic and centralized administrative apparatus vis-à-vis societal interests. The second configuration is a fragmented administration with a low degree of isolation from societal tendencies and a large number of access points for organized interests. A typical example is the administration in the United States of America. The third category is the Swedish model. The latter is defined by a strong tradition of professional bureaucratic administration similar to France on the one hand and implementation based on autonomous authorities, such as in Sweden's labour market policy rather than on hierarchical monocratic administration on the other (Lehmbruch 1987: 22–6). Within this typology, the case of public administration in today's Germany approximates to the Swedish model of decentralized and delegated public administration, although administrative interest intermediation in some policy areas resembles the French model, such as fiscal administration, and the US model, such as public administration in agricultural policy which has long been dominated by interest associations representing German farmers.

Intergovernmentalism

The institutional structure of Germany's federalism emphasizes cooperation and compromise seeking. However, in cooperative federalism policy making tends to be a complicated and time-consuming process comprising many hundreds of committees. In these committees experts are dealing with subject matter that requires cooperation between the federal government and the state governments, or cooperation between the states. This tendency is particularly pronounced in areas in which the federal government and the state government have joint tasks, such as in education, financial planning, regional economic development, science and research, and environmental policy. Policy making in Germany's federalism is indeed to a large extent 'intergovernmental in character' (Smith 1986: 61). The integration of the country into the European Union furthers this tendency.

Two modes of conflict resolution: coexistence of bargaining and majority rule

But policy making in Germany's federalism is not only about the relations between the federal government and state governments. Because the Federal Republic is a party state, partisan factors have also deeply impregnated the relations between federal government and state governments. This further complicates the pattern of compromise seeking and conflict resolution. The reason for this is not difficult to understand: in contrast to bargaining, which dominates the resolution of conflicts between the federal government and the state governments, party competition is dominated by power struggle and majority rule. Thus, at least two opposing modes of conflict resolution are operative in Germany's polity. The first mode is based on bargaining and resembles the techniques of compromise seeking in consociationalism (Steiner and Ertmann 2002). The second mode of conflict resolution resides in majority decision-making and is derived from a pure majoritarian model of democracy.

It is conceivable that both bargaining and majority rule can coexist relatively peacefully. However, tensions, if not blocked decision-making processes, cannot be excluded (Lehmbruch 2000a). Furthermore, the coexistence of bargaining and majority rule is likely to produce other undesired outcomes, such as substantial delays in problem solving, or a long-standing constitutional crisis. But it must be added that the Federal Republic has so far been spared a long-standing constitutional crisis. Moreover, blockades of the decision-making process have so far been the exception in Germany's federalism rather than the rule. Last but not least the architects of the constitution have provided for ways out of a constitutional crisis. These include the role of a potential crisis mediator between Chancellor and parliament falling to the Federal President, and the rules for a state of legislative emergency with respect to a bill according to Article 81 of the Basic Law.

The peculiarities of Germany's federalism

Germany's federalism is in many respects remarkable, if not unique. In contrast to classical federalist theory, German-style federalism has not been a major obstacle to the growth of big government. It has rather been a device which has proved to be compatible with the growth and mainten-ance of an advanced welfare state. Furthermore, in contrast to US-style federalism, political authority in Germany's federalism is not allocated to either one or the other level of government. Political authority is mostly shared by the federal government and the state governments. It is certainly true that the states are mainly responsible for the police, education, and other cultural affairs. But even in these areas they cooperate with each other and occasionally also with the federal government. In many other policy areas, except for the exclusive legislation of the federal government, the states act jointly with the central government. Thus, in contrast to US-style federalism or federalism of the Swiss variety, Germany's federalism leaves little autonomy to its member states. It rather provides nationwide uniform regulation of a magnitude similar to that of a centralized unitary state. It has therefore been labelled a 'unitarian federalist state' (Hesse 1962).

Their limited degree of autonomy may not be equated with powerless-ness of the states. The states in Germany's federalism indulge in consti-tutionally guaranteed participation rights and veto positions at the national level. They are also in charge of most areas of public administra-tion. Moreover, codetermination of the states pertains to most federal legislation and covers also a major part of taxation and public spending. Furthermore, the states have a considerable share of responsibility in plan-ning and in the process of formation of public policy through a wide variety of institutions of cooperative federalism. Examples include the joint decision-making areas[38] and horizontal coordination between the states, such as the Conference of the State Ministers for Education. Thus, despite their limited autonomy and notwithstanding the high level of degree of 'intertwining of policy making' (Smith 1986: 51) between the federal authorities and the state executives, the states in Germany are *de jure* and *de facto* major players in the political process.

The logic of policy making in Germany's federalism

Cooperation between the federation and the states, sharing of power and intertwining of policy making contribute to bridge the vertical and hori-zontal fragmentation of the decision-making process in Germany through a high level of intergovernmental 'interweaving' or *Politikverflechtung*

(Scharpf, Reissert, and Schnabel 1976). As a consequence, the relevant political actors in federal government and in the states find themselves confronted with a wide variety of interdependent decision-making situations. The interdependence minimizes the possibilities and also the attractiveness of solo runs of one or several of the participants. Interdependent decision-making is rather a powerful incentive for extended bargaining and for compromise-seeking problem solving. Within this context non-majoritarian conflict resolution, such as unanimous decisions or supermajorities, prevails over majoritarian decision rules and precludes hierarchical steering. This may dramatically reduce the manoeuvrability of the federalist order (Scharpf, Reissert, and Schnabel 1976) and may strengthen the incentive for maintaining the status quo. The latter solution is particularly attractive for the less wealthy or poor states, because the status quo entails massive redistribution from the federation to the poorer states, from wealthy regions to less wealthy states, and from states with sound budgetary records to Länder with major deficits due to unsound fiscal policy in the past.[39] The status quo incentive, the insistence on consensus-seeking, and massive redistribution from stronger to weaker states with questionable effects on efficiency lie at the heart of the view that Germany's federalism is exaggerated, inflexible, inefficient, and generates political blockades.[40] Consensus seeking may indeed produce protracted problem solving and often generates sub-optimal solutions.

But there exists also a wide variety of examples which point to considerable adaptability of federalism (Wachendorfer-Schmidt 2000, 2003), if only in the form of 'incremental adaptation' (Benz 1999, see also Benz 2002). But even the incidence of protracted problem solving and sub-optimal solutions is not the worst case and is at least partly compensated by achievement such as successful dispersal of political power and political integration of opposition parties (Schmidt 2001d). Non-compliance with the consensus machinery built into the structure of Germany's political institutions after 1949 would have inevitably resulted in a series of blocked decision-making processes over topics of major importance, other things being equal. But that would have inflicted greater harm than compliance with consensus requirements.

2.6 The delegating state: transfer of public policy functions to civil society

Fragmentation of power among the federal government, the states, and local government on the one hand and power sharing between incumbent and opposition parties on the other are trademarks of the post-1949 German polity. In addition, the Federal Republic delegates a wider variety of public policy responsibilities to specialized organs and often to societal associations. Monetary policy, for example, is delegated to an autonomous central bank. That position has long been taken by the German Bundesbank, and has largely been handed over to the European system of central banks since the introduction of the Euro in 1999. Competition regulation is a further example. And so, too, is the self-administration in health care. In health care, a wide variety of medical associations cooperate with health insurance associations in organizing, remunerating, and controlling the delivery of health services. Last but not least the associations of entrepreneurs and labour, the social partners in Germany's industrial relations, are constitutionally entitled to free collective bargaining on wages, working time and organization of the labour process. Delegation of public functions to societal associations or corporatist networks also includes social insurance institutions, such as old age insurance for workers, social insurance for white-collar workers, accident insurance, and the self-administration bodies in labour market policy, above all the Federal Office of Labour (Bundesanstalt für Arbeit) as well as the labour offices at the state level and on the local level (Keller 1999). Moreover, a wide variety of social services of voluntary charitable organizations must be mentioned—from hospitals to care for the elderly and handicapped, and social assistance to the poorest. The voluntary charitable organizations have adopted complex roles. As an interest group and at the same time as a provider of social policy in exchange for the receipt of substantial subsidies from general government, the charitable organizations have gained a unique status in the Federal Republic of Germany (Schmid 1996).

Last but not least, the delegation of public functions comprises a larger transnational component. An increasing part of the delegation has been associated with European integration, which involves substantial transfers of sovereignty rights from the nation state to the European Union. The

Federal Republic of Germany was among the first member states of the European project and has also been one of the most active proponents of European integration. While the merits of European integration are obvious—peaceful exchange and cooperation between countries who often went to war with each other in earlier times are major advantages, to mention just one example—the European Union also generates problems. These include increasing fragmentation of power, less transparency, a major democratic deficit, as well as increased restrictions on the mobility of public policy making in the nation states and often also in the European Union.

The delegation of public functions to interest organizations of civil society is a variable, not a constant. In post-1990 Germany, a significant change occurred in the division of labour between the state and the interest associations: the steering capacity of the social partners in Germany's labour relations is decreasing. Their capacity to manage conflict and, above all, the capacity to adjust social partnership to external economic and social change are lower in the post-1990 period than before. This is exemplified in studies in labour relations such as Bertelsmann Stiftung and Hans Böckler-Stiftung (1998) and Streeck (1999). Decreasing levels of organizational density of trade unions and employers also point to decreasing regulatory power of the social partners. Particularly dramatic is the change in labour relations in East Germany where only half of all enterprises pay wages and salaries in accordance with industry-wide norms of remuneration. There is also a decreasing scope of codetermination of labour representatives in West German and East German enterprises. The causes of the decreasing self-administration capacity of societal associations in Germany's labour relations after 1990 are manifold. They include the exit of enterprises from expensive regulation as the well as the exit of employees to the informal economy. Both trends are largely responses to what is widely perceived as an oversized level of total taxation and an oversized tax wedge, i.e. a major gap between gross and take-home income for the employee. But the exit of enterprises and employees can also be attributed to increasing levels of globalization. Last but not least, the side effects of German unification play a major part. The consequences are important: one of the major components of Germany's social and economic policy—the delegation of public functions to societal associations—is more fragile than before 1990.

2.7 Conclusion: governing in a semi-sovereign democracy

This chapter has explored the structure, the role, and the institutional context of the executive in the political system of the Federal Republic of Germany both before and after unification of the country in 1990. It has been shown that the architects of the post-1949 republic, who were deeply influenced by a process of learning from political catastrophes in the Weimar Republic and the era of national socialism, created a strong Chancellor and—at least in normal times—a weak President. In contrast to this and in further contrast to the powerful role of the President in the Weimar Republic of 1919–33, the role of the Federal President in Germany since 1949 is normally confined to ceremonial functions and other dignified parts of the constitution. According to a widely shared view a 'Chancellor Democracy' has emerged from these structures—in contradistinction to the 'Chancellor Dictatorship' of Bismarck in the German Empire of 1871. This view is not wrong. But the manoeuvrability of the Federal Chancellor and the federal government in general is often narrowly constrained. In contrast to the chief executive in Britain, for example, the federal government in Germany is constrained by the constitution, the law, and a large number of co-governing forces and veto players. Decentralization and highly coordinated federalism also play an important role in this context. So, too, does extensive delegation of public policy functions to expert-led institutions and associations of civil society. Furthermore, a major role is also played by the political parties. It is their dominance, the theory goes, which has created a party state (*Parteienstaat*) in Germany, that is, a state in which most major political decisions are shaped by political parties. But the party state of the Federal Republic is also constrained by dispersal of political power, the existence of multiple co-governing forces, and veto players. Germany's post-1949 political system is thus a very complex one. The type of democracy which these institutional structures generate differs from majority rule in Britain, Sweden, France, or Spain. The result consists of a mixed type of democracy, namely one which is based on majority rule *and* on bargaining, on 'majoritarian' *and* 'consensus democracy', to borrow from Arend Lijphart's concepts (Lijphart 1999), and on 'semisovereignty' (Katzenstein 1987) rather than on full sovereignty. Governing today's Germany thus largely means governing a complex and complicated 'semisovereign democracy' (Schmidt 2002c: 176–79), defined as a demos and a majority in the legislature and the executive, which are tamed by numerous checks and balances, co-governing forces, and veto players.

....

KEY TERMS

- Bundesrat (upper house of federal parliament)
- *Bundesregierung* (federal government)
- Bundestag (lower house of federal parliament)
- cabinet principle
- Chancellor Democracy
- chancellor majority
- concurrent legislation
- consociationalism
- constructive vote of no confidence
- delegating state
- departmental principle
- exclusive legislation
- Federal Chancellor
- Federal Constitutional Court
- Federal President
- federalism
- fragmentation of power
- general policy guideline
- grand coalition state
- intergovernmentalism

- intertwining of policy making (*Politikverflechtung*)
- *Länder* (states)
- minister-president
- parliamentary form of government
- *Parteienstaat* (party state)
- party state
- patronage
- power resources
- presidentialism
- public administration
- semi-presidential system
- semi-sovereign democracy
- taxation
- type of majority (absolute majority/ two-thirds majority/relative majority)
- unitarian federalist state
- unitary state
- upper house of federal parliament (Bundesrat)
- veto player
- vote of confidence

QUESTIONS FOR CHAPTER 2

1 Why has the Federal Republic of Germany come to be regarded as a 'semi-sovereign state'?

2 Is the Federal Chancellor a particularly powerful or a particularly weak chief executive?

3 Why has Germany come to be regarded as a party state?

4 Does Germany's federalism deserve to be called federal?

5 What are the pros and cons of the 'semi-sovereign democracy' in the Federal Republic of Germany?

NOTES

1 But note that in the German states the minister-president is the single leader of the executive.

2 Calculated from Müller-Rommel (1988: 173) and Schindler (1999), i. 1030–59; iii. 4360–1. The first Schröder government (1998–2002) comprised fourteen ministries.

3 Article 69 I Basic Law.

4 Articles 112 and 113 Basic Law.

5 After 1990 it turned out that at least one of the two deputies of the Christian Democratic opposition party who rejected the vote of no confidence seemed to have accepted a large amount of money from the Communist regime in East Germany for the vote against Rainer Barzel, the Christian Democratic candidate for the office of Federal Chancellor.

6 The rules of the game are laid down in Article 68 of the Basic Law: '(1) If a motion of the Federal Chancellor for a vote of confidence is not assented to by the majority of the members of the Bundestag, the Federal President may, upon the proposal of the Federal Chancellor, dissolve the Bundestag within twenty-one days. The right to dissolve shall lapse as soon as the Bundestag with the majority of its members elects another Federal Chancellor. (2) Forty-eight hours must elapse between the motion and the vote thereon.'

7 The reference to Kiesinger as a 'wandelnder Vermittlungsausschuss' is taken from Rudzio 2000: 285–7.

8 This is a constitutional crisis which can emerge from the following situation: when the Bundestag rejects a vote of confidence of the Federal Chancellor, and if the Federal President subsequently does not dissolve parliament, and further, if the Bundestag rejects a legislative act, which the government classifies as 'urgent legislation' (Article 81, Basic Law).

9 Article 115l Basic Law.

10 Article 72 II Basic Law.

11 Article 74 Basic Law.

12 Article 94 I Basic Law.

13 For details Article 95 II Basic Law.

14 The latter includes public expenditure of

central, state, and local government as well as the budgets of social insurance.

15 Calculated from Sachverständigenrat zur Begutachtung der gesamtwirtschaftlichen Entwicklung 2001*b*: 408–12.

16 Ibid. 410.

17 The concept comprises veto players (see Tsebelis 1995) and other highly influential collective actors, in particular actors whose consent to policy change is needed on political grounds although these actors are not institutional or partisan veto players. For example, in social policy trade unions often play the role of a 'co-governing actor'.

18 'A veto player is an individual or collective actor whose agreement (by majority rule for collective actors) is required for a change in policy' (Tsebelis 1995: 301).

19 However, it must be added that unitary centralized states find themselves confronted with hardly less pressing problems in policy making, above all problems resulting from the overcentralized steering of society and economy.

20 Article 21 I Basic Law.

21 See von Weizsäcker 1992; Hofmann and Perger 1992; von Beyme 1993: 197; von Arnim 1997, 2001*a*, 2001*b*.

22 Article 33 II Basic Law.

23 'Empty vessels?', *The Economist*, 24 July 1999: 33–4.

24 More balanced is the distribution of the vote among CDU-CSU and SPD in *Land* elections. The CDU-CSU gained on average 39.50 per cent and the SPD on average 39.54 per cent of the vote in all elections to state parliaments from 1949 to September 2002 (FDP: 7.64 per cent).

25 Calculations based on period from Jan. 1950 to Dec. 2001. Data for Greece and Spain exclude the period of authoritarian rule.

26 A more balanced distribution of power between the Christian Democrats and the

Social Democrats occurred in the state governments, in the Mediation Committee of the Bundestag and the Bundesrat, and—measured by the distribution of party membership—in the Central Bank Council of the German Bundesbank, as well as in the Federal Court of Justice. See section 2.5 below; Bauer (1998); Wagschal (2001*b*: 865, 867, 875, 877–78, 881, 883).

27 Calculation from author's file pooloecd–2005.sav Feb. 2002.

28 Calculation from author's file pooloecd–2005.sav Feb. 2002.

29 Schmidt 1996: table 1; Schmidt 2002*c*.

30 Data for 1950–2001.

31 Calculated from *Der Fischer Weltalmanach 2001*: Table IX and Gunlicks 2000: 285–6.

32 'Republik der Landesfürsten'.

33 The violation of that rule in the Bundesrat's vote on the red-Green immigration law, in which the Bundesrat's president Wowereit (SPD) counted the four decisive votes from the state of Brandenburg as part of the supporters for the law, although these votes were not unanimous, caused a major conflict in German politics in March 2002 and in the subsequent electoral campaign. This decision was declared unconstitutional by the Federeal Constitutional Court in Decembere 2002.

34 Article 51, Basic Law.

35 Schindler 1999, ii. 2430–2; Dästner 2001: 293. These are *zustimmungspflichtige Gesetze* in contrast to simple legislative (*Einfachgesetze*) for which an affirmative vote of the Bundesrat is not mandatory.

36 In the period between November 1990 and April 1996, neither the incumbent coalition in federal government, a coalition of CDU, CSU, and FDP, nor the Social Democratic opposition controlled a majority of the seats in the Bundesrat.

37 The national government, thus, governs without having direct control over the

administration of most of its policies. Administration of public affairs is mainly the responsibility of the *Länder*, or a function of experts' institutions or, alternatively, a task for the so-called *mittelbare Staatsverwaltung* (delegated public administration) in which societal associations and the state interact.

38 Articles 91*a* and 91*b*, Basic Law.

39 Sachverständigenrat zur Begutachtung der gesamtwirtschaftlichen Entwicklung 2001*a*.

40 See, for example, 'Model Vision: A Survey of Germany', *The Economist*, 21 May, 1994: 29–31; see also Henkel 1998; Grimm (2001).

....

GUIDE TO FURTHER READING

ANDERSEN, U., and WOYKE, W. (eds.) (2000), *Handwörterbuch des politischen Systems der Bundesrepublik Deutschland* 4th edn. (Berlin: Bundeszentrale für politische Bildung). Comprehensive collaborative volume on Germany's political system.

HELMS, L. (ed.) (2000), *Institutions and Institutional Change in the Federal Republic of Germany* (Houndmills: Macmillan). Informative collaborative volume on the powers and the political institutions in unified Germany.

KATZENSTEIN, P. J. (1987), *Policy and Politics in West Germany: The Growth of a Semisovereign State* (Philadelphia: Temple University Press). Insightful and influential study of the political institutions and the policy making capacity in post-Second World War Germany until the mid-1980s.

PADGETT, S., and POGUNTKE, T. (eds.) (2001), *Continuity and Change in German Politics: Beyond the Politics of Centrality? German Politics*, 10/2, (London: Frank Cass). Important collaborative volume on political continuity and political change in post-1990 Germany.

SCHARPF, F. W. (1994), *Optionen des Föderalismus in Deutschland* (Frankfurt/ a. M.: Campus). Selection of insightful and influential contributions on German

Federalism's structures and problem-solving capacities.

SCHMIDT, M. G. (1992), *Regieren in der Bundesrepublik Deutschland* (Opladen: Leske & Budrich). Study of the political institutions and political outcomes of governing the pre-1990 Federal Republic of Germany.

——(2002), 'The Impact of Political Parties, Constitutional Structures and Veto Players on Public Policy', in H. Keman (ed.), *Comparative Democratic Politics: A Guide to Present Theory and Research* (London: Sage), 166–84. A comparative study of the impact of political parties, constitutional structures, and veto players on policy outputs and outcomes in Germany and other advanced democracies.

SMITH, G. (1986), *Democracy in Western Germany*, 3rd edn. (Aldershot: Gower). Important contribution to the study of institutions, process, and political culture in the Federal Republic of Germany before unification.

TURNER, L. (1998), *Fighting for Partnership: Labor and Politics in Unified Germany* (Ithaca, NY: Cornell University Press). Analysis of labour relations in unified Germany.

WACHENDORFER-SCHMIDT, U. (ed.) (2000), *Federalism and Political*

Performance (London: Routledge). Important collection of chapters on the structure and problem-solving capacities of federalism in Germany and other countries.

ZOHLNHÖFER, R. (2001), *Die Wirtschaftspolitik der Ära Kohl: Eine Analyse der Schlüsselentscheidungen in den Politikfeldern Finanzen, Arbeit und Entstaatlichung, 1982–1998* (Opladen: Leske & Budrich). Insightful study and stimulating application of the veto-player theory on economic policy making in the Federal Republic of Germany in 1982–98.

3

From Negative Parliamentary Politics to Democratic Parliamentary Government: The Role of the Legislature

Chapter 3 focuses attention on the legislature, one of the classical public powers besides the executive and the judiciary. The structures and political functions of the legislature, above all the national parliament, and its role in articulating and aggregating preferences will be highlighted in this chapter. The questions addressed include the following: what characterizes the structure of the legislature, above all the parliament at the federal level? To what extent is parliament still the 'centre of decision-making' (von Beyme 1997, 2000*a*)? To what extent does parliament fulfil its major functions? Is the Bundestag, as some observers argue, really the most powerful parliament on the continent? Due to the federalist structure of Germany, the study of the role of parliament also requires a closer analysis of the role played by the states and the national representation of the states, the Bundesrat. Like Chapter 2, Chapter 3 again focuses attention on the fact that the majority which governs today's Germany does not govern alone. It is rather power sharing between the Bundestag, the lower house, and the Bundesrat, the upper house of parliament, as well as power sharing between the federal government and the state governments, which structures a large part of the political process in Germany.

3.1 'Negative' and 'positive parliamentary politics'

Political parties played a subordinate role in the constitutional monarchy of the German Empire of 1871. The parties of that time were largely anchored in class-based and religious social milieus or were composed of local notable people. Two of these parties, the Social Democratic Party and the Catholic Centre Party were involved in tough conflicts with the monarchical state. The national parliament, the Reichstag, although elected by vote of the male adult population, was deprived of the power to elect and dismiss government. The Reichstag was thus also seriously constrained in training and selecting qualified political leaders. As a consequence, 'negative politics' prevailed in parliament, to quote Max Weber's critical view of the political process in Imperial Germany (Weber 1984: 486). Weber further argued that parliamentary politics remained subordinate to a bureaucratic mode of domination (Weber 1984: 451–86). Regarding public administration, Imperial Germany was competently managed, Weber conceded. However, the political leadership lacked the quality required for Germany's role as a potential big power in world politics—at least in the period after von Bismarck's dismissal and up to the end of the First World War (Weber 1984, 1988*a*).

The long road to modern parliamentary government

The situation changed dramatically in 1918/19. After the breakdown of the monarchy in 1918 Germany became a member of the club of parliamentary democracies. But parliamentary democracy in Germany remained in many respects severely restrained. A weak parliament characterized the First German Republic. Moreover, constitutional defects made life for parliament from the beginning of the Weimar Republic difficult. Two institutional devices narrowly circumscribed the manoeuvrability of the Reichstag: first, the referendum on controversial issues which the Weimar constitution allowed for, and, second, the directly elected President of the Empire (*Reichspräsident*), the incorporation of what Max Weber had recommended for post-war Germany, namely a charismatic political leader as a counterweight to parliament and a remedy for the loss of the ceremonial functions of the former monarchy.

The breakthrough to modern parliamentary government occurred in Germany in the 1950s. The Basic Law and the formation of the Federal Republic of Germany in 1949 were two of the initial crucial steps towards the rise of a parliamentary government worth its name. However, the Federal Republic of Germany was still under a semi-occupation regime until 1955. Parliamentary sovereignty thus remained restricted, though to a gradually decreasing extent due to the upgrading of the Federal Republic's position in international relations. The period of fully developed, positive parliamentary politics—in contradistinction to Weber's 'negative parliamentary politics'—started in this period. Since that time the Bundestag institutionalized itself as the major German political institution in legislation and agenda setting, as well as control of government and administration. The lower house thus complemented with a certain time-lag the roles it had adopted before the mid-1950s, namely recruiting and selecting political leaders, including the role to elect and dismiss the head of government, interest articulation, interest aggregation, and political communication between the governed and the government.

From negative to positive parliamentary politics

Positive parliamentary politics in the Federal Republic of Germany was designed to be republican in nature, not monarchical. It incorporated a 'parliamentary government with chancellor dominance' (Steffani 1992), that is, a parliamentary system with a powerful role for the Chancellor and a weak position for the Federal President.[1] However, the notion of 'chancellor dominance' should not obscure the interdependence of the head of government and the parliamentary majority. The parliamentary majority is an ally of the Chancellor and needs the support of his government, and the Chancellor is accountable to parliament and dependent on the majority of the members of parliament.

A defining characteristic of modern parliamentary government is a major role for political parties in interest articulation, interest aggregation, policy making, and election and dismissal of the head of government. The distinction holds also for post-1949 Germany (see section 2.5 above). Although they are not omnipotent, the political parties in the Federal Republic of Germany are hegemonic gatekeepers in major dimensions of political life. Recruitment of political leaders, for example, has become mainly a party-driven business. The process of selecting candidates for the lower house, for example, is firmly controlled, if not monopolized, by political parties. While half of the total number of seats in the Bundestag are in theory accessible to non-party candidates, provided they gain a relative majority of the first vote in the electoral districts, the overwhelming majority of the deputies in the lower house of parliament have been party members and have been subject to the respective parliamentary group's discipline of vote.

3.2 The social and political composition of the Bundestag

At the beginning of the fifteenth legislative period (2002–2006), the Bundestag, the lower house of parliament, consisted of 603 members: 598 seats of the total number were basic seats (*Grundmandate*) and 5 excess seats (*Überhangmandate*). Half of the basic seats of the Bundestag are allocated to persons through relative majority votes in constituencies on the basis of the first vote (*Erststimme*), but the allocation of seats to parties in the parliament as a whole is through party lists in each of the sixteen states on the basis of the second vote (see section 5.1 below).

The social structure of the Bundestag

Is the Bundestag, the upper house of parliament, an upper-class or middle-class institution or do the 'have-nots' control the levers of the national assembly? What role is played by social determinants, such as age, occupation, religion, and gender? Regarding the gender composition of the members of parliament in the fifteenth legislative period of the Bundestag (2002–2006), roughly two-thirds of the deputies are male (67.8 per cent). Parliamentary politics thus continues to be dominated by male politicians. However, the proportion of the female members of the Bundestag has increased considerably in recent decades and is among the highest worldwide (Siaroff 2000: 199). The gender gap in parliament, defined as the difference between the proportions of female and male representatives, has dropped from 70 percentage points in 1990–4 to 48 percentage points in the following legislative period, 38 percentage points in 1998–2002, and 36 in 2002–2006. It must be added, however, that the gender gap in political representation varies from one party to the other. The highest share of female representatives in the fifteenth legislative period and, hence the lowest gender gap score, was reported by the two smallest party groups in the Bundestag, the PDS (100 per cent) and the Green Party (58.2 per cent), followed by the SPD (37.5 per cent), the CDU-CSU (22.2 per cent) and the FDP (20.9 per cent).[2]

The occupational background of lower house deputies has changed fundamentally between the first Bundestag (1949–53) and the fifteenth legislative period (2002–2006). While almost half of the parliament in 1949 was composed of manual and lower-level white-collar workers, civil servants (*Beamte*) and higher-level white-collar workers (*Angestellte*) were especially prominent in the fourteenth Bundestag (75.9 per cent). Deputies from occupational groups in the public sector, such as public officials and teachers, alone accounted for 46 per cent of the members of parliament in 1998, whereas white-collar workers from the market sector comprised just 8 per cent of the total. Almost 21 per cent of the deputies were, according to their previous occupational background, self-employed or entrepreneurs.[3] This pattern has not significantly changed in the fifteenth legislative period starting in October 2002.

University education is now a trademark of most Bundestag deputies: 65 per cent of all deputies in the fourteenth Bundestag could pride themselves on a university diploma. There were also 35 deputies who stopped their studies before graduation. Only 47 deputies or 7 per cent of all members of parliament reported as their highest educational grade the upper division of elementary school (*Hauptschule*). Almost 20 per cent of the delegates in the fourteenth Bundestag had passed the doctoral examination. The proportion of those who have received doctoral degrees differs from party to party. The range in 1998–2002 was from 35 per cent in the PDS and 30 per cent in the FDP to 21 per cent in the CDU-CSU, 25 per cent in the Green Party, and 14 per cent in the Social Democratic Party, which turns out to be the party with the strongest links to the working class and voters with lower levels of formal education.[4] The general pattern is that of the increasing importance of highly educated deputies. This trend mirrors also increasing professionalization in the political parties.[5]

Professional politicians, that is politicians who live on politics, are meanwhile a particularly large group in parliament. Germany thus belongs to the group of countries in which an increasing proportion of politicians is tempted to live on politics rather than for politics as a vocation. But there are also many lawyers and teachers among the deputies to the Bundestag. Other major groups of society are under-represented: workers, technicians and natural scientists, the military, the clergy, but also housewives, farmers, and those in business and professional occupations (Conradt 2001: 176–7).

The average age of the members of the fourteenth Bundestag was 50 and it is 48 in the fifteenth legislative period. The members of parliament are on average older than the total population, but parliament is not gerontocratic. A considerable degree of rotation prevents gerontocratic patterns.

The average delegate to the Bundestag spends roughly nine years in office.[6] The proportion of deputies who returned to the Bundestag for another term is lower than in the Congress of the United States of America (Thaysen, Davidson, and Livingstone 1989): 70.2 per cent of the delegates to the fourteenth Bundestag were re-elected at least once, 49 per cent were re-elected three times or more, and every fourth delegate has returned to parliament for another term at least four times. A significant change marks the composition of the fifteenth Bundestag: the total number of 'oldtimers', that is members of parliament with a career of at least six legislative periods, dropped from 75 to 50 in the 2002 election.[7]

Party affiliation

Within the context of a party state, the politically most important distinction among the delegates of the Bundestag concerns party affiliation. Because proportional representation is the electoral formula for lower house elections, the number of parliamentary seats falling to the political parties follows closely the distribution of the votes. The position of the strongest parliamentary party in the fourteenth and the fifteenth Bundestag has been taken by the SPD, with 40.9 and 38.5 per cent of the vote in 1998 and 38.5 per cent in 2002. The position of the second strongest party has been held by the CDU-CSU (35.1 per cent of the vote in 1998 and 38.5 per cent in 2002), followed by the Green Party (6.7 per cent of the popular vote in 1998 and 8.6 in 2002), the Liberals (6.2 per cent of the vote in 1998 and 7.4 per cent in 2002), and the Party of Democratic Socialism (5.1 per cent of the vote in 1998 and 4.0 in 2002) (see Table 6).

The numerical strength of the political parties

The numerical strength of the political parties after the 2002 election to the lower house deviates from the long-term trend. In most national elections the CDU-CSU had gained the largest proportion of mandates, except for 1972, and 1998 and 2002. The SPD held the position of the second largest parliamentary group, except in 1972, 1998, and 2002 when it became the strongest party. The third strongest party in most national elections was the Liberals. The Green Party has been represented in the Bundestag since 1983, and the PDS since 1990. Other small parties gained parliamentary seats only in the 1950s. Among these were the Communist Party, the right-wing Imperial Germany Party (Deutsche Reichspartei), and the Bavarian

| TABLE 6 | Parliamentary seats and political parties in the Bundestag, 1949–2002 | | | | | | |

Legislative period	CDU-CSU	FDP	SPD	Green Party	PDS	Other parties	Parliamentary seats at start of legislative period
1949–53	139	52	131			80	402 (2)
1953–57	243	48	151			45	487 (3)
1957–61	270	41	169			17	497 (3)
1961–65	242	67	190			—	499 (5)
1965–69	245	49	202			—	496
1969–72	242	30	224			—	496
1972–76	225	41	230			—	496
1976–80	243	39	214			—	496
1980–83	226	53	218			—	497 (1)
1983–87	244	34	193	27	—	—	498 (2)
1987–90	223	46	186	42	—	—	497 (1)
1990–94	319	79	239	8	17	—	662 (6)
1994–98	294	47	252	49	30	—	672 (16)
1998–2002	245	43	298	47	36	—	669 (13)
2002–2006	248	47	251	55	2	—	603 (5)

Sources: Schindler 1999, i. 291, 381–2, iii. 4344; *Das Parlament*, 16, 16 Apr. 1999, 11; *Frankfurter Allgemeine Zeitung*, 24 Sept. 2002.

Note: The data on seats include excess seats in brackets.

Party in the first legislative period from 1945 to 1953, the Centre Party in the first and second session, and the German Party from the first to the third session of the Bundestag.

In contrast to the pre-unification period, the parties left of the centre of the political-ideological spectrum, that is, the SPD, the Green Party and the Party of Democratic Socialism, hold more than 50 per cent of the votes and seats. However, the parties left of centre are ideologically and organizationally split, although alliances between them have not been uncommon, at first in the state of Saxony-Anhalt, where the PDS tolerated an SPD minority government in 1996–2002, later in Mecklenburg-West Pomerania, and since 2002 in Berlin.

The new coalitions after 1990, such as red-Green and SPD-PDS, are indicative of, and result from, a high level of variation in the parties' share of the popular vote in the states and changes in coalition behaviour. In state elections in Bremen, Lower Saxony, North Rhine-Westphalia, and Schleswig-Holstein, for example, the SPD's share in the popular vote in the latest state election was equal to or surpassed the SPD's vote share in the election to the fifteenth Bundestag. In contrast to this, the CDU-CSU has been the strongest party in parliament and in government in seven states, measured by the data for October 2002: Baden-Württemberg, Bavaria, Hesse, Saarland, Saxony, Saxony-Anhalt, and Thuringia, while the SPD holds a particularly strong position in government in most of the northern states and in North Rhine-Westphalia. That the party compositions in the states and in federal government differ is at least partly attributable to differences in the share of the vote falling to the Christian Democrats and the Social Democrats in the various regions, but it also reflects changing coalition strategies, such as the leftward movement of the SPD towards the Green Party and the Party of Democratic Socialism since the 1990s.

Concurrent and rival majorities in the Bundestag and the Bundesrat

In contrast to a widely shared belief, concurrent majorities in each of the Bundestag and the Bundesrat have been not frequent. Concurrent majorities (defined as a situation in which those parties which hold the reins of power in federal government control also the majority of the Bundesrat votes, measured by the party complexion of state governments) have characterized the following periods: the Adenauer period from September 1949 to 1963, the Erhard government from 1963 to October 1966, the CDU/CSU/SPD-coalition (1966–69), the first 3 years of the SPD/FDP-coalition (1969–72), the Kohl government from October 1982 to May 1990 and November 1990 to April 1991, and the period from the change in power to the Schröder government in October 1998 until the parliamentary election in the state of Hesse in spring 1999 (Bauer 1998: 92–108, Wagschal 2001b).

More troublesome for the federal government have been rival majorities in the Bundestag and Bundesrat. Rival majorities characterized most of the period of the SPD-FDP coalition in 1969–82, but rival majorities have also shaped politics from May to October 1990, from early 1991 to 1998 in the period of the CDU-CSU-FDP coalition, and from 1999 until the time of writing in October 2002 in the period of the red-Green coalition. In a divided government the opposition party plays the part of a co-governing party, as long as the state governments' deputies in the Bundesrat vote along partisan lines (which is often the case in issues of major policy importance) and as long as the government and the opposition prefer a compromise to a blocked decision-making process (which has been the rule rather than the exception) (Sturm 2001).

Rival majorities include periods in which the opposition party controls the majority of the votes in the Bundesrat, and periods, in which a majority of votes in the Bundesrat depended on support of the states in the middle between the CDU-led states and the SPD-led *Länder*. In these circumstances, a majority in the Bundesrat presupposes support of states with mixed or cross-cutting party compositions relative to the government–opposition cleavage, such as the grand coalition states in Brandenburg, Bremen, and until 2001 in Berlin in the era of the red-Green Schröder government.[8]

3.3 Voting procedures in the lower and upper houses

Majority rule prevails in the voting procedures in the lower and upper houses, but it manifests itself in different forms. Preponderant are absolute and two-thirds majorities. The election of the Federal Chancellor, for example, normally presupposes the majority of the statutory members of parliament, the so-called 'chancellor majority', in contrast to the majority of the deputies present (for details see Chapter 1). In the legislative period 1998–2002, the chancellor majority amounted to 335 of a total of initially 669 seats. The chancellor majority is also required for a vote of confidence in favour of the head of government and for a successful constructive vote of no confidence, which allows parliament to dismiss the Chancellor through the election of a new head of government.

Two-thirds majority

Bills amending the constitution require two-thirds majorities in both the lower and the upper houses.[9] A parliamentary decision to impeach the Federal President for wilful violation of the constitution or any other federal law also presupposes a two-thirds majority of the members of the Bundestag or a two-thirds majority of the votes in the Bundesrat, while the motion of impeachment is filed by at least one-quarter of the members of the Bundestag or one-quarter of the votes of the Bundesrat.[10]

Not all voting procedures in the Bundestag require qualified majorities.

Depending upon the importance of a bill, the constitution prescribes different majorities. For example, a second reading of a bill or the final vote of the Bundestag on a bill, regardless of whether it is liable to the consent of the Bundesrat or not, requires a majority of the votes cast and that a certain quorum is fulfilled.

Moreover, the Bundestag has adopted voting procedures which protect minority rights. For example, a minority comprising at least one-third of the statutory number of the members of parliament may request the procedure of an abstract judicial review from the Federal Constitutional Court.[11] This is a potentially powerful weapon for a parliamentary minority, for example for the opposition party provided that it controls one-third of the parliamentary seats. Minority rights can protect against potential tyranny of the majority. The threshold defined for successful protection of minorities in the lower house is not too high, as long as the protection motives do not clash with party discipline requirements. Simple majority rules in parliament also are not too demanding. They presuppose sufficient discipline in the parliamentary parties to vote *en bloc* on a bill. More delicate is the case of a two-thirds majority. In the Federal Republic, the two-thirds majority requires in practice the formation of an oversized coalition, because none of the political parties normally gains more than 50 per cent of the votes and seats. Moreover, the two-thirds majority presupposes cooperation between governing and opposition parties. The two-thirds majority rule, thus, strengthens the consociational component and the 'grand coalition'–structure in the German polity. It thus necessitates the formation of a formal or informal coalition between the federal government and the majority of the state governments and a coalition of the incumbent parties and the parliamentary opposition (Schmidt 2002b).

German-style consociationalism and the grand coalition state

Consociationalism, that is power-sharing rather than majoritarian democracy, and the grand coalition state may also affect legislation on statute law. As pointed out above, the Bundesrat, the upper house, can veto bills which require an affirmative vote. This is particularly important because almost six out of ten bills and, in practice, most legislation on major domestic issues are bills subject to the mandatory approval of the Bundesrat. In order to prevent the Bundesrat's disapproval of the bill, the federal government and the parliamentary majority must seek a compromise with the upper house. Moreover, the upper house has a qualified veto even in legislation not liable to the consent of the Bundesrat. However, this veto can be overridden by majorities in the Bundestag of a size equivalent to that of the veto majority in the Council. For example, if the veto majority is a two-thirds majority, the Bundestag also needs two-thirds of the votes to override the veto. Thus, the governance of the Federal Republic of Germany through legislation requires in most cases a compromise or even an implicit coalition of the federal government and the majority of the state governments. Particularly in periods of divided majorities in the upper and lower houses, governing Germany also requires a coalition between the incumbent parties and the opposition party, provided the latter manages to toe the party line among the majority in the Bundesrat. This is part of a more general message to be derived from the political institutions in Germany. It is almost impossible in Germany not to be governed by a formal or informal grand coalition of the major established parties, and a formal or hidden grand coalition of federal government and state governments. It is for this reason that the Federal Republic of Germany can be regarded as the embodiment of the 'grand coalition state' (Schmidt 2002b), a German-style consociational democracy.

The Mediation Committee

The institutional core of Germany's grand coalition state is the Mediation Committee of the Bundestag and the Bundesrat.[12] The Committee is charged with formulating a compromise proposal in order to mediate and settle disputes between the lower and the upper house on legislation. Since unification the Mediation Committee is composed of sixteen representatives of the lower house in proportion to the party's share of parliamentary seats and sixteen delegates from the upper house, the Bundesrat.[13] The Committee considers legislative disagreement between the two chambers on appeal from the Bundesrat, the Bundestag or the federal government. Particularly important both in quantitative and qualitative terms has been the role of the Mediation Committee in the first session of parliament (1949–53), and in periods of rival majorities in the Bundestag and the Bundesrat, most notably during the SPD-FDP coalition (1969–82), in the second half of the Kohl era (1990–8) and since 1999 in the period of the red-Green alliance. In contrast to this, the role for the Mediation Committee was more limited in periods of concurrent party political majorities, such as between 1982 and May 1990.

The Mediation Committee has been described as a 'success story' (Bauer 1998: 216). It has indeed been a remarkably efficient and successful compromise seeker and decision maker—mainly through the formation of temporary grand coalitions between the incumbent parties and the opposition as well as through encompassing coalitions between the federal government and the state governments. An overwhelming majority of the mediation procedures were settled in the Mediation Committee through compromise between all or almost all participants. In most cases the Mediation Committee has successfully adopted the role of a mediator and a compromise seeker. Very rarely has the Mediation Committee been used as an instrument for blocking the decision-making process. It has typically been the safety valve in cases of conflict between the Bundestag and the Bundesrat. More than 90 per cent of the proposals of the Mediation Committee were accepted by the Bundestag and the Bundesrat, even if rival majorities in the upper and lower houses existed (Bauer 1998: 215–17).

3.4 The political functions of the Deutsche Bundestag

The role of the Bundestag, the lower house of parliament, has been controversially debated. One theory holds that a previously powerful Bundestag has suffered a substantial loss in power (Agnoli 1968). Others argue that the Federal Chancellor's position became so strong, that 'cabinet stability has been bought at a high price: (...) While avoiding the Scylla of government instability, the Bonn regime fell into the Charybdis of a powerless parliament' (Loewenstein 1959: 93–4).[14] Proponents of a third view regard the Bundestag as more powerful than any other parliament in the political history of Germany. A fourth view sees the power of the Bundestag as second only to the Congress of the United States of America. According to this perspective, the lower house is the main political battleground, the 'centre of decision making' in politics and legislation (von Beyme 1997), and an 'autonomous upper State organ (...) not subject to supervision and directives' (Oberreuter 2000: 90). A fifth view places the Bundestag into the category of a 'reactive legislature' (Mezey 1979: 25), marked by modest policy making power and relatively strong public support in contrast to active, vulnerable, marginal, and minimal legislatures.

Which view is the correct one? An answer to this question can be derived from testing the performance of the lower house of parliament in five dimensions: (1) recruitment and electoral function, (2) legislation, (3) control of government and administration, (4) the role of the Bundestag in articulating and aggregating interests, and (5) the rate of political survival.

3.4.1 Electoral functions and the recruitment of political leaders

In his *Political Writings* in 1917/18 and in his famous 'Politics as Vocation' Max Weber argued that a democratically elected parliament is an arena suitable for the efficient and effective selection of competent charismatic political leaders (Weber 1992: 225). At least partly for this reason Weber raised his voice in favour of democratizing the German Empire after the end of the First World War.

Weberian and post-Weberian views of leader recruitment

The post-Weberian view is more pessimistic on the recruitment functions of parliament. Parliament does not necessarily bring forth highly qualified leaders, as the decline of the Weimar Republic and the rise of the National Socialist German Workers' Party and Adolf Hitler as their leader demonstrated.

In contrast to this, the election of political leaders in the Federal Republic of Germany yielded better results, although complaints about mediocre political leaders have remained as before 1933. Overall, the Chancellors elected by the Bundestag were political leaders with satisfactory, good, and occasionally exceptional levels of performance. A broadly similar pattern emerges from the majority of ministers in federal government. Of course, qualifications of these views are appropriate. Mediocrity is present, although not omnipresent. Due to the dominance of the party state every candidate for the chancellorship and almost every candidate for the post of a federal minister has been a member of one of the rival political parties and has been, thus, liable to polarize the electorate between followers and opponents of his party. Polarization has indeed occurred. Despite the undeniable partisan rhetoric of all Chancellors, the degree to which the heads of government in the Federal Republic wilfully or unintentionally polarized the electorate has mostly been moderate by historical and cross-national standards. Moreover, the polarization effects attributable to the words and deeds of the Chancellors differed: those attributable to the rule of Konrad Adenauer, Willy Brandt, Helmut Kohl, and Gerhard Schröder were larger than those caused by Ludwig Erhard and Helmut Schmidt. The latter two were popular not only among the voters of the incumbent parties, but also among a large group of supporters of the major opposition party.

The effective fulfilment of electoral functions

Overall, the Bundestag has successfully mastered the electoral functions (Saalfeld 1990; Ismayr 2000: 36–7, 195–215). This view is supported by all elections of the Federal Chancellor and the formation of a stable, majority-based government throughout the political history of the Federal Republic. The relatively short time span which the lower house of parliament needs to form a government after a national election is a further positive feature of the Bundestag. The total number of days required to form a government after a lower house election varies from twenty-four in 1969 and 1983 to fifty-eight in 1961. The mean score is thirty-eight days (Schindler 1999, i, 1141–2). This contrasts sharply with the long period required to form a government in more fragmented party systems, such as Italy after many of the post-1945 elections. Moreover, the process of recruiting and electing a Chancellor in the Federal Republic of Germany requires neither lavish consultation nor a mediator, such as the 'informateur' in the Netherlands. Furthermore, most of the chancellors elected in the Bundestag have presided over relatively stable governments over a lengthy period of time. Konrad Adenauer was three times re-elected and remained in office fourteen years, and Helmut Kohl sixteen years. Less successful were the cabinets Erhard, the first Brandt-cabinet, which lost its parliamentary majority in 1972, and the last Schmidt-cabinet which was voted out of office in a vote of no confidence in 1982.

The Bundestag has also been largely successful in electoral functions beyond the election of the government. These include the cooperation of the lower house in the election of the Federal President; the election of the judges of the Federal Constitutional Court; selection of the representatives of the Bundestag in the Joint Committee according to Article 53a Basic Law, that is, the 'reserve parliament' in a state of constitutional emergency;

and election of the representatives of parliament in the Mediation Committee of the Bundestag and the Bundesrat.

Causes of succesful electoral performance

However, a caveat must be added. The success of the lower house in its election functions cannot be attributed to parliament alone. The party system has also been a major conducive factor, most notably due to the presence of ideologically relatively moderate political parties. A further caveat concerns the selection of candidates for the Federal Chancellor's office. The selection is basically a matter of the political parties, above all a matter of the two people's parties in Germany, the CDU-CSU and the SPD. The selection of the candidates takes place outside parliament, mainly in an interplay of the general public, mass media, and party politics and usually several months before the formal election of the Chancellor in parliament. The election of the Chancellor in the Bundestag, thus, in a sense merely ratifies the decision taken outside the parliament. In this respect, it can be argued that the electoral function of the parliament shrinks largely to a 'confirmatory function' (von Beyme 1999: 281), provided that parliament does not resort to rejecting the proposal on the Chancellor.

Within the context of a party state, such as the Federal Republic of Germany, the election of the Federal Chancellor is inevitably a matter of high party politics. And so, too, is the recruitment and selection of political leaders below the office of the Chancellor. In this process, the political parties in Germany have gained a hegemonic, if not a monopoly position. Top-level political positions are, in principle, only accessible to candidates who have successfully participated in a marathon run through one of the major political parties and have demonstrated that they never tire of shaking hands. In contrast to this, the access to political top positions for all other candidates, including candidates from top positions outside politics, is extraordinarily difficult. However, this may impair the openness of the recruitment process for innovation because it often tempts potential candidates to adopt only those innovations which safeguard office seeking rather than policy pursuit, such as a policy of the smallest common denominator or purely populist policy packages.

It is in a sense natural that the political parties are also tempted to apply egocentric criteria to other electoral functions of parliament, including the election of the eight judges of the Federal Constitutional Court for which the Bundestag is responsible. Whether or not the parliamentary parties indulge in that temptation is a controversially debated issue. According to one view, partisan components dominate the search process and the final election of the members of the Constitutional Court. The alternative view is that partisan politicization in the election of the judges is in most cases successfully constrained by institutional safeguards. These include a high majority threshold—a two-thirds majority—and technical-formal requirements, such as formal legal qualification of the candidates and selective criteria on the composition of the Constitutional Court, for example the provision that members of the Court may not be members of the Bundestag, the Bundesrat, the federal government, nor of any of the corresponding bodies of the state. This view is, according to most studies on the Constitutional Court, empirically valid—with the possible exception of a higher degree of party politicization in the first years of the Court, which was founded in 1951 (see Chapter 4).

3.4.2 Legislative performance and the control of government

The Bundestag is the major organ in legislation in today's Germany. No federal law and no constitutional law can be passed without the consent of the majority in the Bundestag. Thus, the Bundestag, the lower house, is indeed 'The Lawmaker' (von Beyme 1997). Regarding the nature of parliament, the lower house in Germany represents a mixture of 'working chamber' ('arbeitendes Parlament') and 'debating chamber' ('redendes Parlament'), to quote Max Weber's distinction between two types of parliament (Weber 1984: 486). In the 'working chamber' the emphasis is placed mainly on committee work, legislation, and the control of the executive, while the 'debating chamber' is chiefly engaged in the process of parliamentary deliberation.

'Working chamber' and 'debating chamber'

The Bundestag comprises both types of parliament, but the character of a 'working chamber' prevails (Ismayr 2000). Quantitative studies have revealed the priority of work in parliamentary committees over parliamentary debates. In the period from 1949 to 1998, for example, 28,407 committee sessions were counted, almost ten times the number of the 2,935 plenary sessions.[15] Other measures of legislative performance support the view of the Bundestag as a productive and efficient parliament. For example, the average annual number of tabled bills amounted to 647 in the first thirteen legislative periods of the Bundestag, and the annual total of bills passed—on average 420—was not dramatically lower.[16] More than half of the bills, about 58 per cent, were tabled by the federal government, about 35 per cent were presented by the Bundestag, and almost 8 per cent by the Bundesrat. The relatively short duration of the legislative process also indicates an assiduous legislative activity, as the average duration across all legislative periods from the date at which a bill is tabled until the promulgation of an act shows. According to this measure, legislative acts span a period of 187 to 266 days.[17]

The overall legislative output of the Bundestag is indeed remarkable— even if many of the bills passed were only of minor importance. But besides less important legislation there have been also legislative acts of major relevance. Examples include legislation in support of economic and social reconstruction of post-war Germany, legislation on integrating Germany into NATO and the European Community, and legislation on the New *Ostpolitik*, that is a policy of détente vis-à-vis the Socialist countries in the era of the Social-Liberal coalition (1969–82). Legislation on social policy must also be counted among the major parliamentary activities in the Federal Republic of Germany. This has resulted in reconstructing, expanding, and later consolidating one of the world's most advanced welfare states. Moreover, German unification has required a massive amount of legislation within a very short period of time. Legislation in broadening and intensifying European integration such as the establishment of the common European currency has also been important.

However, a qualification must be added. The policy on German unification in 1989 and 1990 was mainly the result of the executive's power. The federal government managed to isolate itself largely from the political process as usual and opted for a high-speed policy process with an unusually high degree of centralization and a no less unusually high degree of redistribution mainly in favour of the new states in eastern Germany (Lehmbruch 1990). In this situation, the members of the Bundestag and the Bundesrat found themselves confronted with a difficult choice: to vote in favour of the whole legislation on unification or to reject it altogether, which no one seriously wanted.

Most legislation of the Bundestag concerns statute law and only a small, though important, part of the legislative activities involves amendments to the constitution (Busch 1999). Most of the constitutional amendments were legislated in the period from 1953 to 1957, that is, in the period of a two-thirds majority coalition of CDU-CSU-FDP and the German Party/Federation of the Expellees and Dispossessed (DP-BHE), and in 1966–9, the period of the grand coalition of CDU-CSU and SPD, in which the federal government presided again over a two-thirds majority. The most recent wave of constitutional change was generated by the unification of West and East Germany in 1990 and the legislation required to implement the Maastricht Treaty on the European Union (1993).

Legislation within the shadow of the party state

Legislation in the Federal Republic of Germany takes place within the shadow of the party state. Party political determinants have shaped legislative activity to a very large extent. However, the nature of the impact of parties upon legislation differs. Until the present day, most bills in the lower house are passed unanimously. This seems to indicate high levels of consensus between the parliamentary parties. However, the relative policy importance of a bill makes a difference. Very important bills or important legislative acts, for example, rarely find the opposition party's approval. This is also valid for spending cuts, above all spending cuts in a period prior to an election (Alber 1987: 262). In contrast to this, unanimous approval or near-unanimity is normally achieved only on bills of lesser policy relevance. But it must be added that major exceptions to this rule exist, such as the consensual vote on legislation on German unification and on the Maastricht Treaty, to mention only two examples.

Overall, however, legislation since the 1980s shows a dramatic decline in the proportion of bills that were unanimously passed in the first chamber of parliament. The reasons for this are manifold (Saalfeld 1995). They include increased political polarization between government and opposition parties after the change of power from the Schmidt government to the Kohl government in 1982. That trend has recurred in the 1990s after an interlude of cooperation between government and opposition in legislation on German unification and on the European Union (Schindler 1999, ii. 1954–73). However, a complete picture requires us to take into account the legislative vote in the Bundesrat and in the Mediation Committee of the Bundestag and the Bundesrat. In both institutions cooperative strategies of the political parties have prevailed, but more so in the Mediation Committee than in the Bundesrat (Bauer 1998; Schindler 1999, ii. 2430–1).

On the whole, legislation reflects significant party differences. But the degree to which parties matter in legislation varies from period to period. For example, the high level of political polarization in the 1950s, mainly between the centre-rightist Christian Democratic parties and the leftist Social Democratic Party was replaced by a period of rapprochement between both parties from the late 1950s until the late 1960s. This is the German background of the 'vanishing of opposition'-view and the 'catch-all-party'-hypothesis most forcefully developed in Kirchheimer's contributions (1965 and 1966). However, in contrast to the predicted decline of opposition in West Germany, the cooperation between the larger parties and the grand coalition experiment from 1966 to 1969 turned out to be the overture to a new period of intensified partisan struggle, radical protest movements, and increasingly competitive and confrontational behaviour of the parliamentary parties.

The post-1969 period was a period of intense competition and confrontation between the major political tendencies in the Federal Republic of Germany. But despite increased polarization, the political institutions continued to require a large degree of cooperation, bargaining, and compromise between the government and the opposition party in legislation. This generated contradictory roles for the politicians. Cooperation in legislation and policy making in general on the one hand and confrontational rhetoric and behaviour of the political parties on the other do not necessarily obstruct each other, but they increase the probability of blocked decision-making processes. Moreover, the political costs of cooperative strategies are also increasing: it is difficult for the voters and the party members to understand why the incumbent parties and the opposition should cooperate with each other in a situation which seems to call for confrontation.

The dualism between majority and opposition and 'cooperative parliamentary government'

A further point must be mentioned in this context. Although parliamentary government in the Federal Republic is marked by the dualism between majority and opposition, in contrast to the dualism between parliament and government in a classical constitutional monarchy, the opposition parties can count on a variety of cooperation opportunities in Germany's 'cooperative parliamentary government' (von Beyme 2000a). As pointed out above, an amendment to the constitution requires a two-thirds majority in the Bundestag and the Bundesrat. Constitutional change thus presupposes the approval of the parliamentary opposition party, as long as the government controls less than two-thirds of the parliamentary seats. Furthermore, bills requiring the consent of the Bundesrat are entry doors for the co-government of the opposition, especially when rival majorities exist in the lower and upper houses. Because rival majorities are not at all uncommon in the Federal Republic of Germany, it is also not uncommon in Germany that the opposition party further strengthens the 'co-operative style of opposition activity' (Saalfeld 1990: 77) and produces a 'co-governing opposition' (von Beyme 1989: 350; 2000a: 34).[18]

Co-government of the opposition

This marks a fundamental difference between the Bundestag on the one hand and the US Congress as well as the British House of Commons on the other. In Congress and in the House of Commons co-government of the opposition is only conceivable in a state of emergency, such as in a period of declared war or undeclared war. Co-government between the governmental parliamentary groups and the opposition in Germany is part of normality and is at least partly attributable to the structure of a 'working chamber'. A 'working chamber' offers manifold opportunities for the opposition to cooperate or to withhold support for the government. For example, the parliamentary committees are composed of representatives of government parties and opposition parties in proportion to their respective share of parliamentary seats. Furthermore, a sizeable proportion of the posts of the parliamentary committee's chairman falls to the opposition party. In contrast to the American Congress, in which the winner-takes-all principle dominates parliament as much as it structures the electoral formula, the distribution of parliamentary committee chairmen in proportion to the seat share of the parliamentary parties upgrades the role of the parliamentary opposition parties in the Bundestag.

Co-government of the parliamentary opposition leaves of course an imprint on policy making and policy outputs. But co-government of the parliamentary opposition may take on various forms. One possibility is a formal or an informal grand coalition between the incumbent parties and the opposition party. This has been a rather frequent case in the political history of post-1949 Germany. Legislation on German unification and legislation on Germany's entry to the euro are just two examples. But co-government of the opposition can also result in prolonged stalemate, if not blocked decision making, such as the case of taxation reform demonstrated in the last two years of the Kohl era, that is, in 1996–8 (Zohlnhöfer 2001).

National parliament and feedback from European Law

Since its birth in 1949 the Bundestag has never been fully sovereign in legislation. In the beginning, the Occupation Statute and reserved powers of the Allies constrained the sovereignty of parliament to a large extent (Friedrich 1953). Later on, transfers of sovereignty rights to international and transnational organizations were further indicators of confining restrictions on the sovereignty of parliament. Three additional trends have narrowed the room for manoeuvre available to parliamentary legislation. The first has been the increasing role of the ministerial bureaucracy in designing and initiating legislation (Ismayr 2000: 216–63, 449). This trend largely reflected the rise of 'big government' in Germany, but it is also attributable to the increase in technical complexity of most policy areas and policy instruments. A second trend has been the expanded role that the state governments have gained in legislation via the Bundesrat in exchange for the transfer of sovereignty rights to the federal government, and, in particular, the increase in the absolute number and relative importance of bills subject to approval by the upper house (Lehmbruch 2000a). The third trend lies in the enormous growth of the importance of European law (Weiler 1999). Like other EU-member countries, legislation in Germany is strongly influenced by the feedback from European law (Jachtenfuchs and Kohler-Koch 1996; Leibfried and Pierson 2000). The magnitude of this feedback is impressive (Sturm and Pehle 2001). In 1987, for example, roughly 20 per cent of the bills passed by the Bundestag were transformations of European law into national law. In policy areas marked by a high level of European integration, that percentage share approximated even the 100 per cent mark (von Beyme 2000a: 41). Similar data are reported from the Bundesrat, the representative of the state governments. More than one out of eight agenda topics were due to topics raised by the European Community.[19] Even more impressive are data on the magnitude and density of regulations from the EU. For example, the total number of 12,661 EU decisions with an impact on legislation in Germany in the 1949–98 period, compared with a total of 5,461 bills that were tabled in the Bundestag in this period, is indicative of a major feedback of EU law on the member states (Rudzio 2000: 74; Ismayr 2000: 290–8).

Parliamentary control of government?

Regarding the control of government and administration, the Bundestag has often gained less flattering grades compared with the praise the lower house has received for its electoral function and role in legislation. However, the harsher criticism of the alleged weaker control performance of the Bundestag partly results from a diagnostic error of the division of labour between government and opposition in a modern parliamentary democracy. In a parliamentary democracy, control of government differs fundamentally from controlling presidential government. It differs also dramatically from the control of government through parliament in pre-democratic ages. The major division in the national assembly of parliamentary government as opposed to presidentialism is the division between government together with the majority of the incumbent parties in parliament (or sometimes only the minority) on the one hand and the parliamentary opposition party or parties on the other. This is in marked contrast to the division between government, usually the monarch and its administration, and parliament as a whole in pre-democratic monarchies.

Because the majority in a national assembly of a parliamentary government is *de facto* part of the government, it is normally unlikely that the majority will exhaust the control potential of parliament vis-à-vis government. It is mainly for this reason, that the control functions of parliament will be asymmetrically used by the government parties and the parliamentary opposition.

Whether the parliamentary opposition compensates for the relative loss of control that the coalition between government and parliamentary majority may convey depends upon a wide variety of factors. Of central importance among these are numerical strength, cohesiveness, and the total number of opposition parties in parliament. Following the logic of the veto-player theory, it can be argued that the parliamentary opposition will be the stronger, the larger its numerical strength, the smaller the number of the opposition party, and the more cohesive the opposition, other things being equal. Even more important is the opportunity for the parliamentary opposition effectively to veto legislation or to participate either formally or informally in co-government with the governmental parliamentary groups, such as in the case of a constitutional amendment of the Basic Law or bills liable to the consent of the Bundesrat.

The list of instruments for controlling the government and the administration also includes the submission of a bill passed by the majority of the Bundestag to the Federal Constitutional Court (see Chapter 4). Part of the control instruments is addressing an interpellation to the government via a major interpellation, a procedure which requires the consent of at least 5 per cent of the deputies to the national parliament (*Große Anfrage*), as well as the question raised in parliament by a private member (*Kleine Anfrage*). The arsenal of control instruments comprises also the establishment of a parliamentary committee of inquiry, the organization of parliamentary hearings, and legislative initiatives of the Bundestag as a whole or of a group of deputies. Finally, the 'crown' among the control instruments is to be placed on the constructive vote of no confidence (von Beyme 1993: 273). The vote of no confidence is the most powerful weapon that parliament can employ against the executive in Germany, especially since the Federal Chancellor cannot dissolve parliament and appoint the date of election for the next parliament.

All of these control instruments have been used in the Bundestag on a massive scale and to an increasing extent—mainly by the opposition parties.[20] Some of the control instruments have been used extensively, such as interpellations, others have been employed less frequently, such as parliamentary committees of inquiry, or rarely, for example the vote of no confidence.

3.4.3 Interest articulation and communication function

The Bundesrat, the upper house, manages interest articulation of the state governments and communication between the states and federal government reasonably well. But there is no rule without exception. Articulation and communication in the Bundesrat may be seriously strained by manifest conflicts between governments of different partisan complexion, such as the clash between the SPD-led states and the CDU-led governments over the migration law issue on 22 March 2002 demonstrates. But overall, regarding interest articulation and communication, the upper house performs relatively well.

The extent, however, to which the Bundestag contributes to interest articulation and political communication and the quality of that contribution are disputed. According to one view, the Bundestag masters the core of the articulation function reasonably well, with efficient transformation of mandates into relatively stable majorities as a major asset. Others believe that the role of the lower house in articulating interests and communicating with the citizens deserves less favourable grades. According to an influential view, this is largely due to the contradictory roles facing the deputies of the Bundestag. The delegates find themselves torn between roles which are difficult to combine, especially the roles of a 'constituency champion' and a 'parliamentary star'.[21] Two additional roles aggravate the conflict. The deputy is not only a member of parliament; he or she is also affiliated to a political party and a member of the parliamentary group of that party. Moreover, the deputies to the Bundestag are, according to the constitution, 'representatives of the whole people, not bound by orders and instructions, and subject only to their conscience'.[22] In reality, however, the deputies are part of the party state machinery and are *de facto*, though not *de jure*, subject to tough partisan discipline in voting. Contradictory requirements also stem from the structure of the Bundestag. As pointed out above, the lower house of parliament is a hybrid of a 'working chamber' and a 'debating chamber'. The 'debating chamber' places a premium on rhetorical qualifications, whereas the 'working chamber' requires in particular solid qualifications for expert work in parliamentary committees.

Communication within the structures of the 'debating chamber' is, however, largely shaped by partisan factors. Party politics adds a necessary degree of structured interest articulation, but it often also adds a significant amount of programmatic rigidity and sterile communication to the parliamentary debates. Furthermore, party politics frequently tempts politicians to dichotomize complex issue, to define them in terms of partisan political correctness, and to lay the blame for grievances at the door of their opponent. However, the selectivity and the bias which partisan politics introduces in communication between parliament and the public devalue the dignity and the news value of the parliamentary messages to a significant extent.

The typical member of the Bundestag, thus, finds himself in a dilemma. He or she is confronted with expectations of a 'lone wolf' and a 'hand-to-hand fighter' on the one hand and the role of a party politician, if not party soldier, on the other. The latter qualification is particularly pronounced in practically all parliamentary democracies, because this form of government requires for smooth functioning disciplined parties and disciplined voting by the parliamentary parties.

The members of the Bundestag and the lower house as a whole are therefore in a precarious situation. Representative surveys mirror the delicate situation at least indirectly. Surveys on the representation of the citizens in political institutions, for example, yield only restrained praise for the national parliament. Relatively few respondents believe that the Bundestag represents their interests to a very large extent; 40 per cent see representation of a more moderate degree; and broadly one-quarter believe that the Bundestag does not represent their interests at all (von Beyme 1999: 283). Measured by the level of trust in institutions, the Bundestag also does not gain the best results, even if in this respect it performs better than most other national parliaments (Saalfeld 1990: 84). By the same measure, the Bundestag achieved the fourth rank in 1998, to mention just one point of observation, behind the Federal Constitutional Court, the police, and the judiciary both in West and East Germany (Gabriel and Neller 2000: 82).

However, these survey results must be interpreted with care. Trust scores vary considerably from one point of observation to the other. Furthermore, supporters of the incumbent parties tend to strongly approve of parliament, whereas voters and members of the opposition party usually adopt a far more critical view of what parliament does. Thus, an insider-outsider component contaminates at least part of the picture that surveys convey of the Bundestag. But even after controlling for the insider-outsider effects, the overall message is clear and consistent. In its capacity as an institution of interest representation, the Bundestag receives only moderate grades in political evaluation.

The reasons for this are manifold. The severe standards which voters and the media usually apply to politicians and national assemblies play an important role. But the relatively moderate reputation of the lower house also reflects the increasing difference in the social composition of the people and the Bundestag (see section 3.2). Moreover, mediocrity among the members of the Bundestag may also play a role. Furthermore, the language used by many deputies is ideological, artificial, and inanimate. This repels the audience as much as the widespread know-all manner of most politicians and their tendency to dichotomize complex questions, to moralize issues, and to blame the opponent almost exclusively. The office-seeking and office-maintenance mentality which most members of the Bundestag often display is also unattractive. Office seeking also shapes parliamentary debates: the desired or apprehended effect of a ruling on the electorate is in most cases more important than the argument that speaks for or against a case. Last but not least weaknesses in the publicity of the Bundestag must be mentioned. The parliament has not exhausted the potential for presenting its case convincingly. The publicity function of the lower house, despite considerable improvement in the age of the internet, is not yet fully developed. For example, the Bundestag has rarely resorted to public meetings of the parliamentary committees. Thus, most parliamentary work remains confined to confidential deliberations behind closed doors.

3.5 The most powerful legislative body on the continent?

The role of 'the legislator' (von Beyme 1997) alone turns the Bundestag into a highly influential collective actor. And none of the various pieces of information presented so far lends support to the view of a 'powerless parliament', to quote Loewenstein's pessimistic hypothesis derived from a somewhat premature reading of Adenauer's role as the Federal Chancellor in the 1950s (Loewenstein 1959: 93–4). To classify the Bundestag as a 'reactive legislature' (Mezey 1979: 25), defined as a parliament with moderate policy-making power and relatively strong public support, is more appropriate, even if there exists evidence which points to limited reputation of the parliament (Norton 1990). As far as policy-making power is concerned, the Bundestag, despite its role as the federal legislator, is undoubtedly constrained. Traditional models of parliamentary democracy no longer accurately describe the reality of German-style parliamentary government. Parliamentary processes can be bypassed or subverted by organized interests and institutionalized power structures as well as privileged relationships of highly organized interest groups with the state, as the literature on interest groups, corporatism, and non-decisions suggests (Bachrach and Baratz 1979; Lehmbruch and Schmitter 1982; Reutter and Rütters 2001). Furthermore, the Bundestag is constrained by the increasing role of the judiciary in policy making in the Federal Republic (see Chapter 4). In addition, the Bundestag, like any other parliament, is not in a position to guide dynamic processes such as globalization and the ageing of society. It would also be hopelessly overstrained with moving the unemployment rate, the rate of inflation, or the rate of economic growth to a specific target within a certain period of time. Internationalization and transnational politics, above all the impact of the European Union, rather tend to inhibit the steering capacity of Germany's lower house of parliament. Home-made restrictions are also relevant, as the important role of the ministerial bureaucracy in legislation exemplifies, to mention in passing only the veto position of the federal government against parliamentary decisions which would increase public expenditure or decrease public revenue.[23] Moreover, a situation of deadlock between the governmental parliamentary parties and the opposition, such as in 1972 before and after the vote of no confidence against Chancellor Brandt, may turn the Bundestag into a sleeping giant and prevent parliament from fulfilling its duties as an institution of political guidance and control of government and administration.[24] Finally, a political-constitutional crisis is conceivable in which the role of the Bundestag is drastically restrained by reserve institutions such as a coalition between the federal government, the Federal President, and the Bundesrat in the case of a state of legislative emergency,[25] or the Joint Committee in a state of defence.[26]

Despite undeniable restrictions, the Federal Republic's Bundestag is more influential than the parliaments in all other political regimes in Germany. Moreover, the Bundestag has provided solutions to a wider variety of problems through its legislation than its predecessors, for example by reconstructing and expanding social policy after 1949, by integrating socially weaker groups, and by gradual adaptation to changing international and transnational environments. Last but not least, the lower house is, even if this repeats a message delivered above, the federal 'Lawmaker' (von Beyme 1997). This is a role of overriding importance—even if the Bundestag is situated in a state full of co-governing forces and a wide variety of powerful veto players.

Some spectators however went too far in evaluating the importance of the Bundestag. To argue that the lower house of the federal parliament is perhaps the most powerful legislative body in Europe grossly exaggerates its role (Aberbach, Putnam, and Rockman 1981: 231). The Bundestag is indeed more powerful than the pre-1949 parliaments in Germany, and the expansion of parliamentary services to the deputies the lower house has further strengthened its position. But the Bundestag is not the most powerful parliament in Europe, because the parliamentary majority and the lower house as a whole find themselves confronted with a wider variety of co-governing forces and veto players than most other parliaments in Europe, with the exception of Switzerland (Schmidt 2000: 352–3). The list of co-governors and veto players includes coalition partners, the state governments and the Bundesrat, an autonomous central bank, a powerful autonomous judiciary, delegation of state authorities to societal association, strong self-administration traditions, and membership in the European Union. In the light of these constraints, it can be argued that the parliamentary sovereignty in the Federal Republic of Germany has never been fully supreme.

3.6 Conclusion

Chapter 3 has focused attention on the legislature, above all the national parliament. But due to the institutional idiosyncrasies of today's Germany, the study of the role of parliament also requires a closer analysis of the role played by the states and the national representation of the states, the Bundesrat. Like the preceding chapters, Chapter 3 has again emphasized that the political majority which governs the Federal Republic of Germany does not govern alone. It is rather power sharing between the lower and the upper houses of parliament as well as power sharing between the federal government and the state governments which characterizes a large part of the political process in Germany. Of course, parliamentary government rather than presidentialism is the dominant form of government in Germany, and the Federal Republic of Germany to that extent resembles the British form of government. Like in Britain, the executive of the German federal government is dependent upon the approval of the parliamentary majority. Furthermore, the majority of the deputies in parliament can topple the Federal Chancellor through the election of a successor. This doubtless creates a high level of interdependence between the legislature and the executive. But in contrast to Britain (and also in contrast to many other unitary states), modern Germany is a federal country, composed of the federal government (*Bundesregierung*) and the governments of sixteen member states. These states are powerful entities—both within their own jurisdiction and at the federal level. At the federal level, the states can count on their influential representational body, the Bundesrat. The importance of the Bundesrat is particularly visible in legislation—and in this area it is often as important as the lower house of parliament. For constitutional reasons (which were explained in more detail in sections 2.5 and 3.4.2) legislation in Germany often calls for the formation of unusually broad coalitions made up of the incumbent parties and the major opposition party and between the majorities in the Bundestag and Bundesrat. The political consequences are non-trivial: in contrast to a majoritarian democracy, such as Britain or New Zealand prior to the introduction of proportional representation in 1993, the German polity involves a major non-majoritarian component and transforms the political system of the country into a mix of majoritarian democracy and negotiation democracy.

....

KEY TERMS

- basic seats
- Bundestag (lower house of federal parliament)
- Bundesrat
- co-governing forces
- consociationalism
- debating chamber
- excess seats
- first vote
- legislature
- lower house of federal parliament (Bundestag)
- majority rule
- Mediation Committee between Bundestag and Bundesrat

- negative and positive parliamentary politics
- parliamentary government
- party state
- politics as vocation
- 'politicos'
- presidentialism
- professionalization
- recruitment function (of parliament)
- recruitment of political leaders
- relative majority
- second vote
- two-thirds majority

- upper house of federal parliament (Bundesrat)
- veto player
- working chamber

....

QUESTIONS FOR CHAPTER 3

1 Which social groups are over-represented and which groups are under-represented in the Bundestag, the lower house of parliament?

2 What are the political consequences of the voting procedures in the lower and the upper houses of parliament?

3 Why has the Federal Republic of Germany come to be regarded as a case of symmetric bicameralism?

4 When is the opposition party of the Bundestag in the position of a co-governing actor?

5 To what extent has its Bundestag fulfilled its electoral functions?

6 Is the Bundestag really one of the most powerful legislative bodies on the continent?

....

NOTES

1 See section 2.1.

2 Source: www.bundestag.de/mdb15, 22 Oct. 2002.

3 www.bundestag.de/mdb14/mdbinfo/1322.htm, 26 Mar. 2002.

4 Calculated from www.bundestag.de/mdb14/mdbinfo/132/1324.html, 26 Mar. 2002.

5 Von Beyme (2000*b*), see also www.bundestag.de/mdb14/mdbinfo/1322.html, 26 Mar. 2002.

6 Blickpunkt Bundestag No. 4 (1998): 29.

7 Calculated from www.bundestag.de/mdb14/mdbinfo/1323.html, 26 Mar. 2002; *Frankfurter Allgemeine Zeitung*, 24 Sept. 2002: 1–2.

8 Bauer (1998); *Statistisches Jahrbuch der Bundesrepublik Deutschland*, various issues.

9 Article 79 II Basic Law.

10 Article 61 I Basic Law.

11 Article 93 I No.2, Basic Law.

12 Article 77 II Basic Law; see also Bauer (1998) for an excellent study on the Mediation Committee.

13 Before 1990 the Committee was composed of 11 deputies of the lower house and 11 representatives from the upper house.

14 I follow Saalfeld's translation (Saalfeld 1990: 68).

15 Calculated from Schindler (1999, i. 1638, 2022, iii. 4370, 4372).

16 Calculated from Schindler (1999, ii. 2388–9, iii. 4377).

17 Calculated from Schindler (1999, ii. 2414–15). The data cover the 1949–94 period.

18 In reality, opposition parties tend to mix the two strategies: the conflict-oriented confrontational and the cooperative policy. For a detailed reconstruction of the opposition party SPD in 1982–9, see Gohr 2001.

19 The outgoing president of the Bundesrat, minister-president Kurt Beck, in his report on his presidency on 19 Oct. 2001 in the Bundesrat (*Das Parlament* 44 (2001), 1).

20 See Schindler 1999, i: chapter 6, ii: chapters 9 and 11; Saalfeld 1995; Rudzio 2000: 261.

21 The credit for this distinction goes to Rainer Barzel (CDU) who distinguished between the 'Wahlkreiskönig' and the 'Parlamentsstar'.

22 Article 38 Basic Law.

23 Article 113 Basic Law. This is a major weapon of government against a parliament which tends towards overspending public money. The regulation was added to the Basic Law in 1969, to a large measure in response to coalitions between the parliamentary opposition and sections of the governmental parliamentary parties which had frequently passed legislation with expenditure-raising consequences.

24 The Enquetekommission of the Bundestag on constitutional reform has even concluded that the national parliament in this period 'for several months almost did not exist and was not able to fulfil its duties as an institution responsible for steering and controlling' (Enquetekommission Verfassungsreform des Deutschen Bundestages 1976: 21, translation by the author).

25 Article 81 Basic Law.

26 Articles 115a to 115l Basic Law, which have been among the highly controversial objects of legislation on the case of a constitutional emergency ('Notstandsverfassung') in 1968. The Joint Committee in a State of Defence according to Articles 53a and 115e Basic Law is the 'rump parliament' in the case of a national emergency. Two-thirds of the members of the Joint Committee are deputies of the Bundestag and one-third are members of the Bundesrat. Parliament delegates its deputies in proportion to the relative strength of its parliamentary groups; deputies may not be members of the government.

GUIDE TO FURTHER READING

VON BEYME, K. (1997), *Der Gesetzgeber* (Opladen: Westdeutscher Verlag). Important analysis of the legislation function of the lower house of federal parliament.

ISMAYR, W. (2000) *Der Deutsche Bundestag im politischen System der Bundesrepublik* (Opladen: Leske & Budrich). Comprehensive study of the institutions and the parliamentary process in the lower house.

LEHMBRUCH, G. (2000, 3rd edn.) *Parteienwettbewerb im Bundesstaat* (Wiesbaden: Westdeutscher Verlag). Important study on the relationships between party competition and federalism.

LOEWENBERG, G. (1967), *Parliament in the German Political System* (Ithaca, NY: Cornell University Press). A classic study on the structures, functions, and process of parliamentary government in the Federal Republic of Germany.

NORTON, P. (ed.) (1990), *Parliaments in Western Europe* (*West European Politics*, 13/3) (London: Frank Cass). Presents a wider variety of comparative studies on parliaments.

SAALFELD, T. (1995), *Parteisoldaten und Rebellen: Eine Untersuchung zur Geschlossenheit der Fraktionen im Deutschen Bundestag (1949–1990)* (Opladen: Leske & Budrich.) Instructive analysis of the cohesiveness of parliamentary parties in the Bundestag.

4

'Governing with Judges': The Judiciary, the Court System, and Judicial Review

Policy making in the Federal Republic of Germany takes place within the context of a powerful role for the judiciary and the law (Kommers 1975). In contrast to most other constitutional democracies, Germany's constitution attributes a particularly influential role to the judiciary (Kommers 1997*b*). In order to take proper account of that role, this chapter looks at the organization of the judiciary, the court system, the Federal Constitutional Court, and judicial review. Furthermore, it explores in more detail the extent to which the judiciary affects the political process and the substance of policy making in the Federal Republic.

Constitutional democracy

The Federal Republic is a member of the family of constitutional democracies (Freedom House 2001). In this family of nations the judiciary, representing one of the three powers beside the executive and the legislature, holds a central position. In contrast to the common-law tradition of the Anglo-American system of justice, Germany's judicial system follows the Roman law tradition. Rather than relying on precedents from prior cases as in the common-law system, the legal process in Germany is based on an extensive system of legal codes. Within this tradition, specific cases are judged against the standards laid down in these legal codes. In contrast to most other constitutional democracies, the judiciary in the Federal Republic of Germany plays a particularly powerful role in legislation and policy making—not least due to a Federal Constitutional Court, which is renowned for an unusual abundance of competences (Stone Sweet 2000; Wahl 2001). From this follows, it will be argued in this chapter, a further massive restriction of parliamentary sovereignty—in contradistinction to the exclusive sovereignty of parliament in a majoritarian democracy, such as Britain. It will be further pointed out that the constraints on parliamentary sovereignty have major consequences for Germany's party state. Although the political parties play an important part in the Federal Republic, the room for manoeuvre available to them tends to be more narrowly circumscribed by the judiciary than in most other democracies.

The dominance of the judiciary reflects a deep-seated process of political learning in post-1945 West Germany and, after the accession to the Federal Republic in 1990, also in the Eastern part of Germany. The central position of the judiciary can largely be attributed to the anti-totalitarian spirit of Germany's Basic Law, but it also mirrors the founding fathers' choice of a constitutionalized democracy instead of an unconstrained democracy. Moreover, the emphasis placed on the judiciary and the claim that the law should be supreme reflect the effort of the founding fathers and the motivation of most of the politicians to guard the new republic against a government in which politics was in command, such as in the National-Socialist period (1933–45) and in East Germany's socialist state (1949–90).

4.1 Regulating the judiciary

A superior role for the judiciary is enshrined in the Basic Law of Germany's Second Republic.[1] Following classical constitutional theories of the division of state powers, the founders of the Basic Law have explicitly distinguished between three powers—legislative power, executive power, and the judiciary. Furthermore, they have related each of these powers to specialized institutions of the state. The judiciary has accordingly been linked to the body of independent judges. Division of powers, dispersal of power resources, and fragmentation of state authority in order to forestall authoritarian or totalitarian rule have been a leitmotif of the constitutional design for Germany's Second Republic. A further leitmotif has been the condition that legislation shall be subject to the constitutional order and that the executive power as well as the judiciary shall be bound by law and justice. The Federal Constitutional Court, the Bundesverfassungsgericht, one of the major political innovations in Germany and one of the world's most powerful constitutional courts, embodies the institutional core of the superiority of the law.

The judiciary as guarantor of the rule of law

In order to safeguard the constitution against authoritarian or totalitarian politics, the architects of the Basic Law have placed the judiciary in the position of a genuine third state power and a guarantor of the rule of law. Moreover, the founding fathers conceived of the judiciary as an institution of strength equivalent to, if not superior to, that of the legislature and the executive. The indicators of the importance of the judiciary are manifold. They include the constitutionally enshrined independence of the judiciary and recourse to the court should any person's rights be violated by public authority. In addition, judicial review and administrative review play a major part. Judicial review, that is, rule of judges of the constitutional court on the constitutionality of laws and regulation, is a major part of the Constitutional Court's competences. The growing importance of judicial review in the Federal Republic has been accompanied by a similar growth in judicial review of administrative acts (administrative review), that is, the rule of judges on the legality of government actions, usually those of the executive branch.

Moreover, the Basic Law stipulates an ambitiously defined rule of law which goes beyond the limits of a liberal law state. The target is a state defined by the rule of law and social justice, a *sozialer Rechtsstaat* in the terminology of German constitutional policy. According to the federal constitution, the German polity must conform to the principles of a 'republican, democratic and social state under the rule of law'.[2]

Regarding the organization of the court system, the founders of the constitution entrusted the judiciary to professional experts, that is, professional full-time judges, not elected lay judges, such as in the earliest democratic states in ancient Greece. Moreover, the constitution provides that the organization of the judiciary is the monopoly of the state. This is in marked contrast to the division of judicial power between various centres in state and society, such as the agrarian upper class and the military, for example, or among lay judges and party soldiers, such as in the 'socialist judiciary' of the communist German Democratic Republic. Furthermore, Articles 93 and 94 of the Basic Law lay down the principles of a powerful Federal Constitutional Court with comprehensive rights in judicial review.

Independence of the judges is part of the constitutionalization of the country. A ban on extraordinary courts, a ban on double punishment and legal guarantees in the event of deprivation of liberty are further stipulations defined in the constitution. Part of the constitutional democracy in post-1949 Germany has also been due process and recourse to the courts for everyone.[3]

Civil rights and political rights

These norms are derived from the charter of fundamental rights in the constitution.[4] The charter comprises the civil rights and the political rights in the West European and North American tradition of constitutional democracy. The rights are premissed on the assumption 'that certain liberties of the individual are antecedent to organized society and beyond the reach of governmental power' (Kommers 1997a: 203). Moreover, the basic rights in the constitution are rooted, as the Federal Constitutional Court has emphasized, in a value-oriented order based on the concept of human dignity, the constitution's highest legal value. The concept of human dignity has repeatedly been employed by the Federal Constitutional Court 'as an independent standard of value by which to measure the legitimacy of state actions as well as the uses of individual liberty' (Kommers 1997a: 203). Compared with the Weimar Republic, the basic rights in the constitutions of the Federal Republic of Germany are much more broadly defined and are far better protected. These include advanced legal protection against the violation of individual rights by legislative power and administrative acts. Constitutional complaint and institutional safeguards of democracy, such as a ban on an unconstitutional party and forfeiture of basic rights, are also part of the protective shield for the political and social order.

4.2 The court system

Organizationally, the judicial system in today's Germany consists of the courts in the states, the federal courts, and the Federal Constitutional Court, the German equivalent to the Supreme Court. In the process of unifying West and East Germany, the East German states have substituted the legal order and the judiciary of West Germany for the 'socialist judiciary' of the German Democratic Republic (Raschka 2000). The period of organizational adaptation of East Germany to the West German judiciary lasted until 1994. Since that time the Federal Republic of Germany has had a uniform and integrated judicial system in both west and east. And since that time the long-standing tradition of a highly politicized authoritarian judiciary in East Germany has been replaced by a judiciary of the rule of law type. A state based on the rule of law has been widely welcomed in the new German states as a major security provider. But there were also opponents to the rule of law. Most of the supporters of the old socialist regime raised their voice against adaptation to the West German judiciary. But critical voices came also from spokesmen of the citizens' protest movement in the late German Democratic Republic: 'We wanted justice, but we've got only the rule of law'[5]—instead of getting real justice, defined in substantial terms and including social justice and equality, one had received, it was argued, nothing but procedural justice.

The judiciary in Germany's Second Republic reflects the federalist structure of the country. All lower and intermediate courts of appeal are within the jurisdiction of the states, while courts of final appeal are federal courts. The division of labour between federation and states leaves considerable latitude to the latter. For example, the states control administration and staffing of the judiciary. They also control the training of judges to a large measure. Moreover, the states are the employers of most of the judges. In contrast to this, federal law specifies the structures of the courts and regulates the organization of the federal courts. In addition to the regular courts, responsible for ordinary civil and criminal cases, there are separate judicial hierarchies. These consist of administrative courts, finance courts, labour courts, and social courts as well as separate courts for judges and for soldiers. Each of the judicial hierarchies is headed by a federal court. These are the Federal Administrative Court in Leipzig (in earlier times in Berlin), the Federal Finance Court in Munich, the Federal Labour Court in Erfurt, the Federal Social Court in Kassel, and the Federal Court of Justice (the Bundesgerichtshof) in Karlsruhe, the highest court with jurisdiction in civil and criminal matters. Responsiblity for constitutional matters lies with the states and the federation. The states have a constitutional court of their own, with the exception of Schleswig-Holstein and two East German states. The highest court in Germany's judiciary is the Federal Constitutional Court, the Bundesverfassungsgericht.

The total number of jurists in the Federal Republic of Germany is relatively small when compared with the executive power. Approximately 21,000 judges were counted in 1998. About 75 per cent of them were judges in one of the regular courts (*Ordentliche Gerichte*). Roughly 5,000 judges served in one of the courts of specialized jurisdiction. About 500 judges sat in the various federal courts. Associated with the courts in 2001 were approximately 5,000 public prosecutors (*Staatsanwälte*), 101,000 lawyers (*Rechtsanwälte*), 9,000 attorneys (*Anwaltsnotare*), and about 1,700 notaries (*Notare*) (Statistisches Bundesamt 2001: 358).

4.3 The Federal Constitutional Court

Autonomous constitutional courts are a valid indicator of a vital democracy of the Western tradition. But the non-existence of a constitutional court is by no means an exclusive sign of an authoritarian state or a totalitarian regime, as the British case demonstrates. And not all democracies can pride themselves on a constitutional court with encompassing authorization, as Switzerland shows. The Swiss tradition of a constitutional court is the tradition of a severely constrained court which lacks the power of judicial review of federal legislation. In contrast to this, the Federal Republic of Germany is a country with an extraordinarily powerful Federal Constitutional Court.

The origin and structure of the Federal Constitutional Court

Germany's Federal Constitutional Court is the product of learning from catastrophes. In the light of the decline of the Weimar Republic, the seizure of power by the National-Socialist German Workers' Party in 1933, Germany's totalitarian past in the 1933–45 period, and the rise of Soviet-style socialism after the Second World War in the eastern part of the country, traditional parliamentary and judicial safeguards of democracy were regarded after 1945 as insufficient. At least partly for this reason the founders of the Basic Law created with the Federal Constitutional Court 'a national constitutional tribunal' (Kommers 1997a: 200). The major purpose of the Federal Constitutional Court has been to protect citizens against unlawful interventions of state powers, to safeguard the constitutional and legal order of the country, 'to supervise the judiciary's interpretation of constitutional norms, to enforce a consistent reading of the constitution on the other branches of government, to resolve conflicts between branches and levels of government, and to protect the basic liberties of German citizens' (Kommers 1997a: 200).

Organizationally, the Federal Constitutional Court consists of two senates or chambers with mutually exclusive jurisdiction and personnel. Nowadays each senate is composed of eight judges. Until 1956 twelve judges were sitting in each senate and thereafter ten until 1962. The First Senate was originally responsible for reviewing the constitutionality of laws and resolution of constitutional doubts arising out of ordinary litigation. The Second Senate was mainly in charge of more politicized issues, such as abstract judicial review, a potential battleground between government and opposition, and disputes between branches and levels of government. Due to the overload of the First Senate a major part of the First Senate's functions were later transferred to the Second Senate.

In contrast to the US Supreme Court whose justices are appointed for life, the justices of the German Federal Constitutional Court are appointed for a single term of up to twelve years (and less than twelve years in the case of retirement which is mandatory at the age of 68). Appointment for life was abolished in 1961. Re-election is not allowed in order to minimize office-seeking temptations for the judges and to prevent electoral cycles in the choice of judges, the selection of cases put in front of the Constitutional Court, and the decisions of the Court. Moreover, strict qualification requirements must be met by the candidates for one of the prestigious posts of constitutional judge. These requirements rigorously limit the potential partisan factor in the process of selecting and electing constitutional judges: fundamental prerequisites to the election of a candidate are his or her formally testified qualification to hold judicial office and an age of at least 40.

The selection of the judges of the Federal Constitutional Court

Half of the sixteen members of the Federal Constitutional Court are chosen by the Judicial Selection Committee of the lower house of parliament with a two-thirds majority. The other half are chosen in the upper house. Due to the central role of political parties in the legislature, party political factors play an important role in choosing and appointing the judges of the Federal Constitutional Court. It cannot be ruled out that this results in overt party politicization of the Constitutional Court. But the requisite expertise and autonomy of the judges have been a major barrier against overt party politics in the process of selecting judges and in the decisions taken by the Court. Other constraints on overt party politics have produced outcomes of similar quality, for example the two-thirds majority required for the election of the judges. As long as none of the political parties controls two-thirds of the seats in parliament and the upper house, the two-thirds majority requires extended bargaining between the government and the parliamentary opposition parties. *De facto* the two-thirds majority also necessitates compromise seeking between the Judicial Selection Committee of the Bundestag and the Bundesrat. In political terms, the consensus requirements stipulated by the methods of selecting and appointing the judges of the Federal Constitutional Tribunal thus also presuppose cooperation between government and opposition and—though not *de jure*—cooperation of the minority and the majority in the Bundesrat. That recruitment of constitutional judges has been strongly influenced by party-political factors has been controversially debated. According to one view, a too strong role of the party state is embodied in the present regulation. Supporters of this view argue that there is 'considerable open political "horse trading" and occasional conflicts in the selection process' (Conradt 2001: 235) of the constitutional judges. Others have added that the party political component needs to be cushioned by the cooperation of the Federal President in the process of selecting constitutional courts (von Weizsäcker 2001).

The Federal Constitutional Court and the party state

At least numerically, the party state has a significant impact on the composition of the Federal Constitutional Court. Roughly two-thirds of the constitutional judges have been members of one of the established political parties—a marked contrast to the low nationwide party membership density. According to data collected in a survey of party-state structures in Germany, 28.5 per cent of all judges of the Constitutional Court in 1951–2000 were members of the CDU-CSU. A slightly higher proportion fell on members of the SPD (34.2 per cent); 3.4 per cent of the judges were party members of the FDP, and one-third were not affiliated to one of the political parties. Modest differences exist between the party affiliation of judges in the First and the Second Senate of the Court. For example, the share of

SPD members among the judges in First Senate has exceeded the SPD members' proportion in the Second Senate (38.7 versus 29.7 per cent) (Wagschal 2001*b*: 881).

The selection of the judges and the composition of the Federal Constitutional Court, thus, highlights Germany's character as a party state and manifests at least partly significant partisan impacts on the judiciary. These impacts are reinforced, for example in some of the SPD-governed German states, by the amalgamation of the Ministry of Justice and the Ministry of the Interior, such as in North Rhine-Westphalia, Mecklenburg-West Pomerania, and Bremen.

However, selection of the constitutional judges and the composition of the Federal Constitutional Court do point not only to a party-state component, but also to a strong impact of the regional states, the *Länder*. The recruitment of judges, for example, has been notorious for significant differences between the Bundestag and the Bundesrat. The Bundesrat, as an administrative and executive-oriented institution and a counterweight to party politics, has indeed often 'preferred high-level civil servants with excellent records in state administration' (Conradt 2001: 235). In contrast to this, the Bundestag has tended 'to nominate active politicians and judges from other federal courts' (Conradt 2001: 235).

Moreover, the impact of political parties on the Constitutional Court should not be overestimated. Despite the important role of the parties in the selection of candidates for the Federal Constitutional Court, 'outstanding judges' were appointed (von Beyme 2000*a*: 410; von Beyme 2001*a*: 497). Trends in recruitment patterns support this view. Professionalization has become more important in the process of recruiting constitutional judges: 'Compared to the first generation of judges in the early 1950s, the number of judges with professional experience in politics and economics have declined significantly. At the same, the total number of judges with a career background in administration, judiciary or academia has increased' (Helms 2000*b*: 88). Moreover, party affiliations of judges may play a role in highly controversial cultural issues, such as abortion and biotechnological engineering or reproduction medicine. But in many other cases, judges' deliberations and decision making in the Federal Constitutional Court do not significantly vary with party affiliation. Judicial self-restraint and professional ethos protect quite effectively against overt partisan influence (Benda 2001: 12). Rule adjudication in cases which the opposition party has brought to the Constitutional Court broadly support this view (Stüwe 1997, 2001).

The powers of the Federal Constitutional Court

Cross-national comparison demonstrates that the Federal Constitutional Court is a particularly powerful constitutional tribunal (Landfried 1988; Goetz 1996). The powers of judicial review of the Court have rightly been classified as 'sweeping' (Kommers 1997a: 200). Moreover, the Federal Constitutional Court has fully used its authorization and has indeed 'developed into an institution of major policy making importance' (Kommers 1997a: 200; see also Volcansek 1992).

The founders of the constitution have equipped the Federal Constitutional Court with extensive jurisdiction, subject to appeal from judges, federal government, state governments, one-third of the members of the Bundestag, and in the case of a constitutional complaint also the appeal of everyman, provided that all other legal means are exhausted. The authorization of the Federal Constitutional Court includes competence for binding decisions in the case of litigation between constitutional organs, such as constitutional conflicts between the federal government and the states. The authorization also includes ruling on constitutional complaints, the right to decide on banning unconstitutional political parties, and impeachment of the Federal President.

Judicial review

A substantial part of the competence of the Federal Constitutional Court resides in judicial review, the power to review legislative and executive acts and to nullify unconstitutional ones among them. Judicial review is a major weapon in legislation and in the politics of lawmaking. Judicial review upgrades the role of judges in legislation and policy making. It also engenders strong interdependence of the judicial and legislative branches and functions of government. Furthermore, judicial review results in 'governing with judges' and 'governing like judges', because constitutional courts place the political process of lawmaking inexorably 'in the shadow of constitutional review' (Stone Sweet 2000: 202). This trend has been exacerbated by the two types of judicial review in force in German constitutional law, namely 'concrete judicial review' and 'abstract judicial review' (Kommers 1997b: 13–14, 18, 28). Concrete judicial review allows judges to petition the Federal Constitutional Court to review constitutional questions arising out of a pending case. Politically more sensitive is the case of abstract judicial review. Abstract judicial review means asking the Court to rule on a constitutional issue arising out of a federal or a state statute. The Basic Law authorizes the federal government, a state government, and also one-third of the members of the Bundestag, and thus for example the members of a larger opposition party, to petition the Constitutional Court directly in this matter. The authorization has major political implications. It creates a unique opportunity mainly for the state governments, but also for opposition parties in the lower house of parliament—provided the opposition controls at least one-third of the seats—to attack legislation of the federal government through submitting the case to the Constitutional Court. The opportunity has been seized, although with mixed consequences. The appeals of the state governments to the Federal Constitutional Court have been relatively successful, particularly when the division of labour between the states and the federation was at stake; the appeals of the opposition parties significantly less so (Stüwe 1997).

Judicial review is one of the most important activities of the Federal Constitutional Tribunal. However, constitutional complaints outrank judicial review in quantitative terms. Most of the cases brought before the Federal Constitutional Court (96 per cent of the total)[6] consist of constitutional complaints concerning violations of fundamental rights and freedoms guaranteed by the Basic Law. Although they tend to overload the Court, constitutional complaints have been among the most popular institutions of the Constitutional Court. It is the access to the Court which the constitutional complaint offers for everyone that makes the difference.

On the limits of the Federal Constitutional Court

The Federal Constitutional Court is a powerful court. But it is a reactive court, not a proactive one. A ruling of the Federal Constitutional Court requires prior appeal from authorized institutions and authorized individual actors. Authorization to petition the Court is defined in the constitution. The right to petition varies from procedure to procedure and from target group to target group (see Table 7).

Concrete judicial review, that is review of the compatibility of statutory law with the constitution, presupposes appeal from a court. No other institution or actor is entitled to demand concrete judicial review. In contrast to this, abstract judicial review can be demanded by the federal government, the state governments, or one-third of the members of parliament. Abstract judicial review focuses attention mainly on constraining the executive and the majority of the legislature.

Constitutional complaints, to mention a third major procedure, give access to the Court for every citizen, provided that he or she is violated in his or her basic rights. Constitutional complaints are mainly supposed to protect the citizen against violations of his or her rights by state powers.

Finally, the banning of unconstitutional political parties, to mention the fourth item in a longer list of procedures (see Table 7), is regarded as a vital instrument for the self-defence of democracy. Those authorized to demand the banning of a political party are the Bundestag, the Bundesrat, the federal government, and, in certain circumstances, state parliaments.

4.4 The political impact of the Federal Constitutional Court

The Federal Constitutional Court is a reactive court, not an active one. But when petitioned, the Court makes binding decisions of the highest authority. In the view of many, a conservative stance is characteristic of the Court's policy. Others emphasize a liberal stance as the major characteristic of the Court's ruling. Supporters of a third view point out a more pluralist pattern of the decisions taken in the court.

Government of constitutional judges and by constitutional judges

Although considerable disagreement exists on the details of the court's stance in policy making, it is uncontroversial that the Federal Constitutional Court, through its decisions but also thanks to the legislator's anticipation of judicial review, has been a major determinant of public policy. The judges of the Federal Constitutional Court ruled on many issues of major importance, and the Court is famous for an impressive record of constitutional interpretation in a wide variety of important matters. The Court's constitutional interpretation includes the treaties on the foreign policy of détente vis-à-vis the Eastern European states inaugurated by the SPD-FDP coalition in 1969, the so-called *Ostpolitik*. The judges of the Constitutional Court have also decided on abortion law, industrial democracy, and the constitutionality of the route to German unification,

TABLE 7 **The Federal Constitutional Court: procedures, authorization to appeal, and targets of the Court's rule**

Procedure	Institution or actor authorized to appeal to the Federal Constitutional Court	Target of Court's rule
Abstract judicial review (Article 93 I No. 2 Basic Law)	Federal government, a state government, one-third of members of the Bundestag	Legislature
Ban on a political party as unconstitutional (Article 21 II Basic Law)	Bundestag, Bundesrat, federal government, state parliaments	Unconstitutional parties
Complaints against decisions of the Bundestag on the scrutiny of elections (Article 41 II Basic Law)	Among others: members of the Bundestag	Protection of democracy
Concrete judicial review— compatibility of statutory law with the Constitution (Article 100 Basic Law)	Each court of justice	Legislature, judiciary
Conflicts between organs of the state (Article 93 I No. 1 Basic Law)	Bundestag, Bundesrat, federal government, Federal President, members of parliament	State organs
Constitutional complaint (Article 93 I No. 4a Basic Law)	Everyman	Legislature
Constitutional complaint against violation of local self-administration (Article 93 I No. 4b Basic Law)— provided that the issue is not part of the competences of a state constitutional court	Local government and confederations of local governments	Legislature
Constitutional dispute between federation and states on Article 72 (concurrent legislation) (Articles 93 I No. 2a, No. 3, 84 IV 2 Basic Law)	Federal government and state governments	State organs
Constitutional dispute within a state (Article 99 Basic Law)	Organs of a state	State organs

TABLE 7	Continued		
Forfeiture of basic rights (Article 18 Basic Law)	Bundestag, federal government, state governments	Violators of basic rights
Presidential impeachment (Article 61 Basic Law) and impeachment of justices (Article 98 II, V Basic Law)	Bundestag, Bundesrat	Executive and judiciary

to mention only a few examples. In its role as guardian of the constitution, the Court has been a major policy maker, and also in its role as 'a protector of human rights, and an adjudicator of German federalism' (Helms 2000*b*: 84). Among the ruling of the Court the decision to nullify the plan of the Adenauer government to establish a national pro-governmental television station deserves major attention. That decision also marked the beginning of a series of rulings in support of safeguarding and extending the freedom of opinion and the freedom of the press.

The Constitutional Court has also declared two extremist parties unconstitutional: in 1952 the Socialist Reich Party, a follow-up organization of the National-Socialist Party, and in 1956 the German Communist Party. Moreover, the Court is currently examining the constitutionality or non-constitutionality of the Nationaldemokratische Partei Deutschlands (NPD). Massive intervention in public financing of political parties and no less massive intervention against liberal abortion laws in 1975 and in 1993 have also been landmark cases. Moreover, a decision of the Federal Constitutional Court on electoral law in 1990 fundamentally shaped the political landscape in East Germany. The Court's ban on the application of the 5 per cent clause to all of Germany in the first Bundestag election after unification in December 1990 opened the route to national parliament for the PDS (see section 5.1 below). The Court's ruling on gender issues and family policy is also worth emphasizing. The Federal Constitutional Court has actively promoted equal status for men and women in family law and in the society as a whole. Moreover, the judges of the Constitutional Court have strongly advocated social protection for families with children and single parents, as the famous ruling of 2 April 2001 on financing care for the elderly demonstrated. Advocacy of gender equality has been part of a larger recurrent topic of the Constitutional Court's ruling, namely: safe-guarding and extending civil rights, strengthening the status of the citizen vis-à-vis public administration, and emphasizing the importance of civil liberties of the citizens. That emphasis has encouraged one of the observers to argue that Germany's Federal Constitutional Court is 'a late realization of a liberal 19th-century dream' (Blankenburg 1996: 308).

Several times the Federal Constitutional Court has been an explicit pol-icy maker. It has even adopted the role of *the* major policy maker, most notably in issues that the political parties put in front of the Court in order to avoid a political stalemate. A major example is the ruling on whether the participation of the Federal Army in out-of-NATO-area missions is consti-tutional, as in the case of NATO's military attack on Milosevic's Serbia in response to the Kosovo War in 1999.

The 'Karlsruhe Republic'

Although undoubtedly not a 'cemetary of laws declared as unconsti-tutional' (von Beyme 2000*a*: 417), the Federal Constitutional Court has classified almost 5 per cent of the bills passed into law by the Bundestag as invalid or incompatible with the Basic Law (Schindler 1999, ii. 2495–511, iii. 3064–5). Furthermore, the Court is often petitioned to rule on major legis-lative acts. For example, 40 per cent of the key laws in von Beyme's study on the Bundestag as the major lawmaker in Germany were put before the Constitutional Court in Karlsruhe (von Beyme 1997: 426).

The Federal Constitutional Court is not only one of the most powerful institutions in the Federal Republic of Germany, it is also highly popular. Most public opinion polls show high levels of reputation of, support for, and trust in, the Court. As regards reputation, support, and trust, the Federal Constitutional Court outperforms all other political institutions (Gabriel and Neller 2000: 82). In contrast to the Weimar Republic, neither the highest Constitutional Court nor the court system as a whole can now be reproached with 'Klassenjustiz', that is administration of justice based on class bias. And although politicians sometimes find it hard to accept the rulings of the Court, above all when the constitutional judges indulge in judicial activism (Ehmke 2001), the political class has taken good care not to bypass the decisions of the Federal Constitutional Court. This does not preclude harsh criticisms of the Court. Konrad Adenauer, for example, occasionally classified a ruling of the Constitutional Court as 'wrong'. And in a bitter conflict between the Adenauer government and the Constitutional Court on the issue of a constitutional appeal against German rearmament, Adenauer's Minister of Justice, Thomas Dehler gave vent to his anger in private through conceding that he personally 'would love to blow up the whole Constitutional Court' (Blasius 2002: 12). But these were local outbursts of frustration over an otherwise widely respected and politically highly influential Constitutional Court.

How deeply the reputation of the Court has been anchored can be guessed from the high trust scores and the esteem enjoyed by the Constitutional Court at home and abroad (Badura and Dreier 2001). The Federal Constitutional Court has even become one of Germany's 'most successful export products' (Kerscher 2001: 4), especially in the new democracies of the post-1989 wave of democratization in central and eastern Europe.

Without the ruling of the Federal Constitutional Court the Federal Republic would probably be different from today's Germany. Today's Germany has been so deeply impregnated by the Federal Constitutional Court that the label 'The Karlsruhe Republic', as suggested by the official speaker on the 50th anniversary of the Court in Karlsruhe, Gerhard Casper (2001: 10), is not too far fetched. The Federal Republic without the Constitutional Court probably would have been marked by steeper power hierarchies, less press freedom, and a lower level of civil rights (Kerscher 2001)—and wider room for manoeuvre for policy makers.

Judicialization

It is less difficult to establish the most visible effects of the Federal Constitutional Court. There exists general agreement that the ruling of the judges in the Court has strengthened the position of the judiciary to a degree unprecedented in Germany's history. Moreover, the establishment of a specialized Constitutional Court possessing powers of concrete and abstract judicial review has generated an expansionary dynamic which resulted in 'judicialization' of lawmaking and, at the same time, 'politicization' of constitutional review (Landfried 1994; Stone Sweet 2000). That process has been under way in almost all European constitutional democracies except for Britain where the sovereignty of parliament impeded a breakthrough of the judiciary in a magnitude similar to that of the continental European countries. But the simultaneity of 'judicialization' of lawmaking and 'politicization' of constitutional review had a particularly profound impact in Germany, where the post-totalitarian spirit and the preference of the founding fathers for powerful checks and balances were particularly manifest in granting a dominant role to the judiciary. The overall outcome of the latter in the Federal Republic of Germany has not only been growing interdependence of the legislature and the Constitutional Court, but also the domination of the political by the law, if not supremacy of the law (Maier 1999: 6).

This involves massive judicial constraints on the legislature and the executive. The Constitutional Court has also not hesitated to push policy makers into a direction more compatible with the basic stipulations of the constitution and the Court's view of the Basic Law, such as the protection of marriage, families, and children. For example, the Federal Constitutional Court has insisted on upgrading family policy and support for families with children in particular, but it has also focused attention on single parents. Moreover, the Constitutional Court's roles include, in the words of its former President, Jutta Limbach, the role of 'a lobby in favour of disadvantaged social groups'.[7] Furthermore, the Constitutional Court has been praised from a civic rights perspective for its protection of human rights. From the perspective of empirical or realist democratic theory, much can also be said in favour of the Constitutional Court's role as an effective and prestigious guardian of a constitutional democracy.

A 'contre-gouvernement'?

However, according to critics a considerable price has to be paid for the achievement of an independent judiciary and powerful Federal Constitutional Court. Proponents of unconstrained democratic rule, for example, regard judicial review with suspicion and construe it as an unwarranted constraint on the popular will. In a similar vein, supporters of a model of majoritarian democracy, of judicial restraint, and the full sovereignty of parliament are critical of the important role played by the Federal Constitutional Court. Technocrats could add to this that the judges of the Constitutional Court have unnecessarily relieved parliament, government, and the opposition of responsibility in a wide variety of highly controversial issues. And from a policy-oriented perspective, the Constitutional Court has been criticized for exhibiting pronounced judicial activism, adopting an overtly political role, usurping the legislative power and policy-making prerogatives of parliament and government, and for not exercising sufficient judicial restraint.[8] Judicialization, that is, the 'expansion of the province of the courts at the expense of politicians and/or administrators' (Sunkin 1994: 125) occurs also in the Federal Republic of Germany.[9] And not infrequently the Federal Constitutional Court adopts the roles of a 'participant in government' (Papier 2000: 15), a 'parallel government' (Helms 2000b: 94), and now and then also the position of a 'reserve legislator' (Wefing 2001a: 58) and an architect of general policy guidelines (Helms 2000b: 92). Ruling on abortion law, taxation, and family policy are major examples of the latter tendency.

It may be exaggerated to argue that the Constitutional Court is in charge of the long-term political decisions, while the federal government in Berlin is responsible only for day-to-day business. But it can hardly be denied that judicial review is, in reality, 'governing by judicial means' (Helms 2000b: 92). Moreover, the importance of many review procedures may turn judicial review into 'governing with judges' and 'governing like judges' (Stone Sweet 2000: 202). Undoubtedly a court with a wide variety of competences, as Germany's Federal Constitutional Court, is inevitably 'a policy maker' (Landfried 1994: 122) either through binding decisions or through anticipation of the Court's ruling on the part of the lawmaker (Kommers 1997a). Many factors have been conducive to governing by judicial means. Among these, the legalistic tradition in the Federal Republic's political culture is one factor. According to this tradition, judicial decisions are more valuable than decisions taken by the parliamentary majority. The relevant determinants also include the widespread inclination of the political class to anticipate decisions of the Federal Constitutional Court or to postpone decisions on controversial issues until the Court has put forward a ruling. The case of out-of-area missions of the Federal Army in 1994 is a major example. However, 'governing by judicial means' has also been influenced by the Court itself, for example through substituting active judicialism for judicial restraint at least in some issues.

Despite its powerful role the Federal Constitutional Court is not the incarnation of a genuine 'contre-gouvernement' (Wildenmann 1969). As long as the Federal Constitutional Court remains a passive court, it can only adopt the role of a veto player. Moreover, the Court is rarely in the position of an agenda setter, that is, an actor who controls the political agenda in order to maximize goals important for him. Furthermore, the Federal Constitutional Court is not only a subject in the political process; it can also become an object of political strategies designed by government and opposition. There is a temptation for politicians to exploit the Court for partisan purposes, such as in the selection of judges. The party state component is not absent from politics and policy of the Federal Constitutional Court, as Wagschal (2001b) has shown.

Achievements and problems of the supremacy of the law

The pros and cons of the Federal Constitutional Court are part of a larger topic, namely: achievement and problems of the claim that the law should be supreme in Germany. The major achievement is clearly this: the establishment of an autonomous Federal Constitutional Court, the relatively high level of independence of the judiciary, as well as the importance of administrative review have transformed the Federal Republic of Germany into a state in which the law is omnipresent. From this follows a high level of legal security throughout the country and a climate conducive to a 'law- and court-minded people' (Conradt 2001: 228). This is no mean achievement in a country which has long been exposed to, and has suffered from, the supremacy of the political, such as in the National-Socialist era (1933–45), in East Germany's Socialist state (1949–90), in the period of belligerent occupation between 1945 and 1949, and, albeit to a lesser extent, in the period from 1949 until the Germany Treaty in 1955 (Friedrich 1949, 1953; Jarausch and Sigrist 1997).

The dominant role claimed by the judiciary has generated stabilizing effects, such as high levels of certainty and predictability, but it has also been conducive to side effects and problems. The reduction of organizational overload of the courts due to the large number of proceedings is long-overdue homework for the judiciary. Long waiting periods and the long duration of legal proceedings are part of the overload syndrome. And so, too, is the indirect influence on Court rulings of the so-called 'Third Senate', the nickname for the scientific staff of the Federal Constitutional Court. It is to a large extent the 'Third Senate' which predetermines a substantial part of the decisions taken by the Constitutional Court without being properly legitimized to do so.

Furthermore, language barriers between professional jurists and ordinary citizens have aggravated communication between the judiciary and the people. In addition, a gap exists between the qualification profile of most jurists and the type of social, economic, and political problems addressed in court proceedings. Regarding complex political-economic problems, above all problems with complex trade-offs and problems which cut across departmental boundaries, the training of most judges is not sufficient. A lack of expertise in real-world political and social processes, insufficient sensitivity for trade-offs, a deficit in basic macroeconomics and micro-economics, and lack of expertise in evaluating the social, political, and economic costs and benefits of judicial choices—all these factors often result in costly decisions. The adjudication of labour law and social law offers abundant examples.

In addition, handing a substantial proportion of political power to elected or non-elected judges is not to everybody's liking. For those who prefer a strong parliament elected by a sovereign people, 'governing with judges' (Stone Sweet 2000: 202) resembles oligarchic rule by a few experts who meddle in politics, thwarting the will of the people. But the counter-hypothesis also deserves to be considered: a democracy without a constitutional state, independent professional judges, and judicial and administrative review would almost certainly be plagued by wildly fluctu-ating majorities, tyranny of the majority, abuse of power by scheming politicians and arrogant bureaucrats, and violation of minority rights.

It must be added, however, that the judiciary, like all other state powers in today's Germany, is circumscribed by narrowly defined institutionalized checks and balances. A massive constraint also lies in the construction of a passive constitutional court: as mentioned above, the Federal Consti-tutional Court is not allowed to intervene in legislation on its own initia-tive. Jurisdiction of the Court requires prior appeal from those authorized to petition the constitutional judges. A more active role was denied to the Court in order not to place the judiciary in a hegemonic position among the state powers. Thus, the Federal Constitutional Court may now and then behave as if it were a 'contre-gouvernement' (Wildenmann 1969), but it has also been constrained by powerful checks and balances. A further barrier is to be found in the lack of direct power of the Constitutional Court. The Court has no big bureaucracy, no revenue-raising ability, and no police force or army at its command—and thus no way to enforce its rulings. If other branches of government ignored the ruling of the Constitutional Court, the Court would be powerless.

In addition judicial power is under close scrutiny. In addition to this scrutiny is the impeachment of a judge, a powerful legal weapon. When a federal judge intentionally infringes the principles of this Constitution or the constitutional order of a State, the Federal Constitutional Court may decide by a two-thirds majority upon the request of the Bundestag that the judge be dismissed.

Further checks and balances exist below the level of constitutional law. Intra-organizational devices provide checks and balances on the judiciary, such as the provision that the courts shall be composed of several judges. Unanimity and near-unanimity also exert a major influence in constraining the power of the judiciary. In addition, organizational separation of the various branches of the judiciary is part of the checks and balances. And so, too, is judicial self-restraint as long as it is respected. Furthermore, the Federal Constitutional Court may be regarded as a limping constitutional organ, largely because the legislature rather than the court itself is in charge of regulating the organization and the proceedings of the Court. Even more important is that the legislature may change the rules of the game through constitutional change or legislation below the level of constitutional change.

National law and European law

Last but not least the judiciary of the Federal Republic of Germany is not the only judicial player in town. The Federal Republic of Germany has been born as a penetrated system and has grown up as a 'semisovereign state' (Katzenstein 1987). Part of the external semi-sovereignty has been due to the transfer of sovereign powers to intergovernmental institutions and transnational institutions, such as the European Community. As far as the European Community is concerned, the Federal Republic of Germany participates in a multilevel system comprising the member states, transnational institutions, and subnational levels of government. This involves a more or less reduced scope for action at the level of the nation state and an increasing role for European policy making inclusive of a major feedback loop from European law on the law of the member states (Weiler 1999).

The relationship between EU law and law in the member state is conflict-ridden. A major part of the conflict concerns gains and losses of sovereignty and democratic control. The conflict also reflects major differences in legal traditions, such as the difference between the common-law countries (with the United Kingdom as the major example) and the civil-law countries, among these the Romance family (with France as the core country), the Germanic family (with Germany as the core), the Nordic family, and, after the opening of the EU to the Eastern parts of Europe, the socialist and post-communist family of nations. The core of the conflict consists of a potential clash of the process and substance of European integration on the one hand and fundamental norms in national law on the other, such as the basic rights of the German constitution and constitutionally enshrined institutional idiosyncracies, such as Germany's federalism (Bach 2001). This conflict also played a major role in the position adopted by the German Federal Constitutional Court vis-à-vis the Community and the European Court of Justice. While the European Court of Justice regards European law as supreme, the Federal Constitutional Court claims supremacy for the national law and accepts European integration subject to compatibility with fundamental norms of the national law. The Federal Constitutional Court further argues that Germany's participation in the European community presupposes that the EU is bound to the democratic rule of law and social and federal principles, as well as to subsidiarity as a leitmotif for the division of labour between government and non-statist organization, and provides a protection of fundamental rights essentially equivalent to that of the Basic Law in Germany.[10] Under these circumstances, the Federal Republic of Germany may delegate sovereign powers to the European Community, provided the Bundesrat consents. Thus, the Federal Constitutional Court regards the member states and their parliaments as the 'Masters of the European Treaties'. This is not totally free from institutional egocentricity: as long as the member states and their parliaments remain Masters of the European Treaties, the Federal Constitutional Court in its role as guardian of the Constitution and incarnation of the supremacy of the law vis-à-vis the political is also superior to the Masters of the European Treaties.

4.5 Conclusion

Policy making in the Federal Republic of Germany takes place within the context of a powerful role of the judiciary and the law. It is therefore hardly possible to understand the political institutions and the political process in the Federal Republic of Germany without considering the important part played by the judiciary. It is also almost impossible to explain the political process and policy making in Germany without taking proper account of the role played by the Federal Constitutional Court. Due to a particularly powerful role which the constitution attributes to the judiciary and, above all, to the Federal Constitutional Court, the Federal Republic is a major example of a political system in which elected government coexists with 'governing with judges' and not infrequently also with 'governing by judges'. This finding adds further support to the view that politics and policy making in the Federal Republic of Germany take place within the context of a particularly wide variety of checks and balances, co-governing forces, and veto players. It is largely for these reasons that political will formation and political decision making in today's Germany are highly complicated and complex processes and differ to a considerable extent from politics and policy in a more centralized majoritarian democracy with a more limited role for the judiciary.

KEY TERMS

- abstract judicial review
- administrative review
- Basic Law
- ban on unconstitutional parties
- Bundesverfassungsgericht (Federal Constitutional Court)
- civil rights
- concrete judicial review
- constitutional complaint
- constitutional democracy
- 'contre-gouvernement'
- division of power
- dispersal of power resources
- fragmentation of state authority
- Federal Constitutional Court
- forfeit of basic rights
- 'governing with judges'
- impeachment
- judicial review
- judiciary
- 'Karlsruhe Republic'
- party state
- political rights
- rule of law
- 'socialist judiciary'
- sozialer Rechtsstaat
- totalitarianism/totalitarian regime

QUESTIONS FOR CHAPTER 4

1 What are the pros and cons of the view that the Federal Republic of Germany represents a case of 'governing with judges'?

2 Can the Federal Constitutional Court be conceived of as a 'contre-gouvernement'?

3 To what extent does the federalist structure of the state affect the court system in the Federal Republic of Germany?

4 What are the major pros and cons of the supremacy of the law in the Federal Republic of Germany?

5 What are the major political functions of the judiciary in the Federal Republic?

NOTES

1 Article 20 III and Articles 92–104, Basic Law.

2 Article 28 I Basic Law.

3 Articles 92–104 Basic Law.

4 Articles 1–19 Basic Law.

5 'Wir wollten Gerechtigkeit und haben den Rechtsstaat bekommen!'

6 7 Sept. 1951 to 31 Dec. 2000. Of the 132,002 cases brought to the Court, 126,962 were constitutional complaints, 3,288 fell into the category of abstract and concrete judicial review, 5 were related to a ban on unconstitutional parties, and 1,747 concerned other cases, such as constitutional conflicts between the federal government and the states. *Source:* Bundesverfassungsgericht (www.bundesverfassungsgericht.de).

7 *Der Spiegel*, 30 (2002), 54.

8 See, for a selection of views critical of the Constitutional Court, Landfried 1988, 1994. Judicialization is also a perennial topic in the press, see, for example, Zuck 1999; Wefing 2001a: 58.

9 The examples include the ruling of the Constitutional Court on the abortion issue in 1993, and decisions with major fiscal implications, such as the costly rulings on the *Familienlastenausgleich* 1998, that is, the Compensation of the Burden Shouldered by Families.

10 Article 23 Basic Law.

GUIDE TO FURTHER READING

AVENARIUS, H. (2001), *Die Rechtsordnung der Bundesrepublik Deutschland*, 3rd edn. (Bonn: Bundeszentrale für politische Bildung). Overview of the judiciary, constitutional law, and statute law in Germany.

GOETZ, K. H. and CULLEN, P. J. (eds.) (1994), *Constitutional Policy in Unified Germany, German Politics*, 3/3 (London: Frank Cass). A collection of studies in continuity and discontinuity in constitutional policy in pre- and post-1990 Germany.

KOMMERS, D. P. (1997), *The Constitutional Jurisprudence of the Federal Republic of Germany*, 2nd edn. (Durham, NC: Duke University Press). The most comprehensive study in English on constitutional jurisprudence in post-Second World War Germany.

LANDFRIED, C. (1984), *Bundesverfassungsgericht und Gesetzgeber* (Baden-Baden: Nomos). Pathbreaking study of direct and indirect relationships between the Federal Constitutional Court and public policy making.

——(ed.) (1988), *Constitutional Review and Legislation.* (Baden-Baden: Nomos). International comparison of constitutional review and legislation.

STONE SWEET, A. (2000), *Governing with Judges: Constitutional Politics in Europe* (Oxford: Oxford University Press). Important study of the process of upgrading the role of the judiciary in Germany and other European states.

WEILER, J. H. H. (1999), *The Constitution of Europe* (Cambridge: Cambridge University Press). Pathbreaking analysis of the impact of European law on the member states of the European Union.

5

....

Linking People and Political Institutions

Chapter 5 discusses the link between the people and political institutions. What are the major intermediary institutions between the people and the government? Which type of electoral formula shapes the transformation of votes into parliamentary seats? How is the party system structured? What drives voting behaviour, and what are the outcomes of voting? To what extent are state–interest group relations corporatist in nature, and to what extent pluralist? What role do representative democracy and direct democracy play, and to what extent is the democratic order in Germany shaped by majoritarian and non-majoritarian systems? Finally, who belongs to the political elite, and what characterizes the recruitment patterns, the attitudes, and the belief systems of the political leaders before and after unification? These are the major questions addressed in this chapter.

5.1 More than proportional representation only: the electoral system

The Federal Republic's electoral formula is a two-track proportional representation on the basis of universal suffrage for citizens of German nationality (Jesse 1990; Nohlen 2000). Before 1970 all citizens above the age of 21 were entitled to vote and since then all citizens aged 18 or above have been able to vote. Since 1953 the special feature of the electoral system for elections to the lower house of the federal parliament has been that each voter may cast two votes, in contrast to one vote in the first Bundestag election in 1949. The first vote is for a constituency candidate in single-member districts; the second vote is for a political party. Before 1953 60 per cent of all seats in the lower house were direct seats and 40 per cent were allocated according to the party lists. Since 1953 half of the basic seats (*Grundman-date*)—656 in the fourteenth legislative period of the Bundestag (1998–2002) and 598 in the fifteenth legislative period—are allocated through relative majority vote in the single-member districts, and the other half through party lists in each of the sixteen states of the Federal Republic.

First vote and second vote

The decisive vote is the second vote, not the first. The reason is that the distribution of the second vote largely determines the final percentage of parliamentary seats each party will receive,[1] while the first vote determines which candidates get those seats. The second vote prescribes proportional representation, whereas the first vote adds a personalized component to the electoral formula. The outcome consists of 'personalized proportional representation'. The constituency seats won by a party's candidates are deducted from the total due to it on the basis of the second vote. If a party wins more direct seats than it is entitled to under proportional representation, it retains these 'excess seats' (*Überhangmandate*). The size of parliament increases accordingly, for example in the 1998–2002 legislative period from 656 to 669 seats. Since 1985 the transformation of votes in seats follows the Hare-Niemeyer formula of mathematical proportions, a method of calculating slightly more favourable for smaller parties than the d'Hondt formula which was in force until 1985.

Five per cent clause

The 5 per cent clause is a further restriction on proportionality in the electoral formula for elections to the Bundestag. According to the 5 per cent clause, only parties with at least 5 per cent of the votes or, alternatively, three constituency seats through relative majority in the first vote win rights to a proportional share of seats, that is, they can use their second vote.[2] Lower hurdles were in force in the early 1950s, such as 5 per cent of the votes not nationally but only in one state before 1953, and one constituency seat rather than three before 1956. Furthermore, two temporary exceptions from the electoral formula were in effect in the 1990 Bundestag election, the first all-German election after unification. The exception was based on a ruling of the Federal Constitutional Court which demanded fair treatment for both West German and East German parties. In the 1990 election, a political party was required to secure the 5 per cent minimum in either the West German electoral area or in East Germany. The further exception in the 1990 election designed to assist the new East German parties was the right of the parties to combine their electoral lists and, thus, to form alliances in the various states. It was basically due to these exceptions that the PDS, the follow-up organization to East Germany's Socialist Unity Party, and the Alliance of East German Greens and East German Citizen Democrats gained parliamentary seats in 1990, although they received less than 5 per cent of the national vote.

Disproportionality of votes and seats

The degree of disproportionality of votes and seats in the electoral system of the Federal Republic is low by international standards. For example, electoral disproportionality between seats and votes[3] in Bundestag elections in the second half of the twentieth century was four times smaller than the disproportionality between votes and seats in elections to the British House of Commons in the same period (Lijphart 1999: 162). Although the 5 per cent hurdle has reduced higher levels of fractionalization (Capoccia 2002: 179), it has not blocked access for new parties, as the rise of the Green Party in the 1980s and the ascent of the PDS after 1990 demonstrate. The German electoral system is, thus, an interesting formula for contributing to stability through moderate defractionalization and keeping at the same time access for minorities and new parties open, provided that the minorities and new parties surpass a critical threshold in voter support. It is at least partly for its capability in achieving 'a good balance between a defragmenting impact ... and respect for political minorities' (Capoccia 2002: 171), that the electoral system of the Federal Republic has served as the model of reference for electoral reform elsewhere, such as in New Zealand's reform of the electoral system in 1993, which substituted the German electoral formula for the majority system.

Electoral systems and election outcomes in the states

Most scientific studies on elections and electoral behaviour in post-1949 Germany have focused on the elections to the Bundestag. That perspective is well founded, because the lower house of the federal parliament is the centre of legislation in Germany. But the focus on the Bundestag elections can underestimate the importance of federalism and ignore the impact of elections in the states on the composition of the state governments and the party make-up of the Bundesrat, parliament's upper house (section 2.5 above). The electoral systems in the states of the Federal Republic of Germany differ from the rules of the game in Bundestag elections, but they differ mostly in nuance and detail, not in substance (Korte 2000: 74–8). Proportional representation, not majority rule, is standard in all states. And all of the electoral formulas in the states provide a 5 per cent hurdle in order to restrict the access of small parties to parliament—except for two parties of ethnic minority in Schleswig-Holstein (*Südschleswiger Wählerverband*) and Brandenburg, where the hurdle does not apply to the *Sorben*, a Slavic minority. The major contrast to the electoral formulas for Bundestag elections concerns the length of the legislative period. Contrary to the four year legislative period in the Bundestag, most state parliaments have opted for five years. The exceptions from this rule are the states of Bremen, Hamburg, Hesse, Mecklenburg-West Pomerania, and Saxony-Anhalt with a four-year legislative period.

In contrast to the broadly converging electoral formulas in the states, party preferences and election outcomes vary widely. For example, the political division in 2002 between the CDU-CSU-dominated south of the country and the mostly SPD-run north catches the eye. Furthermore, the CDU-CSU vote in elections to state parliaments in 1998 to 2002 varied from 22.0 per cent in Saxony-Anhalt to 56.9 per cent in Saxony. In contrast to this the SPD vote in this period spanned the difference between an all-time low of 10.7 per cent in Saxony to 47.9 per cent in Lower Saxony.

The election outcomes in the German states have major impacts on national politics and policy. First, the numerous state elections create a climate of permanent electoral campaign. Second, election outcomes in the states can result in rival majorities in the Bundestag and Bundesrat, such as since 1999 until the time of writing (October 2002). This constellation of political forces reinforces the consociational elements and strengthens the grand coalition components in the architecture of Germany's polity.

5.2 Political parties and party systems

Even if a wide variety of political parties have participated in national elections, the centre of the party system has been the struggle between the two major parties—the Christian Democrats and the Social Democrats. Notwithstanding remarkable changes in the total number and the patterns of interaction between the parties, the party system in the Federal Republic has basically been an alternating system, with at least three parties on the one hand and coalitions as the most typical form of government on the other.

The structure and transformations of the party system

The party system of the Federal Republic of Germany has undergone major transformations (Gabriel, Niedermayer, and Stöss 2001). A large number of relevant parties and, hence, a relatively high degree of fragmentation on the one hand and dominance of the Christian Democratic parties on the other marked the German party system at the federal level after the first national election in 1949 as well as in the early 1950s. Later, from the late 1950s to the late 1970s it turned into a highly concentrated party system with a pronounced centrist drive and a truncated ideological spectrum dominated by two large parties—CDU-CSU and SPD—and a smaller liberal party. In this period, the Liberals were the kingmakers, whose coalitional policy determined whether the CDU-CSU or the SPD gained access to the centre of power (Stöss 1984). The rise of the Green Party in the 1980s and the ascent of the PDS in East Germany have again resulted in a higher level of fragmentation, although fragmentation is still moderate when compared with the Weimar Republic. Nevertheless, the increase in the total number of relevant parties substituted a more complex, fluid, and open post-unification party system for a stable, more exclusive pre-unification party system (Roberts 1997). A higher potential for the rise of new parties, such as the Party of the Rule of Law-Offensive (Partei Rechtstaatlicher Offensive) in the 2001 election in Hamburg, is part of this trend. Even more important are the instability and the asymmetry of the post-1990 party system (Kielmansegg 2002). It is more unstable because the vote shares falling to the various parties and the dealignment of voters make the formation of stable parliamentary majorities more difficult than before. Moreover, the post-1990 party system is asymmetrical because the coalition options are unevenly distributed—in contrast to the symmetry in the preceding period. The key position is held by the SPD, because the Social Democrats are potential coalition partners of all other relevant parties. The second position is taken by the Liberals, a potential coalition partner of both the CDU–CSU and the SPD. All other parties, including the Christian Democrats, can count on fewer potential coalition partners at the federal level: the CDU–CSU on the liberals (and potentially also the SPD), and the Green Party and the PDF on the SPD.

A large number of parties and a complex cleavage-structure character-ized the West German party system in the first and second legislative period (1949–53 and 1953–7). The major cleavages at that time were based on class and religion, but they also comprised, albeit to a lesser extent, centre–periphery differences, anti-communism versus communism, and disparity between the native population versus refugees and expellees. The 1950s, however, were a period of rapid economic, social and political change. The transformation was driven by high economic growth rates, rapid social change, the secularization as well as the social and economic integration of most weaker social groups through rapidly expanding job opportunities and expansive social security, including the integration of most of the 11 million refugees and expellees from the Eastern areas of the former German Reich, the Soviet Occupation Zone, and the German Democratic Republic. The transformation of West Germany's post-war society and economy was conducive to a rapidly declining number of political parties and a simplified cleavage structure dominated mainly by religion and class (Falter and Schumann 1994).

The process of concentration in the party system also reflected genu-inely political determinants. Among these, the political mobilization of broad voter coalitions by the CDU-CSU and the SPD, the two mass integration parties with a structure bordering on a 'catch all party' (Kirchheimer 1965) deserves attention.[4] An alternating party system with three parties emerged from the concentration process and dominated party politics at the federal level in the 1960s and 1970s. These parties were the CDU-CSU, a people's party of centrist complexion in economic and social policy and centre-right or conservative outlook in many other policy areas, the SPD, a centre-left people's party of social reform with close links to the labour movement, and the FDP, a smaller liberal party, which held a position as the pivotal party at that time.

The transformation of the German party system did not stop there. Notwithstanding its high degree of concentration in the 1960s and 1970s, the party system has proved to be more open to newcomers than predicted by its critics. The rise of the Green Party in the 1980s points to the first major change. German unification generated a further major change in the party system, with the rise of the PDS in the East German states since the first all-German national election in 1990 and the resulting weakness of the Liberals and the Greens in East Germany as the major trends.

From pluralistic fragmentation to near 'polarized pluralism'

The German party system has moved from pluralistic fragmentation to 'low fragmentation', 'moderate pluralism', and a more polarized system after unification, to borrow from Sartori's typology of party systems (1976: 127). However, peculiarities of the German case must be added to Sartori's typology. In contrast to Italy, the classical case of polarized pluralism, polarization in Germany's party system is relatively moderate and asymmetrical. It is relatively moderate, because anti-system parties, such as the German Communist Party and the ultra-rightist National-Socialist German Workers' Party (NSDAP) in the Weimar Republic, have been weak or non-existent in post-1949 Germany. Moreover, German-style polarization is asymmetrical, because a relevant party of the radical right, such as the Italian Alleanza Nazionale, is missing (Betz and Immerfall 1998). The post-1949 German radical right is organizationally divided into various small parties, including the Republicans and the National Democratic German Party, the NPD. None of these parties has managed to jump over the 5 per cent hurdle of the law on elections to the lower house of the federal parliament up to the time of writing in October 2002.

The Federal Republic of Germany is also a country without a secular-conservative party of the type of the British Conservative Party since the late 1970s. The position of a secular-conservative 'rightist party' (Castles 1982, 1998) has thus been empty in the German party system since 1949. This is of major importance for a better understanding of public policy in the Federal Republic. The absence of a major party of the right and the non-existence of a market-oriented conservative party on the one hand and the presence of the two large people's parties of Christian Democratic and Social Democratic complexion with ambitious social policy programmes on the other have created a party system highly conducive to expanding and maintaining an advanced welfare state even in economically hard times (Schmidt 1998: 75–112, 168, 172–3; Klingemann and Volkens 2001).

A unified state with a divided party system

Post-1990 Germany is a case of a unified nation. In contrast to the period before the collapse of the Berlin Wall, post-1990 Germany is no longer divided into a democratic capitalist western part and an authoritarian socialist regime in eastern Germany. But unified Germany is based on a divided electorate (Dalton 1996a, 1996b), a divided party system (Poguntke 2001), and a divided political culture (Kolinsky 2001). In contrast to the relatively homogeneous party system before 1990, the post-unification party system is dual in nature, with a major division between the western and the eastern parts of the country (Padgett and Saalfeld 1999). The West German party system replicates its structures of the 1980s. It is basically a four-party system with two large parties—CDU-CSU and SPD—and FDP and the Greens as the smaller parties. Radically different is the party political landscape in East Germany. The East German party system approximates to a new three-party system—with the CDU, SPD, and the post-communist PDS as the three major players of broadly similar strength. In further contrast to West Germany, the East German Liberals and Greens, squeezed between the three larger parties and a considerable fringe party vote of 8.6 per cent in the late 1990s, must content themselves with 'a marginal existence' (Padgett 1999: 91). Unified Germany thus has only two truly national parties—the Social Democratic Party and the Christian Democratic Party—while all other major parties are more or less regional tendencies: the Bavarian CSU, the East German PDS, and the West German Liberals and the West German Greens. The two party systems in reunified Germany mirror a divided German electorate with a far greater proportion of non-aligned voters in the east, and an east–west division in the political culture. The latter manifests itself most visibly in a much stronger demand of the East German electorate for a powerful role of the state vis-à-vis the market and in a significantly higher dissatisfaction in the east with the way democracy works (Fuchs 1999; Roller 1999).

Alternating government

In contrast to 'uncommon democracies' (Pempel 1990) in which one party dominates political life and monopolizes government, such as Japan under the rule of the Liberal Party and Italy until the dissolution of the Democrazia Cristiana in 1994, the party composition of German federal government has varied considerably. Changes in power have also been common in the states (Schmidt 1980; Bauer 1998). The major changes in power at the level of federal government were the replacement of the CDU-CSU-led governments from 1949 to 1966 by a grand coalition of CDU-CSU and SPD in 1966, followed by the 1969 government takeover of the SPD-FDP coalition, the substitution of a CDU-CSU-FDP coalition for the Schmidt government in 1982, and the change after the 1998 Bundestag election from the Kohl government to a red-Green coalition. Among the changes in power in the states, the formation of new coalitions, for example red-Green coalitions, such as in North Rhine-Westphalia, and a SPD/PDS-coalition, such as in Mecklenburg-West Pomerania in 1998 and in Berlin in early 2002, deserve particular attention because both coalitions demonstrate a dramatic increase in the coalition options of the SPD, while those of the major opponent, the CDU-CSU, remain more or less constant. No less important have been other changes in power: the loss of Hesse to a CDU/FDP-coalition in 1999 has been as painful for the SPD as the loss of Saarland in 1999 to a CDU-single party government, and the loss of Hamburg to a coalition of CDU, Liberals, and the 'Schill party', that is, the Partei Rechtsstaatlicher Offensive in 2001. Hardly less galling were the losses for the Christian Democratic Party, when they were ousted from a grand coalition with the SPD in Mecklenburg-West Pomerania in 1998 and in Berlin in 2001. Particularly painful for the red-Green federal government was the election in Saxony-Anhalt in April 2002 which resulted in a change in power from an SPD minority government to a CDU-FDP coalition and in a majority of CDU-CSU-controlled seats in the Bundesrat, the upper house of parliament (see Table 5).

These changes are part of a broader pattern: Germany's party system in the post-unification period exhibits more 'complexity, fluidity and openness' (Padgett and Saalfeld 1999: 5). The key indicators include a declining percentage of the vote for the two largest parties, an increasing number of parties, a change in coalition formation albeit with an asymmetry due to larger coalition options for the SPD and stable or declining options for the CDU, with the Liberals and the SPD as potential candidates. Dealignment is also part of the new pattern (see section 5.3).

Policy positions of the major parties in unified Germany

The policy positions of the major parties in the Federal Republic of Germany differ considerably (Laver and Hunt 1992; Gabriel, Niedermayer, and Stöss 2001).[5] Moreover, they differ to a larger extent than before unification, because the political-ideological spectrum after 1990 is wider than before unification (von Alemann 2000). Measured by the left/right placement of party supporters for example, PDS supporters are the most leftist of all voters, and the supporters of the *Republikaner* the most rightist (Dalton 2000: 307–9). Green voters and SPD supporters position themselves to the left of the centre on the political-ideological spectrum, and the FDP voters and the Christian Democratic voters more to the right, although not too far from the SPD. However, the differences and the commonalities that exist between the various parties vary from one policy area to the other, but also from sub-period to sub-period.

The Christian Democratic parties

The Christian Democratic parties, that is, the CDU and its Bavarian sister organization the CSU, two separate, distinct parties, are the major representatives of religiously affiliated voters, the old middle classes, land-owning classes and property owners, farmers and entrepreneurs, and residents of rural areas and small towns. But the Christian Democrats can also count on the support of the rank and files of public servants, non-socialist wage earners in the private sector economy, old age pensioners, and generally voters from lower-income classes.[6] A trademark of the Christian Democratic policy profile has been the 'Social Market Economy', that is, a market economy governed by private ownership, competition law, and social policy. Characteristic of the CDU-CSU has also been the support for a societal order based on Christian norms and values, including the commitment for employers and the state to care for their dependants. Rejection of excessive individualism, critique of collectivistic regimes, and disapproval of anti-clericalism on the one hand and preference for subsidiarity as an organizing principle of domination and the division of labour between state, market, and family on the other have also been at the top of Christian Democratic preferences. As a mass integration party of the supra-confessional, inter-class, and pragmatic reformist variety, the

Christian Democratic parties have long approximated to the 'catch-all party' more closely than their rivals (Schmidt 1985).

The policy positions of the CDU-CSU reflect its heterogeneous social constituency. As a party that embraces different denominations, the Christian Democratic Union has rightly been described as 'a new attempt to unite practising Catholics and Protestants in a modern Centrist party, mainly in reaction to their experience of Nazism' (Klingemann 1987: 296). Furthermore, the policy profile of the CDU-CSU has been marked by the combination of market capitalism and 'social capitalism' (Hartwich 1970; van Kersbergen 1995). Idiosyncracies have also characterized the organization of the Christian Democratic parties. In the 1950s and 1960s, the CDU was mainly 'a party of local and regional notables, with a small and largely inactive membership' (Pulzer 1999: 128) and a loosely coupled association for electing the Chancellor, a *Kanzlerwahlverein*. But during the opposition period from 1969 to 1982, the CDU rapidly transformed itself into a highly organized modern people's party with a larger and more active membership (Schmid 1990).

A heterogeneous social constituency, pragmatism, and conservatism closely linked to Christian Social values on the one hand and endorsement of market- *and* state-driven economic modernization on the other have characterized the Christian Social Union (CSU), the Bavarian sister organization of the Christian Democratic Party. Since 1963, the CSU has been the single governing party in Bavaria, a large state in the south-eastern part of Germany. In contrast to the CDU, the CSU places emphasis on regional, that is Bavarian interests. This includes massive support for Bavarian agriculture, industry, and culture, support also for the ordinary man, a determined conservative stance on civil rights issues, a pronounced pro-federalism view and—as a consequence—a more critical position vis-à-vis the European Union than most other parties in Germany. Populism, and, if required, active state intervention to a magnitude which parallels French and Swedish traditions have also been among the political instruments which CSU governments have frequently used. The latter comprises an active stance in social policy and includes support for favourite projects of the unions, such as regional Alliances for Jobs, and endorsement of subsidies to charitable organizations, above all religious-based charitable organizations. Part of the CSU rule in Bavaria is an astonishingly high level of party penetration of society on the one hand and state-led transformation of a former agrarian state to a wealthy industrial and post-industrial state on the other (Mintzel 1977; Hanns Seidel Stiftung 1995). Originally, the CSU has been a classical example of an *Honoratiorenpartei*, that is a party dominated mainly by notables and prominent and wealthy citizens of a town, but it rapidly turned into a well-organized mass integration party with an exceptionally broad electoral base, large membership, and remarkable success in acquiring and maintaining political power. Compared with all the parties in the Federal Republic, the CSU can pride itself on the best proxy to the Kirchheimerian 'catch-all party' (Kirchheimer 1965). Last but not least, popular if not charismatic political leaders, such as Franz Josef Strauß and Edmund Stoiber, have been a further key to the remarkable electoral success of the CSU in Bavaria and—via the alliance with the CDU in the Bundestag—also in politics at the federal level.

The German Social Democratic Party

The SPD is the oldest political party in modern Germany and the one with the longest democratic tradition. Originally, the SPD embodied mainly a secularized class-based mass integration party rooted among non-Catholic and non-communist workers. In the post-1949 period, the SPD gradually transformed itself from an anti-capitalist mass integration party to a moderate centre-left party of social amelioration. The programmatic transformation of the former party of the working-class movement culminated in the adoption of a programme of moderate social reform in the 1959 congress in Bad Godesberg, and in the formation of a grand coalition with the CDU-CSU at the federal level from 1966 to 1969.

The SPD gains votes from different social constituencies. Among these, trade union members among blue-collar workers are of central importance for the SPD. There is no social group with a higher proportion of SPD voters than unionized blue-collar workers. But that social class is declining in absolute and in relative terms. Increasingly important for the political fate of the SPD today is therefore the recruitment of voters outside the core of the working class. These voters outside the proper proletariat include private-sector employees and public servants, most notably the growing proportion of white-collar workers, not forgetting the social income earners such as old age pensioners and the unemployed, housewives, single parents, and materialists as well as post-materialists (Lösche and Walter 1992; Walter 2002).

Social justice, social equality, and employment policy as well as a policy of détente and peace in international affairs have been among the trademarks of the SPD. Unlike liberal and market-oriented conservative parties the SPD has been a party in favour of big government and active state interventionism. And if an incarnation of a pro-welfare state is called for, the first choice would be the German Social Democratic Party (Gohr 2001). The policy profile of the Social Democrats also includes a pro-labour and a pro-trade-union stance, support of corporatist cooperation between government and organized interest groups, and promotion of other forms of negotiated democracy beyond the channels prescribed in constitutional law and statute law, such as round tables and councils of various sorts. Furthermore, many Social Democrats, above all post-materialist partisans, regard the emphasis on citizen participation and environmental protection as the most natural inclination of a modern leftist party. Last but not least, a strong pacifist faction has been one of the trademarks which differentiate the SPD from the CDU-CSU, the alternative people's party.

The Free Democratic Party (FDP)

The Free Democratic Party regards itself as the legitimate heir of the German liberal tradition. Part of this tradition has been the division between progressive liberal and national-conservative tendencies (Kaack 1976). The latter tendency is more inclined to coalitions with the Christian Democrats, the former tends towards alliances with the Social Democrats. The FDP is asymmetrically located between the CDU-CSU and the SPD. The Liberals, it has been argued, are for 'people who found the CDU too close to the churches and the SPD too close to the trade unions' (Soe 1985: 124). The primary political goals of the FDP, it has further been pointed out, are to be found in the 'preservation of individual freedom, the reunification of Germany, the rejection of Socialist planning and of clericalism' (Klingemann 1987: 297). However, that picture needs to be complemented by differences between the FDP and the bigger parties. In contrast to both the CDU and the SPD, the Liberals, as an avowedly pro-market party, are not partisans of social income earners, such as old age pensioners. Furthermore, the FDP are not partisans of the trade unions, but rather opponents of labour. As an advocate of private enterprise, the FDP is positioned closer to the CDU-CSU than to the SPD and the Green Party on economic issues, not to mention the PDS. However, in most civil rights issues, the SPD and also the Green Party rather than the culturally conservative CDU-CSU are the more natural coalition partners for the Liberals (Lösche and Walter 1996).

The shift from the social liberalism of the late 1960s and 1970s to the economic conservatism in the 1980s and 1990s resulted in upgrading the interests of economically well-off groups in the programmatic profile of the FDP. The emphasis on economically wealthy groups reflects a major part of the voter base of the FDP, albeit not the complete electoral base of the Liberals. It is also for this reason, that the self-portrait of the FDP as a 'party of the higher income groups' ('Partei der Besserverdienenden') in the 1994 campaign for the parliamentary election deserves to be rated as a one-sided slogan which verges on political suicide. This self-portrait has nourished harsh criticism from the left, such as the view that the Liberals seek to 'make the rich richer and the poor poorer'.[7] In reality, the potential social constituency of the Liberals is much broader and comprises in principle social groups which strive for economic and political freedom as well as for the predominance of secular views.

Measured in cabinet seat shares, the FDP has been spectacularly successful both compared with its rivals in Germany and with liberal parties outside the Federal Republic. In most of the post-1949 period, the FDP has held the position of a numerical and 'ideological balancer' (Soe 1985: 115), if not a 'kingmaker' in Germany's polity. In most of the Bundestag elections it ultimately depended on the Liberals' choice whether the CDU-CSU or the SPD gained access to the reins of power. This largely accounts for the astonishing length of the FDP's participation in federal government.

The Green Party—Bündnis '90/Die Grünen

The Green Party, that is, Bündnis '90/Die Grünen, is an offspring of the value change from priority for materialist policy goals to a mixed pattern of materialist and post-materialist goals (Müller-Rommel 1993; Raschke 2000). At the same time the Green Party can be regarded as the product of political protest against the 'politics of centrality' (Smith 1976) and the pronounced centrist orientation inherent in Germany's party system of the late 1950s, the 1960s and the 1970s (Padgett and Poguntke 2001). Ecological issues, gender equality, protest for peace, internationalism, and the endorsement of civil rights issues have been major concerns of the Green Party, although the party does not have a monopoly in these issue areas. The German Greens advocate mostly left-wing oriented post-materialist policies, with a major emphasis on environmental protection, phasing out of atomic energy, citizenship, and extreme liberal regulation of migration, but they are also the spokespeople of civil liberties including massive protection of minority rights. Internal strife includes conflicts between fundamentalists, that is, proponents of an uncompromising ecologist and pacifist stance in policy, and advocates of a reformist, moderate approach to policy making and coalition building with centre-left or liberal parties. The merger between the West German and the East German Greens in 1993 has strengthened moderate tendencies within the Green Party. A similar effect resulted from participation in government, most notably participation in the red-Green Schröder government since 1998.

The Green Party's voter base has its centre in the New Politics movements. A particularly large proportion of its voters and party members come from the better-educated groups among service sector workers and professionals.

The Greens transformed themselves from a grass-roots movement and an 'antiparty-party' into an established party (Lees 2000). Regarding organizational structure, the Green Party remains a coalition of decentralized groups and factional tendencies. In contrast to the well-organized classic mass integration parties, the Green Party is a relatively loosely coupled party confederation of partly converging, partly diverging tendencies. Although the Green Party in the Federal Republic has remained a relatively minor electoral force (Mair 2001; Müller-Rommel and Poguntke 2002), it has been more successful in shaping public policy than Green parties in most other countries. Mainly due to the coalition with the Social Democratic Party since 1998 the Greens have had a major impact on public policy. Examples include the phasing out of nuclear energy and the strong impact of the Greens on the 'internationalist' oriented reforms of citizenship and immigration law in the Schröder government from 1998 to 2002. But part of their destiny has also been a process of 'banalization of green politics', to quote Isabelle Durant, a Green minister in the Verhofstadt government in Belgium (1999–).[8] Banalization of green politics has two sides: one is a diffusion process which results in the adoption of ecology on the part of most other parties; the other side is that 'the doctrine of greenery itself has lost its rebellious tinge and become unfashionably conventional'.[9]

The Party of Democratic Socialism (PDS)

In contrast to other political parties in Germany, the Partei des Demokratischen Sozialismus (PDS) is a radical socialist party. The PDS is the follow-up organization of the Socialist Unity Party, the communist state party of the German Democratic Republic. According to its party programme, the PDS is a post-communist party. However, more detailed analysis reveals heterogeneous profiles. First of all, the PDS is almost exclusively an East German party, with all four of the directly elected Bundestag seats in 1998 and the 2 seats in 2002 in East Berlin, the former capital of the German Democratic Republic. In contrast to this, the role of the PDS in West Germany remains insignificant. The PDS, thus, expresses a new regional cleavage in Germany. Second, the PDS is composed of different factions from protest movements to radical democratic socialists and orthodox communists of the Stalinist and Leninist tradition. Its rank and file also includes supporters of the former German Democratic Republic, especially the East German intelligentsia and party faithful. Similar to the SPD and the Communist Party of Germany before 1933, the PDS is the only party in unified Germany which represents a 'community of fate and a culturally embedded social movement' (Winkler 1994) in almost all domains of political and social life. And as a regional protest party with strong links to the theory and practice of socialism GDR-style, the PDS benefits from economic problems and disappointed expectations in the process of unification. The PDS vote can therefore at least partly be regarded as an indicator of disappointment with the impact of unification.

Policy distances and coalition strategies

According to a widely shared view of the 1960s, the policy distance between the major parties in the Federal Republic of Germany was declining considerably (Kirchheimer 1965, 1966). In this view, Kirchheimer's proposition of the 'waning of opposition' and the prediction of the rise of 'catch-all parties' seemed to come true (Agnoli 1968). Studies of party manifestos have supported Kirchheimer's view in so far as they mirrored the major role of consensus-oriented behaviour in Germany's party system (Klingemann 1987: 321). The difference between the extreme poles were indeed smaller in the pre-unification party system in Germany than in most other constitutional democracies and in the Weimar Republic (Thomas 1980; Laver and Schofield 1990: 240–66)—not least due the weakness of communist tendencies and rightist parties (Betz and Immerfall 1998).

However, the 'catch-all-party' hypothesis and the 'vanishing of opposition' view have overestimated the degree to which the parties actually succeeded in transforming themselves to 'omnibus parties'. More detailed analysis shows that reduced ideological difference resulted from two different processes: the first of these was the disappearance of radical parties on the right, such as the Sozialistische Reichspartei, the follow-up organization of the National-Socialist German Workers' Party, and the German Communist Party on the left. The second trend is the decreasing ideological distance between the two major parties, CDU-CSU and SPD. That latter trend, however, resulted from two opposite trajectories: the CDU moved from a centre-right to a centre position in several policy areas, such as social policy and family policy, while the SPD turned from centre-left to a centrist position, for example in economic policy. Moreover, the waning-of-opposition view overestimated the decline in party differences and underestimated the potential for re-polarization. Furthermore, the waning-of-opposition view veiled the continuity of significant policy differences between the German political parties. For example, economic policy divergence manifests itself as an inter-bloc difference between the centre-left, left, and the Green parties on the one hand and the centre-right parties as well as the Liberals on the other. Most civil rights issues however, such as abortion and citizen participation, create major divisions between the Social Democratic Party, the Liberals, and to some extent also the Greens on the one hand and the conservative stance of the Christian Democratic parties in these issues on the other.

Coalition patterns

This asymmetry in policy differences indicates different coalition possibilities in Germany. In most civil rights issues the Social Democratic Party has been closer to the Liberals and has been a more natural coalition partner for the FDP than the Christian Democratic parties. In economic policy and other issues concerning the division of labour between the state and the private market economy, however, the natural coalition is a Christian Democratic-Liberal alliance. But this is valid only as long as the

SPD sticks to its traditional policy position. If the SPD however chooses a business-friendly policy, such as in taxation in 1999 and 2000, and adopts a restrictive fiscal policy stance, such as in 2000 and 2001, changing coalition options are conceivable, including a SPD-FDP coalition. For the Green Party, the most natural coalition partner, though not the ideal one, is the SPD, due to the emphasis of the Social Democrats on social equality including gender equality, but also due to the greater willingness of the SPD to take part in an anti-nuclear energy policy. The SPD is also the most natural coalition partner of the PDS, although the PDS's foreign policy stance tends towards neutrality, if not anti-NATO and anti-USA positions.

In contrast to most of the English-speaking nations and majoritarian democracies in general, coalitions have been the typical form of government in the Federal Republic of Germany. However, the German coalition pattern of the post-Second World War period is also at variance with that of many other democratic states outside the world of the majoritarian democracies. A wider range of variation has marked the coalitional status of the federal governments. The dominant coalition type has been a surplus majority government. Minimum winning coalitions have been in power over a somewhat shorter period (1969–72, 1976–82, and 1987–91). Exceptions rather than the rule were single-party governments (1960–1) and minority governments (November 1962, November and December 1965, and September 1982) (see Table 1).

Moreover, government at the federal level and in the states has been characterized by a wide variety of coalition types. Coalitions between all parties prevailed in the immediate post-war period. When the Cold War began, all-party coalitions were replaced by coalitions which excluded the Communist Party, and later on, by surplus majority or minimum winning coalitions of different political composition. Although a clear trend towards centre-right-liberal coalitions or, alternatively, centre-left-liberal governments had emerged in the 1950s, grand coalitions of the CDU and the SPD have been a familiar phenomenon both at state level and in 1966–9 also in the capital of the Federal Republic, at that time Bonn.

The rise of the Green Party in the late 1970s and 1980s also affected coalition politics. Since the 1980s the environmentalists of the Green Party entered into permanent or temporary coalitions with the Social Democratic Party in eight states. Hesse was first (1984–7 and later in 1991–9), followed by Berlin (1989–91), Brandenburg (1990–4), Lower Saxony

(1990–4), Bremen (1991–5), North Rhine-Westphalia (1995 until the time of writing in October 2002), Schleswig-Holstein (1996 until the time of writing), and Hamburg (1997 until September 2001).

The formation of an SPD-FDP coalition in 1969 and the conflict-oriented strategy of the incumbent parties and the opposition party, the CDU-CSU, marked the end of the era of rapprochement between the Christian Democrats and the Social Democratic Party. Increasing political polarization in the party system also resulted from controversies over new politics issues and new social movements in the 1970s and 1980s, most notably the environmentalists, the anti-nuclear-energy movement, and the peace movement, while the women's movement remained weak in Germany. In this period, political conflicts were intensified to a degree which resembles the bitter disputes of the early 1950s between the Christian Democratic parties and the SPD.[10] However, owing to rival majorities in the Bundestag and the Bundesrat, with the social-liberal coalition in power at the level of the federal state (1969–82) and the opposition party in control of the majority of the seats in the Bundesrat, the higher level of polarization in the period had to be reconciled with the requirements of cooperative politics inherent in Germany's Federal Republic. This resulted in confrontation *and* cooperation, and, thus, in coexistence of competition, partisan struggles, and majority rule together with consensus formation through compromises or unanimity in decision-making. The outcome consisted of a unique confrontation-and-cooperation game and a co-governing opposition party most notably in legislation subject to an affirmative vote of the Bundesrat (Schmidt 1978; Bracher, Jäger, and Link 1986; Lehmbruch 2000a).

5.3 Voting: more volatile than before

Voter turnout in the Federal Republic of Germany is high. The average turnout in the Bundestag elections from 1949 to 2002 amounted to 85 per cent of those entitled to vote—approximately four percentage points above the average turnout in national elections in all democratic member states of the Organization for Economic Cooperation and Development (OECD) in the period from 1949 to 2002,[11] not to mention the low turnout in US presidential elections (57.5 per cent) and the Swiss Nationalrat elections

(54.4 per cent). A somewhat lower average turnout than in national elections has been reported from state parliament elections in Germany in the period from 1949 to September 2002 (75.7 per cent). But turnout in the elections of the state parliaments rarely declines below the 60 per cent threshold. These data indicate that conventional political participation, above all voting, is deeply anchored in the political culture of the Federal Republic of Germany.

Regarding the average share of the popular vote in all Bundestag elections from 1949 to 2002, the CDU-CSU has been the strongest party, with 43.7 per cent of the valid votes cast, while 37.6 per cent of the popular vote went to the SPD, the second strongest party. About 9 per cent of the votes fell to the Liberals. The Green Party, which made an entrance on the parliamentary stage in the late 1970s in state parliaments and in 1983 in the national parliament, mobilized between 2 and 9 per cent. Other small parties attained a lower share of the popular vote. In the early 1950s, the German Communist Party, the GB/BHE (Unified Germany Federation/Bloc of the Expellees and Dispossessed) and regional parties, such as the Bavarian Party, won between 4 and 6 per cent of the votes. And in the Bundestag elections since 1990, the PDS gained between 2.4 and 5.1 per cent of the Second Vote (see Table 8).

However, the long-term average veils major differences between subperiods. For example, the overall balance of power between the major political parties, CDU-CSU and SPD, and between political-ideological families of parties has changed considerably. In terms of electoral strength, the non-leftist parties, mainly Christian Democrats and Liberals, surpassed the group of the leftist parties until the 1990s. And with the exceptions of 1972, 1998, and 2002, the CDU-CSU outmatched the SPD as far as the percentage share of the popular vote was concerned.

Until the mid-1990s German voters had been less inclined to adopt centre-left or leftist positions than the electorate in many other democracies, such as Sweden, Norway, and Austria. Moreover, in contrast to nations with strong centre-right or right-wing tendencies, such as the USA, Australia, and Ireland, the Federal Republic of Germany has long been rather representative of a position in the middle group. But that changed gradually as the ratio of the non-leftist and the leftist vote shows. The ratio of the vote for the major non-leftist parties and the vote for the major leftist parties changed from 1.82 in 1957, indicative of a solid lead of the

TABLE 8	Party vote in Bundestag elections, 1949–2002

Year	CDU-CSU	FDP	Greens	SPD	PDS	Others	Turn-out	Total share of the major non-leftist parties	Ratio between major non-leftist and major leftist parties	Percentage point difference between CDU-CSU and SPD vote
1949	31.0	11.9	0	29.2	0	27.9	78.5	42.9	1.23[a]	1.8
1953	45.2	9.5	0	28.8	0	16.5	86.0	54.7	1.76[b]	16.4
1957	50.2	7.7	0	31.8	0	10.3	87.8	57.9	1.82	18.4
1961	45.4	12.8	0	36.2	0	5.6	87.7	56.2	1.61	9.2
1965	47.6	9.5	0	39.3	0	3.6	86.8	57.1	1.45	8.3
1969	46.1	5.8	0	42.7	0	5.4	86.7	51.9	1.22	3.4
1972	44.9	8.4	0	45.8	0	0.9	91.1	53.3	1.16	−0.9
1976	48.6	7.9	0	42.6	0	0.9	90.7	56.5	1.33	6.0
1980	44.5	10.6	1.5	42.9	0	0.5	88.6	55.1	1.24	1.6
1983	48.8	7.0	5.6	38.2	0	0.4	89.1	55.8	1.27	10.6
1987	44.3	9.1	8.3	37.0	0	1.3	84.3	53.4	1.18	7.3
1990	43.8	11.0	5.1	33.5	2.4	4.2	77.8	54.8	1.34	10.3
1994	41.4	6.9	7.3	36.4	4.4	3.6	79.0	48.3	1.00	5.0
1998	35.2	6.2	6.7	40.9	5.1	5.9	82.2	41.4	0.79	−5.7
2002	38.5	7.4	8.6	38.5	4.0	3.0	79.1	45.9	0.97	0.0
Mean 1949–2002	43.7	8.8	6.2	37.6	4.0	6.0	85.0	52.3	1.29	6.1

Key: CDU-CSU: Christlich Demokratische Union/Christlich Soziale Union. SPD: Sozialdemokratische Partei Deutschlands. FDP: Freie Demokratische Partei. PDS: Party of Democratic Socialism. Green: Die Grünen and since 1993 Bündnis '90/Die Grünen. Ratio between major non-leftist and major leftist parties: sum of CDU-CSU vote and FDP vote divided by sum of the vote for SPD, Greens, KPD, and PDS.

[a] 1.47 if the KPD vote (5.8 per cent) is excluded.
[b] 1.90 if the KPD (2.2 per cent) is excluded.

Source: Statistisches Bundesamt (ed.), *Statistisches Jahrbuch für die Bundesrepublik Deutschland* (various issues). Party vote is measured as a percentage of the total Second Vote (*Zweitstimme*).

non-leftist parties, to 1.0 in 1994, indicative of parity between the two party camps, 0.79 in 1998, and 0.97 in 2002 (see Table 8). The 1998 Bundestag election, thus, stands out as the first national election in Germany in which the parties to the left of the centre gained the majority, while the non-leftist parties declined to a historically unprecedented minority position comprising 41 per cent of the vote, an all-time low in the political history of the Federal Republic of Germany. In the national election in 2002 the left of centre parties maintained their lead, although only by a narrow margin.

The changing ratio of the non-leftist and the leftist vote reflects substantial underlying shifts in voting behaviour. Like electoral behaviour in other advanced democracies, voting in the Federal Republic is mainly shaped by three classes of determinants: social structure including cleavages; socio-psychological factors, such as party identification, perception of issues, issue competence of parties and evaluation of candidates; and value orientation such as left-right scale placement and materialism/post-materialism (Klingemann and Kaase 2001). All three factors have changed significantly over the last few decades.

The impact of social structures and cleavages on voting

The impact of social structures and cleavages on voting since the 1960s has been marked by both continuity and discontinuity. Region, type of economic activity, age, and gender, for example, continue to influence voting behaviour, as the data on the 2002 election to the Bundestag suggest (Table 9). The CDU-CSU and Liberals won a narrow majority among West German voters, while the majority of East German electorate voted in favour of the SPD and the PDS. The SPD has become the strongest party among female voters, while the CDU-CSU holds the position of the strongest party among male voters. Furthermore, in 2002 most voters of older age groups again preferred the Christian Democratic Party, while a larger proportion of the younger age groups voted in favour of the left-of-centre parties. Among economically active voters, the CDU-CSU attained the relative majority in the 2002 election, closely followed by the SPD. In the 2002 election, the SPD gained relative majorities among blue-collar workers, white-collar workers, and the unemployed, while the CDU-CSU mobilized the relative majority of the old age pensioners and the absolute majority of the votes among public servants, farmers, and the self-employed (see Table 9).

Cleavage voting has also remained an important determinant of voting. Religion and class have been the major cleavages in the Federal Republic. For example, unionized workers vote mainly in favour of the SPD. In contrast to this, entrepreneurs as well as the self-employed prefer the

| TABLE 9 | Voting behaviour in the Bundestag election 2002 |

Social category	SPD % vote	CDU-CSU % vote	B90/ Green Party % vote	FDP % vote	PDS % vote	Others
Total vote	38.5	38.5	8.6	7.4	4.0	3.0
Region						
East	39.8	28.3	4.8	6.4	16.8	3.9
West	38.3	40.8	9.4	7.6	1.1	2.8
Gender						
Male	36	40	8	8	4	4
Female	41	36	10	7	4	3
Age						
18–29	38	33	10	10	4	5
30–44	40	34	11	8	4	4
45–59	38	40	9	7	4	2
60+	38	45	5	6	4	2
Economic activity						
Economically active	37	38	10	8	4	3
Old age pensioners	40	44	4	6	5	2
Education	38	28	16	10	5	3
Unemployed	41	27	9	6	10	7
Occupation						
Workers	44	37	4	7	4	4
White-collar workers	41	35	10	7	4	3
Public servants	33	41	14	6	3	3
Self-employed	21	51	11	13	3	2
Farmers	19	66	3	6	4	3
Trade union membership						
Member	51	27	9	5	5	3
Non-member	36	41	9	8	4	3
Denomination						
Catholic	30	52	8	7	1	2
Protestant	44	36	8	8	2	3
No denomination	40	25	11	8	11	5
Religious affiliation						
Strong	18	70	5	5	0	2
Moderate	33	50	7	7	1	2
Weak or none	43	36	10	8	1	2

TABLE 9	Continued					
Social category	SPD % vote	CDU-CSU % vote	B90/ Green Party % vote	FDP % vote	PDS % vote	Others
Highest level of education						
Elementary (*Hauptschule*)	44	41	4	6	2	3
Ordinary level (*Mittlere Reife*)	37	39	7	8	5	4
Grammar school (*Gymnasium*)	38	34	13	9	4	3
University diploma	30	34	18	9	7	2

Sources: Forschungsgruppe Wahlen (2002), *Bundestagswahl. Eine Analyse der Wahl vom 22. September 2002* (Mannheim: Forschungsgruppe Wahlen): 7, 9, 51, 56, 63, 66, 67. Data were derived from an exit poll on 22 Sept. 2002 (N = 20,561).

Christian Democratic parties and the Liberals. Religion also continues to matter a great deal in voting. Most Catholics vote for the Christian Democrats, while the SPD is the strongest party among Protestants and among voters not belonging to any denomination. Although the bitterly fought struggle between Roman Catholicism and Protestantism ended in the twentieth century in Germany, religious affiliation still makes a difference. Religiously affiliated voters, both Catholics and Protestants, are far more likely to vote for the Christian Democratic parties than religiously non-affiliated groups. The latter prefer non-religious parties, such as the Liberals, the Green Party and the SPD. Overall, religion continues to be more important in shaping voting behaviour in Germany than class (Falter and Schoen 1999), while class cleavage indicators point to a more moderate impact on class on voting behaviour in Western Germany (Falter and Schoen 1999; Gallagher, Laver and Mair 2001).

Although cleavage voting continues to play a significant role in voting in Germany, a caveat must be added. The relative magnitude of the sectors in society in which cleavage voting occurs, such as unionized workers on the one hand and groups with strong religious affiliation on the other, is gradually declining. From this follows the declining relative importance of cleavage voting for the vote as a whole, other things being equal. One major trend concerns a potential core constituency of the SPD, namely unionized manual workers in the industrial sector of the economy.

Though still economically more important in Germany than in most other OECD member countries, that sector has declined in relative importance in West Germany and since 1990 to a truly dramatic extent in East Germany. At the same time, the rise of the service sector economy poses difficult problems for unions. The unions find it far more difficult to organize labour in the private service sector than in the industrial sector of the economy.

However, a relative decline has also marked the core constituency of the CDU-CSU, namely the self-employed and religious voters of both Catholic and Protestant denominations. This has been largely due to ongoing socio-economic development and continued secularization.

The discussion of cleavage-based voting would be incomplete without mentioning regional determinants of voting behaviour. The case of the Bavarian Party in 1950s and most notably the CSU throughout the whole history of the Federal Republic of Germany exemplifies the important role of regional determinants of voting. Unification established a further regional cleavage, namely a cleavage between the West German part of the country and East Germany, the area of the former German Democratic Republic. This cleavage manifests itself in a coalition between 16.8 per cent of voters and the PDS in East Germany in 2002 and the weakness of the PDS, if not its non-existence, in the western part of the country.

The relative importance of cleavage-based voting has declined as has the importance of party identification. This is one of the key variables in the socio-psychological approach to the study on voting. Time series data taken from the *Politbarometer*, a monthly survey conducted by Forschungsgruppe Wahlen since 1977, reveal a significant trend: the proportion of non-aligned voters in West Germany (measured by absence of party identification) increased from broadly 20 per cent in 1977 to 34 per cent in 1998. The proportion of party identifiers has declined correspondingly from 80 to 66 per cent. These trends continued after 1998. Non-identification with parties is particularly pronounced in East Germany where almost 50 per cent of the electorate is not aligned with one of the political parties (Schmitt-Beck and Weick 2001). The data on party identification reflects a higher proportion of volatile voters than in the decades before the 1980s (Falter and Schoen 1999).

Like most other advanced democracies, the Federal Republic of Germany is, thus, positioned on a road towards 'parties without partisans'

(Dalton and Wattenberg 2000). That means diminishing involvement in electoral politics. For those who do vote it results in more volatility in their voting choices, openness to new political appeals, and less predictability in their party preferences. The reaction on the part of the political parties can be no less dramatic: the political parties feel tempted to adapt to the uncertainties by strengthening their internal organizational structure, and attempting to partially isolate themselves from the ups and downs of the electoral market. As if they were to implement the predictions in Kirchheimer's 'catch-all-party' theory (Kirchheimer 1965), the political parties, above all the larger parties with encompassing social consti-tuencies, feel tempted to substitute centralized, professionalized electoral politics with short time horizons for ideology driven politics (von Beyme 2000*b*, Dalton and Wattenberg 2000).

It must be added, however, that the proportion of voters with party identification is still high in the Federal Republic of Germany. Further-more, the aggregate data on party identification must be interpreted with care, because the trend at the macro-level should not obscure massive change at the micro-level. Non-partisanship rarely lasts long. Only 20 per cent of the West German voters did not identify with one of the political parties throughout the whole period from 1984 to 1998 (Schmitt-Beck and Weick 2001). All other voters changed at least once from non-identification to party identification. That means that the trend towards 'parties without partisans' has remained so far more moderate in the Federal Republic.

Issue competence and party leaders

Significant changes have also marked two further key determinants of voting: issue competence and party leaders. The policy positions of the parties differ to a considerable degree. So, too, do the perceptions of policy distances between the political parties and the awareness of issue com-petence of the various political tendencies. According to the *Politbarom-eter*, the Christian Democratic parties have usually been regarded as the most competent party in policy areas such economic policy, law and order, and defence. In contrast to this, the public has regarded the Social Demo-cratic Party as more potent in softer issues, such as social security, social justice, citizen participation, and a détente-oriented foreign policy vis-à-vis Eastern Europe in the period of the Cold War. But there have also been remarkable fluctuations in the perception of issue competence. In the first two years after the Bundestag election in 1998, for example, the SPD super-seded the CDU-CSU as the most competent party in economic policy, but lost that lead afterwards. Regarding competence in job creation and fighting increasing taxation, however, the Christian Democrats have traditionally surpassed the SPD (Forschungsgruppe Wahlen 2002).

The popularity and the reputation of the major candidates of the parties also vary widely. In the 1950s and in the first half of the 1960s, the lead of Christian Democratic candidates over candidates of the Social Democratic opposition party was unequivocal. Above all the popularity of Konrad Adenauer, the first Chancellor in the Federal Republic of Germany, strengthened the position of the CDU-CSU-led government in the 1950s. Significantly less popular was Ludwig Erhard, the former Minister of Economic Affairs and Federal Chancellor from 1963 to 1966, and Kurt Georg Kiesinger, who presided over the grand coalition of CDU, CSU, and SPD in the 1966–9 period. Helmut Kohl, the fourth Christian Democratic Chancellor, in power from 1982 to 1998, was largely popular only in his own party—with the major exception of German unification policy in 1990, in which his leadership was widely praised both among Christian Democratic followers and a larger segment of Social Democratic voters. The popularity of chancellors from the ranks of the SPD has also been mixed. Helmut Schmidt was popular both among supporters of the SPD and the CDU-CSU. He embodied electorally the most successful candidate of the SPD. Next to him came Schröder, above all in 2000 and 2001. In contrast to Schmidt and Schröder, Willy Brandt, Chancellor in 1969–74, had a more diverse impact on the electorate. He succeeded in mobilizing SPD voters and potential allies, particularly voters of the younger age groups. However, Brandt's emphasis on a policy of détente vis-à-vis the socialist states and numerous ambitious and costly social reform projects polarized the electorate into pro- and anti-Brandt camps.

Changes in value orientation

Changes in value orientation, a further key determinant of voting be-haviour, also had an impact on voting in Germany. This pertains above all to left/right scale placement and materialism versus post-materialism. The changes in left/right scale placements can be attributed at least partly to unification effects. East Germany's voters tend towards a somewhat more leftist placement than their West German counterparts—a favourable condition for a leftist party such as the PDS. A second major change in value orientations concerns the change from priority for materialistic values to more emphasis on post-materialist ones. That shift in values resulted in upgrading of ecological issues, environmental protection, conventional and unconventional political participation, gender issues and emancipation from traditional authority. As regards the party system, the major impact of the value change has been the rise of the Green Party (Müller-Rommel 1993), but it involved also the rise of environmental protection as a policy goal for most other parties. The rise of the Green Party posed a particularly difficult electoral challenge for the SPD and the FDP, because these parties lost a not insignificant proportion of potential votes to the ecological party.

Social structural determinants, including cleavages, continue to matter in voting. But they do so to a decreasing extent. So does party identification, which is also declining, albeit from a relatively high level. The consequences of declining cleavage voting and declining party identification are undoubtedly grave. One of these consequences is that voters from traditional social constituencies of the parties are less important in relative terms for the total vote than before. For example, religiously affiliated voters accounted for not more than 14 per cent of all CDU-CSU voters in 1994, and only 11 per cent of the SPD vote in 2002 can be attributed to unionized blue-collar workers and 9 per cent to unionized white-collar workers (Forschungsgruppe Wahlen 1994, 2002: 59). But because party identification still matters to a large extent, it is premature to argue that socially structured partisanship would be confined to the traditional core milieu of the parties and would leave the party system subject to sharp swings in electoral behaviour. In the face of a large proportion of party identifiers—more than 65 per cent of the voters—it is also questionable whether elections are won or lost more often than before 'through shifts of electoral allegiance amongst unattached or weakly attached voters' (Padgett 1999: 93). This may be the case, but it is not the whole story of the factors that decide the outcome of an election.

However, the changes in socio-structural determinants of voting and in party identification have resulted in 'more unpredictability of the voter' (Falter and Schoen 1999: 468), a larger proportion of 'floating' or 'volatile' voters, and more complexity, fluidity, and openness than in periods of stronger cleavage voting and higher levels of party identification. It follows from this that voting in Germany is influenced to a larger degree by a wider variety of determinants than cleavages, traditional party alignment, and stable party identification. This means in general more importance of medium-term and short-term determinants of voting, such as salient issues, perception of candidates, performance profiles, media fitness of candidates and events, although not necessarily more importance of rational calculation (Falter and Schoen 1999: 468). Among the short-term determinants of voting, media effects and the effects of electoral campaigns of the parties play a major and probably increasing role (Schmidt-Beck 2001).

A further consequence of the increasing importance of short-term and medium-term factors lies in mounting uncertainty and growing stress for the political parties. Each political party finds itself confronted with more uncertainty than in the old days when voting was to a larger extent structured by deeply anchored social conflicts, cleavages, and higher levels of party identification. When competing for votes, the political parties are faced with more stress than before: their job is to invest more resources in mobilizing voters without precisely knowing how to achieve this end.

5.4 Partly pluralist, partly corporatist: organized interest groups and interest intermediation

5.4.1 Organizational density

The Federal Republic's record of membership in political parties is not outstanding: 1.7 million citizens or about 3 per cent of the voters were counted as members of a political party at the end of the twentieth century (Statistisches Bundesamt et al. 2002: 164–5). Party membership in Germany is very low by international standards (Mair and van Biezen 2001). But as far as the density of societal associations and interest groups is concerned, the Federal Republic of Germany outnumbers most other democracies (Armingeon 2002: 223, 229). The higher density of societal associations and interest groups is part of a long tradition. Germany has been famous for the tradition of 'a densely organised society' (Conradt 2001: 130).

Associational man

The older roots of a densely organized society can be traced to the corporate guilds of the Holy Roman Empire of the German Nation, while the younger heredity is to be located in the nineteenth century, above all in the German Empire of 1871. Max Weber, for example, regarded the 'astonishing, hitherto unknown incidence of the associational man' as one of the major characteristics of Germany's society in the beginning of the twentieth century (Weber 1988*b*: 422). Weber echoed the rise of a wide variety of associations in the period after the foundation of the German Empire of 1871—a process fuelled by the rise of the welfare state, protectionism and industrial conflicts between labour and employers (Reutter 2001*b*: 76). A century later, Weber's 'associational man' seems to be virtually omnipresent. According to *Eurobarometer* data, 63 per cent of Germans have been members of a non-religious association or an interest group in the 1990s, a higher proportion than in France (53 per cent), Italy (48 per cent), Greece (24 per cent), and the United Kingdom (61 per cent), but lower than in the Nordic countries (Reutter 2001*a*: 16). About 544,000 associations were counted in Germany in the early twenty-first century.[12] Most of the associations centre their activities on socio-cultural purposes; 40 per cent of the total consists of local sport clubs. Almost 20 per cent focus on recreational activities, among them numerous singing societies; 13 per cent of the associations serve charitable purposes. For these purposes several million citizens cooperate in an honorary capacity (Schmid 1996; Klein 2001). Moreover, two-thirds of Germans are members of one of the two major churches of the country: 26.8 million or 32.7 per cent of the total population were affiliated to the Protestant church in 1999, while 27.0 million citizens or 33 per cent of the total population are members of the Catholic church. The Muslim population, the third largest religious group, comprises roughly 3.0 million or 3.7 per cent of the total population (Statistisches Bundesamt et al. 2002: 171–4). Almost all Catholics live in the western parts of the country. Only 800,000 Catholics reside in eastern Germany, originally a Protestant country, which, due to rigid state-led secularization in 1949–90 has turned into 'one of the most "de-Christianized" regions in Europe' (Berndt 1998: 302), where two-thirds of the population do not belong to any church.

The 'Big Four'

Compared with the total number of associations, the proportion of political interest associations is relatively small. According to estimates political interest groups number roughly 5,000. Precise data are available only for central associations registered in the Bundestag.[13] The total number of central associations was 1673 in 1998 (Sebaldt 2000). Among these were older and younger interest groups, highly specialized interests, and a surprisingly large number of associations of more general interests, as well as politically less important organizations and very important ones (Bührer and Grande 2000; Sebaldt 1997). Among the latter, the 'Big Four' (Edinger 1986: 183–94)—big business organizations, labour organizations, churches and farmers' interest groups—continue to be influential players at least in some policy areas.

Among the business associations the Confederation of German Employers' Associations (Bundesvereinigung der Deutschen Arbeitgeberverbände, BDA), the Federation of German Industries (Bundesverband der Deutschen Industrie, BDI), and the Deutsche Industrie- und Handelstag (DIHT) have played major roles throughout the history of the Federal Republic (Bührer and Grande 2000). The BDA is the head organization of the German employers' associations in all sectors of the economy. It pursues social policy matters of general interest to the employers. Through cooperation with the trade unions in negotiating wage and salary agreements, the BDA is a major pillar of industrial relations. In contrast to the BDA, the BDI is the umbrella organization of the trade associations in Germany. Membership, which is voluntary, has covered roughly 80 per cent of the total number of industrial enterprises (Mann 1994: 41). The BDI acts mainly as the spokesman of the entrepreneurial interests in the industrial sector of the German economy and is widely perceived to be an influential interest organization of the employers. The BDI has even been regarded as one of the most effective lobbies, if not the most influential and effective voice of business in German politics (Sontheimer and Bleek 1999: 205). The third major organization of business in Germany is the DIHT. The DIHT is responsible for the national representation of the Chambers of Industry and Commerce in the Federal Republic of Germany. It is to the association of those local public law corporations with compulsory membership to which the government delegates the competence for vocational training and regulation of occupational standards and practices.

Organized labour comprises 9.7 million members or roughly 30 per cent of all employees, all of them associated to unions of different occupational composition and political outlook (Statistisches Bundesamt et al. 2002: 167). The labour organizations include the Beamtenbund, the German Federation of Civil Servants, the German Salaried Employees Union (DAG), an organization composed of white-collar workers which is meanwhile a member of *Verdi*, Germany's big service sector union, and the Christian Trade Union Federation of Germany. But the centre of Germany's organized labour both in terms of absolute numbers and relative importance is to be found in the Federation of German Trade Unions, the Deutsche Gewerkschaftsbund (DGB) and the member unions of this Federation (Armingeon 1988). The DGB is the umbrella organization of ten trade unions, among them the Industrial Metal Workers' Union (IG Metall), one of the world's most powerful unions with more than 2.7 million members in 2000 (Statistisches Bundesamt et al. 2002: 167).

The secularization of German society has reduced the influence of the Protestant and the Roman Catholic church, the third among Edinger's 'Big Four'. But despite reduced influence, both churches can still count on roughly 27 million members each. Moreover, churches and state continue to remain relatively closely related, rather than being separated, as in the United States of America. For example, the Protestant and the Roman Catholic church continue to be financed mainly through a church tax collected by the government via a surcharge levied on income tax. In addition, both the Protestant and the Roman Catholic church are often directly involved in the policy process. Appointees of both churches have regularly participated in government planning committees that deal with social-cultural topics, such as family law, education, gender issues, social policy, and poverty. By law, both the Protestant and the Roman Catholic church take part in the supervisory board of public broadcasting and television.

The fourth interest group among Edinger's 'Big-Four' is the 'Green Front', the farmers' interest groups. Among these, the German Farmers' Association (Deutsche Bauernverband) holds a particularly important position. The German Farmers' Association defines itself as the major representative of the professional interests of the agricultural and forestry sectors and the 1.0 million workers who earn their income in these or related areas (*Der Fischer Weltalmanach* 2000: 244). The Farmers' Association, the dominant actor in the 'agrarian trinity'[14] of the German Farmers' Association, the Association of Agricultural Chambers (Verband der Landwirtschaftskammern) and the Raiffeisenverband, an association in banking, mortgage loan, and retailing, is one of the best-organized interest groups in Germany. The German Farmers' Association has long been regarded as a prime example of successful 'capture' of the state administration and as a major example of 'a dukedom of an interest group' (Reutter 2001b: 87). But even the German Farmers' Association and the 'Green Front' as a whole found themselves exposed to the tide of change generated by the rise of post-materialism and alternating government. The political impact of the 'Green Front' varies with the political complexion of government. Most favourable for the 'Green Front' has been a government in which at least one of the major parties of the farmers participated: the Christian Union parties and the Free Democratic Party. In contrast to this, governments without these parties, such as the red-Green coalition in the federal government since 1998, mean reduced access for the farmers' interests.

The 'Big Four' still make a great difference in politics. However, Germany's interest group system is more diversified and pluralist in nature than in preceding decades (von Alemann 1987; van Deth 2000). Moreover, some of the associations outside the 'Big Four' have gained a more important role, such as the interest groups in health care. Furthermore, not all of the 'Big Four' have remained as important as in the first two or three decades of the Federal Republic. The influence of both the Protestant and the Roman Catholic church, for example, has gradually waned over the last decades not least due to declining church attendance and decreasing numbers of church weddings, both indicators of a steady secularization of German society (Statistisches Bundesamt et al. 2002: 172–3). In addition, the influence of the agricultural interest groups has decreased parallel to the declining economic weight of the agricultural sector. Agricultural interests have been confronted with a further decline since January 2001, when the Federal Ministry for Agriculture, traditionally the stronghold of the farmers' interest group, was headed by Renate Künast, a politician from the ranks of the Green Party which focused attention on consumer protection and ecological agriculture rather than on the representation of traditional agricultural interests. Furthermore, the rise of numerous interest organizations which represent post-materialistic issues and more general interests, such as environmental protection, points to significant flexibility and adaptiveness in the interest group system—in marked contrast to the theory of latent interest groups (Olson 1965).

5.4.2 Interest associations and political parties: commonalities and differences

Like political parties and mass media, interest associations act as intermediaries between the citizens and collective political institutions. Interest groups campaign for candidates and make themselves the spokesman of a cause. They provide information to public officials, seek to persuade policy makers, and advance policy alternatives. Furthermore, interest groups contribute to interest articulation and interest aggregation. However, most interest associations represent highly specialized interests. And in contrast to most political parties, the large majority of interest groups promote particularistic interests of more or less narrowly defined segments of society. Interest groups are therefore far more likely to maximize narrowly defined egoistic interest and to risk the violation of the public interest. Furthermore, interest associations do not systematically recruit and appoint public policy makers. Most important of all, interest groups, albeit ambitious in influencing the course of public policy, do not strive to run government and therefore avoid public accountability.

Interest groups may occasionally contest elections as a strategy to influence political parties, but in order to influence government policy they normally rely on campaigning and lobbying methods. Moreover, politically relevant interest groups are usually also represented in a variety of public or semi-public arrangements. Thus, for example, all major social and economic interest groups in the Federal Republic of Germany are formally represented in parliamentary consultation procedures. This includes participation in the hearings of the Bundestag and legally mandatory hearings concerning federal legislation or federal government orders. In addition, interest groups participate in advisory councils and committees of federal ministries. There are also a wide variety of informal contacts between federal ministerial officials and top representatives of interest associations. Participation of interest groups also includes parliamentary

institutions. Thus, for example, a wide variety of parliamentary committees in areas such as social policy, economic policy, and agriculture are
dominated by Members of Parliament associated with trade unions,
employers' associations, and farmers' associations. Moreover, interest
groups participate in the delivery of public policy and in implementing
political decisions at least in some areas, for example health care and the
regulation of industrial-technical standards. The administration of monetary compensation for losses on the part of the expellees and refugees
from East German and Eastern European areas (*Lastenausgleich*) also
involved to a large extent the bureaucracy of the interest association of the
expellees and refugees. Furthermore, Germany's comprehensive system of
codetermination rights for labour representatives to participate in plant-
level decision making and in management boards of industrial enterprises,
has been conducive to social partnership-style industrial relations, but it
has also increased the potential for patronage through the creation of a
wide variety of posts for representatives of the unions. In a similar vein, the
Chambers of Agriculture are dominated by the German farmers' associations just as the Chambers of Industry and Commerce are dominated by
employers' associations.

Firm links also exist between the major political parties and the major
social, cultural, and economic interest groups. The most obvious indicators of these links are—first—the extent to which functionaries of the
interest associations are represented in the political parties and in the
parliamentary factions of the various parties and—second—the frequency
of contacts between members of parliament and interest groups. It is not
too difficult to identify the major alliances (von Alemann 1987): the SPD is
the partisan ally of labour, while most ecological associations count on the
Green Party as the major representative organization. Most representatives
of business, both from big business and small business, find their natural
coalition partner in the Christian Democratic parties and the FDP. The
representatives of agriculture and forestry as well as refugee and expellee
organizations have most often seen the Christian Democratic parties as
their natural allies. The position of the two major churches is more mixed,
although conservative policy preferences in education, family law and
other socio-cultural issues have made the CDU-CSU more attractive for
the Catholic church than other parties. In contrast to this, the Protestant
church has at least partially been the ally of pacifist social movements, such

as the peace movement of the 1980s, while the Green Party cooperates closely with environmental and other citizens' initiatives.

5.4.3 A state governed by interest groups?

The debate on the political role of interest groups has long been centred on the division of power between the government and organized interests, and on possible incompatibilities of particularistic interests and the common interest on the other. That participation in forming the political will of the people may turn an interest group into a potentially influential political actor is hardly controversial. However, a wide variety of analysts argue that highly organized interest groups, especially producer group associations, have acquired a too powerful position or even a co-governing status of dubious legitimacy (Hennis and Kielmansegg 1977). The corporatist Alliance for Jobs, for example, which the red-Green Schröder government established in 1998, provokes diverse responses. For example, experts in the study of corporatism regard the participation of trade unions and employer associations in the Alliance for Jobs as a potentially rational strategic partnership between government and interest organizations for the purpose of improving coordination and, if possible, problem solving in economic and labour market policy. Others however doubt the rationality and the integrity of the actors involved and question the legitimacy of interest group participation in a policy process for which only those elected by the people and sent to parliament should be responsible. These observations and data on close networks linking interest groups together with the state apparatus and political parties have nourished the view that the Federal Republic of Germany may become a case of political domination by interest associations, a *Verbändestaat* (Eschenburg 1955; Forsthoff 1971: 119).

Competing theories

Whether Germany is heading towards political domination by interest associations is controversially debated. According to one school of thought, the relative autonomy of the state apparatus vis-à-vis particularistic interests is safeguarded. Others point to a large influence of interest groups on the political process and argue that the high level of organizational density in Germany makes a major difference. Germany's associations and interest groups undoubtedly do matter a great deal in social, economic, and political life. The German economy would follow a different trajectory if neither trade unions nor employers' associations existed. The 'associational man', to quote Max Weber again, is nowadays to be found almost everywhere—in public discourse, formal deliberation of legislative proposals, parliamentary consultation, and decision making as well as in administration and implementation of public policy. It would be unrealistic to expect that the omnipresence of the 'associational man' makes no difference. Furthermore, the Bundestag is famous for the presence and impact of influential interest associations in parliament (Reutter 2001b: 94). Among these, the proportion of pressure groups in social policy areas on the one hand and cultural affairs, science, and religion on the other is increasing, while associations in economic and labour market policy areas are decreasing in relative terms (Reutter 2001b: 94–6).

Channels of influence

Studies on interest associations, such as Streeck (1981), von Winter (1997), and von Alemann and Wessels (1997), consistently point to the influential role of interest groups. Interest groups play a part in parliamentary recruitment and appoint group representatives to the numerous permanent councils and ministerial advisory commission in the states, at the level of federal government and—to an increasing extent since the 1980s—in the European Community (Van Schendelen 1993). Furthermore, experts in comparative politics argue that German interest groups do matter more than interest groups in other countries. Compared with the United States of America, interest associations in Germany, the theory goes, are 'more inclusive, more tightly organised, and occupy a more privileged position in public policy processes than their American counterparts' (Edinger 1986: 184). Edinger also pointed to a further noteworthy difference: American policy makers 'may pay attention to the demands of interest groups' spokesmen if they wish', but German officials 'are legally bound to do so' (1986: 187–8). The difference is that in Germany, as in most European countries, but in contrast to the USA, 'institutionalised rules for the functional representation of pluralist interests allow pressure groups to bypass the political parties and inject themselves directly into policymaking' (Edinger 1986: 188). Numerous laws and administrative regulations thus give formal sanction and encouragement to the practice of direct contacts between interest groups and agencies of the state. Examples include the attachment of consultative bodies to governmental institutions. Even more important is the requirement of administrative procedures of the ministries of the federal government that, when they draft a bill for submission to the legislation process, they must consult the official representatives of the relevant peak interest organizations. This requirement indeed approximates to a 'magna charta of pressure groups' influence' (J. Weber 1976: 77).

But at the same time no single interest association can count on a majority position among the lobbyists. Furthermore, the view that bypassing the political parties and injecting themselves directly into policy making enhances the role of interest groups misses a major constraint of politics in a party state. Within a party state, bypassing parties may count, but gaining access to parties is decisive, above all access to incumbent parties and therefore to the decision-making process. Thus it is perfectly rational for most interest groups to seek to establish firm direct contact with the political parties.

The view that German interest groups matter a great deal is largely uncontroversial in the comparative literature on pressure groups and linkages between interest groups and the state. Whether they matter more than the interest groups in other countries, however, is contentious. It may well be the case that a pluralist system of interest associations, such as in the United States of America, creates more scope for pressure groups at the levels of local, state, and federal government. But it can also not be ruled out that a high degree of tripartite coordination between government, employers, and unions may provide a wider variety of participation opportunities to interest groups than a pluralist mode of interest intermediation, the dominant mode of state–interest group relations in the English-speaking democracies. Because Germany is a country with a corporatist tradition (Wehler 1995: 662–80), co-administration and co-governance of interest groups together with the state or sectors of the state apparatus are far from common in the Federal Republic (Siaroff 2000).

Corporatist and pluralist interest intermediation

The German experience is part of a larger pattern: the nature of interest group politics differs across democratic states (Reutter and Rütters 2001). The exact combination of campaigning and lobbying methods used by the interest associations to exert influence varies from one political system to the other. In the United States of America, for example, interest associations pay particular attention to influencing Congress. In Britain, where power is concentrated in the executive branch of a centralized state, interest groups usually place greater emphasis on influencing ministers and civil servants. In a decentralized federalist system, however, such as in Australia or Canada, influencing parties, parliaments, and government at the state level counts most.

Furthermore, the literature has suggested various typologies of interest intermediation between organized interests and the state (Schmitter and Lehmbruch 1979). One of these typologies resides in the distinction between two ideal types of relations between organized interests and the state, one corporatist in nature, the other pluralist in character. The corporatist ideal type emphasizes the involvement of associations in public policy formation and implementation. The networks between the state and organized interests may involve delegation of public tasks to private or parapublic interest groups. This can turn the interest groups into 'auxiliary bureaucracies' of the state and thus relief government (Lehmbruch 1999: 94). But the networks may also involve joint partnership of the interest groups and the state in policy formation and implementation, such as in the case of a deal comprising sound macro-economic management and labour acquiescence (Cameron 1984). The corporatist pattern tends to go along with the representational monopoly of one peak association as the major representative of a particular sector or occupational group.

In contrast to this, a pluralist pattern of interest intermediation between the state and organized interests is characterized in an ideal-type fashion by a larger number of competing interest groups and a high degree of relative autonomy on their part vis-à-vis the state. Moreover, within the framework of pluralist interest intermediation, the emphasis is often on pressure group politics, including a conflictual style of lobbying. Furthermore relations between the state and the interest associations are bilateral rather than tripartite or multipartite, and tend to be confined to consultation short of institutionalized participation in the policy process. Pluralist interest intermediation may take on different roles, from the virtual capture of the state by organized interests to the exploitation of an interest group by the state and exchanges between the state and an interest group, such as privileged treatment of an interest group by public officials in exchange for a service for the government, for example the provision of detailed information on a policy area.

Ideal types differ from real types. No country conforms to either ideal type. But approximations exist. There is, for example, agreement in the literature that Austria most closely approximates corporatism. There is also widespread agreement that most of the English-speaking democracies, most notably the United States of America, approximate the pluralist ideal type. In contrast to this, colonization of the state administration, instrumentalization of an interest group by the state as well as exchange between organized interest and public bureaucracies have occurred in all these countries.

Measured by scales of corporatist interest intermediation, Germany is positioned in the middle between pluralist arrangements and corporatism.[15] Germany is thus partly corporatist, partly pluralist. Notwithstanding the coexistence of corporatist and pluralist arrangements, the corporatist patterns of interest intermediation have been discernible, both with respect to tripartite relationships between the government, labour, and capital, such as in labour market policy, but also regarding the delegation of public tasks to societal associations, such as in old age insurance and health care, and in agricultural policy. The corporatist networks are part of a long-standing division of labour between the state and societal organizations. Part of this tradition is the delegation of a wide variety of public policies to half-autonomous, half-public institutions supervised by public authorities. Prominent examples include the social insurance institutions introduced by social legislation in Germany in the 1880s. Social insurance institutions are organizations in which representatives of labour and capital cooperate, both of them licensed by the state. The examples comprise also corporatist administration of unemployment insurance and selective labour market policy, as typified by the Federal Employment Office (Bundesanstalt für Arbeit). Organizationally, the Federal Employment Office is based upon a tripartite network comprising representatives of the state, labour organizations, and employers' associations. State-licensed self-administration in health care and the delegation of welfare services to charitable organizations are further examples of the delegating state. And so, too, is free collective bargaining between organized labour and employers' associations over wages, working time, and the organization of labour.[16]

Although Germany is a state with significant corporatist traditions, the Federal Republic of Germany is not a case of fully developed Austrian-style corporatism. Moreover, Germany's interest group landscape is 'much more pluralist and dynamic than any textbook description of neo-corporatism' (Sebaldt 2000: 202), because individual lobbying and a wide variety of bilateral exchanges between interest groups and government play a major role. European integration exacerbates the pluralist character and works against corporatist arrangements, because the dominant mode of interest group coordination and consultation between the European Union and interest groups is pluralist and may even turn into disorganized pluralism, if not 'anarchical pluralism' (Sebaldt 2000: 202). It must be added that capture of the state administration by interest groups has also not been unknown in Germany, as agricultural policy mainly in the 1950s and 1960s demonstrated. In addition, the federal administration of social policy reminds the observer of effective colonization mainly by unions, pro-welfare state political parties, and interest groups of the welfare state clientele. But it must be added that social policy proved to be autonomous enough to change policy in periods of reduced economic growth rates, rising unemployment, and rising old age dependency ratios, as various cutbacks in social programmes testify (Siegel 2002).

Indicators of corporatist and pluralist interest intermediation, such as Schmidt (1982b: 135), Lehmbruch (1984), and Siaroff (2000), provide useful data on the comparative location of Germany. However, they do not sufficiently reflect the prominent part played by the delegation of public functions to interest groups in Germany. Indicators of corporatism or pluralism, thus, underestimate the extent to which networks between the state and interest groups shape political and social life in the Federal Republic.

Rejecting the 'Verbändestaat' hypothesis

Despite the important role played by the delegation of state authorities and the relevance of interest groups in policy formation and implementation, Germany cannot be regarded as a state politically dominated by interest groups (*Verbändestaat*). Interest groups are numerous and occupy privileged positions at least in some important policy areas. But they are neither omnipresent nor omnipotent. Of course, unions matter a great deal in social policy and labour market policy, to mention just two examples. Most governments therefore avoid social policies which might provoke sustained protest from the unions or, alternatively, seek to buy off protest through compensation of the unions in other policy areas.

Furthermore, interest groups play a much less important role in policy areas governed by experts, such as monetary policy. And even in policy areas in which interest groups control a strategic position, such as in social policy or labour market policy, they seem to be less influential than their counterparts in countries with the highest scores on the corporatism scale, such as Austria and the Nordic countries. In addition, although most governments shy away from a major conflict with the unions, some of them risk major conflicts with labour, such as the Kohl governments in the 1980s and in the period 1995–8.

These observations lend support to the view that the power resources of the 'Big Four' among Germany's most influential interest groups are also more limited than has been expected. This receives further support from the observation that none of these interest groups meets the criteria of a highly influential collective actor, namely influential policy advice, voting power, market power, and organizational power. The Bundesverband der Deutschen Industrie (BDI) may be an influential policy adviser, but it lacks voting power. Conversely, the German Trade Unions Confederation may be an influential supplier of votes, but it lacks power in managing the economy and cannot control the total number of jobs offered in the private or in the public sector. The two major churches are morally influential institutions, but their capacity to control members and to influence societal values is decreasing not least due to secularization. And despite the important influence of the farmers' associations on agricultural policy, the total number of jobs in agriculture has declined over the last decades. Moreover, farmers' associations suffered further losses in influence when Renate Künast, a representative of the Green Party, became the first Green Federal Minister for Agriculture and Consumer Protection in 2001. In addition, none of the interest groups, regardless of whether it belongs to the 'Big Four' or not, is a constitutional veto player, defined as an actor whose consent is constitutionally mandatory for policy change. Whether legislations change course is therefore not dependent upon the explicit consent or refusal of a particular interest group. This is not to deny that interest groups can be very powerful, but it helps to place them in perspective. Furthermore, whatever power resources an interest group may command, it does not possess sufficient power to effectively guide the policy making process. The interest groups' potential for effectively blocking policy making and implementation may be large but their potential for constructive policy making remains weak, not to mention the capacity for inter-sectoral coordination and mobilization of political support inside and outside parliament.

Three further observations can be marshalled against the view that Germany is ultimately governed by pressure groups or at least mainly a dependent variable of interest groups. First, the emergence and success of a wide variety of citizen initiatives and new social movements, such as the peace movement and the ecologists, testifies to the existence of demand that the established interest groups have not met. Secondly, the weakness of interest associations in the East German economy needs to be taken into account. Thirdly, the gradual decrease in problem-solving capacities on the part of societal associations throughout Germany speaks against the view that Germany is a state which is politically dominated by interest groups. Membership in interest groups plays a lesser role in East Germany than in West Germany. The organizational density of enterprises in East Germany, for example, is significantly lower than that of West German firms. Not more than 36 per cent of East Germany's enterprises were members of employers' associations in 1994, and the data for the post-1994 period do not point to alternatives. Moreover, gradual erosion of associational problem solving has also characterized West Germany. That trend is indicated by the decline in the organizational density of the BDA, as reflected by the decrease in the total number of members as a percentage of the total number of potential members from 66 per cent in the 1960s to 43 per cent in the mid-1990s (Abromeit 2000: 613). Data published by the trade unions are also indicative of decreasing organizational density, a decline which reflected broadly the average trend in industrial relations (OECD 1997: 71).

These data show that Germany continues to be a state full of organized interests. But it is not a state controlled by interest groups. Despite the presence of a wide variety of interest groups and notwithstanding the power resources of the interest associations, the Federal Republic of Germany is not to be equated with a *Verbändestaat*, that is a state captured and exploited by egoistic interest groups. Societal associations remain powerful institutions in the Federal Republic, although they are less centralized and less encompassing than predicted in Katzenstein's formula of a sharp contrast between decentralized power in the public sector and centralized society (Katzenstein 1987: 23–35). Last but not least Germany is neither mainly corporatist nor chiefly pluralist. Regarding the distribution of labour between the state and major interest groups, the predominant mode of interest intermediation is rather partly corporatist, partly pluralist.

5.5 Representative government and the not so frequent use of referenda

A wide variety of intermediating organizations provide the institutional linkage between the people and the government in the Federal Republic of Germany. These linkages include political parties, interest groups, mass media, and parliamentary elections. The latter comprise national elections, elections in each of the sixteen states and in local government, as well as elections to the European parliament. The frequency of elections creates a climate of a permanent electoral campaign in Germany's political system and this may impair the elasticity and adaptability of the polity because electoral campaigns normally place a premium on short-term-oriented office seeking rather than long-term-oriented policy pursuit. But citizen participation in Germany is not confined to electoral politics. Participation opportunities also exist in political parties, interest groups, social movements, innumerable interest associations, and in numerous forms of unconventional participation, such as petitions, demonstrations, and Internet-based political communication. Moreover, self-administration in schools, universities, judicial institutions, and social insurance institutions provides additional participation opportunities. Furthermore, company-based codetermination of employees has also contributed to a high level of participation in the Federal Republic of Germany. Compared with other established democracies, the opportunities to participate are numerous in post-1949 Germany—and more numerous than in majoritarian democracies, such as Britain and the Nordic countries (Schmidt 2000: 373–5).

No nationwide plebiscites, but direct democracy prospers in the states and in local government

Despite a high level of political participation, there is no role for nationwide plebiscites in the Federal Republic. Germany's democracy is effectively a pure representative government—in contrast to the referendum democracy in Switzerland. However, three caveats must be added to the classification of Germany as an exclusively representative democracy. The first concerns the plebiscite which the constitution prescribes for delimitation of state boundaries in the states involved.[17] In practice, plebiscites on boundary changes have been confined to the vote on the three-states merger of Baden, Württemberg-Baden, and a region called Württemberg-Hohenzollern in 1952, and the unsuccessful ballot on the fusion of Brandenburg and Berlin in 1996. The second caveat concerns a functional equivalent of direct democratic arrangements: lower house elections often turn into an informal plebiscite on the candidates for the office of the Chancellor. The third caveat is related to direct democracy in the states, the *Länder*, and in local government. While nationwide plebiscites are precluded in the Federal Republic, direct democracy is well established in the states and in local government. The post-1990 period even witnessed an 'expansion of direct democracy' (Scarrow 1997: 451), above all in the new East German states.

Direct democracy in the states concerns mainly popular initiatives and optional referenda on legislative acts. That the Bavarian constitution also provides a referendum on the dismissal of parliament is the exception rather than the rule. But like all other states, Bavaria has excluded fiscal policy from the reach of direct democracy in order to keep the political agenda free from undesirable voting results on the size, trend, and structure of public finances.

Direct democracy in Germany is strongest in local government. The main plebiscitary institution is the direct election of the mayor. A particularly wide range of direct democratic arrangements characterizes the states of Bavaria and Baden-Württemberg. In both states the direct election of the mayor is complemented by other plebiscitary mechanisms, such as the popular initiative and referenda on local policy issues.

At the level of the federation, however, democracy means almost exclusively representative democracy. This is not a trademark of Germany alone. Predominance of representative institutions is widespread in modern democracies. Examples include India, Japan, the Netherlands, and, at the level of the federation, the United States of America.[18]

A significantly more important role is attributed to direct democracy in a second group of nations, comprising among others Australia, Denmark, France, Ireland, Italy, and New Zealand. Italy's constitution, for example, contains an optional referendum on legislation, a referendum on constitutional amendments, and a popular initiative. But it must be added that most plebiscitary institutions in these countries are non-binding popular initiatives or consultative mechanisms, or empower a constitutional organ to petition the people. These institutions do not transform the demos into the sovereign ruler. Often the demos remains 'a figurehead in the political chess game played by the actors of a representative democracy' (Kielmansegg 1996: 3). This indicates the possibility that the representative mode of democratic decision making can prevail even in countries with influential plebiscitary elements.

The undisputed leader in direct democracy is Switzerland. No other country offers its citizens more opportunities to participate in politics. These opportunities include obligatory and optional referenda on constitutional changes and simple legislation as well as the popular initiative. Plebiscitary institutions are part of the Swiss *raison d'état*. Moreover, plebiscitary institutions pervade not only politics at the federal level of Switzerland but also politics in the states, the *Kantone*, and in local government. Regarding the total number of national referenda (311 referenda in the period 1945–98 for example), Switzerland is far ahead of other countries. Switzerland is followed by Italy, with 47 referenda, New Zealand (26), Australia (24), Ireland (21), Denmark (15), and the French Fourth and Fifth Republics, with 12 referenda. Spain (five referenda) and Sweden as well as Greece—four plebiscites each—take the next positions, ahead of countries in which one referendum or two referenda were held in the period of observation, such as Austria, Belgium, Finland, Great Britain, Norway, and Portugal (Butler and Ranney 1994; Schmidt 2000: 360).

Explaining the absence of nationwide plebiscites

Why does plebiscitary democracy hardly play any role at the federal level in Germany? Part of the answer resides in the existence of numerous alternative modes of political participation, including European, national, state, and local elections as well as elections in the various self-administration corporations such as universities and social insurances. No less important has been the impact of the Weimar Republic's decline in the early 1930s and the rise of National Socialism. The view that the plebiscitary elements of the Weimar Constitution, especially the direct election of the President and the institution of a referendum, contributed to the decline of Germany's First Republic and the rise of the NS state was almost uncontroversial among the founders of the Basic Law. Largely uncontroversial also was the conclusion that the institutions of the Federal Republic in Germany should be made immune against potential destabilizations of the kind experienced in the Weimar Republic. Part of the therapy were the election of the Federal President in the Bundesversammlung as opposed to a direct election, a powerful role for the Chancellor, and constructive votes of no confidence in order to guarantee stable transfers of power from one Chancellor to the other as well as the renunciation of other plebiscitary institutions, except for the case of territorial delimitation.

Further support for the critical view of plebiscites stemmed from the experience of the three national referenda held in the National-Socialist period (1933–45), and the four plebiscites in the communist German Democratic Republic. The three referenda in the Nazi era concerned the approval of Germany's withdrawal from the League of Nations in a popular vote on 11 November 1933, the affirmative vote on the transfer of the President's office to Hitler on 19 August 1934, and the plebiscite in favour of the union of Germany and Austria of 10 April 1934 (Samples 1998: 26–7). These referenda were major examples of the manipulative mobilization of support for the National-Socialist leadership in post-1933 Germany and the acclamation of Hitler as a charismatic leader (Kershaw 1998, 2000). Manipulation and acclamation also characterized the four plebiscites held in the Soviet Occupation Zone and the German Democratic Republic. These were the referenda on the People's Congress of 1949, the issue of remilitarization in 1951, the Peace Treaty in 1954, and the new constitution of the German Democratic Republic in 1968 (Samples 1998: 35–6).

Evaluating direct democracy

The experience of plebiscites as a device for manipulative mobilization and acclamation nourished the view that direct democracy is mainly a 'premium for demagogues', to quote Theodor Heuss, the first Federal President in post-1949 Germany. While this view is still widely shared among the political generations socialized in the interwar period and in the Second World War, later generations have adopted a more relaxed interpretation of the potential misuses of direct democracy. Plebiscites are nowadays widely regarded as 'cures with by-effects' (Di Fabio 1998: 127) rather than premiums for demagogues, provided they are given in proper doses. For example, direct democracy takes the democratic principle 'government by the people' more seriously than any other form of democracy, as long as minority rights remain guaranteed. Positive results in favour of direct democracy can also be seen in the experience of countries in which full democracy prevails, such as Switzerland. Moreover, regarding the experience of the conservative and integrative functions of the plebiscite in modern Western countries, Switzerland can again be invoked as an example: full Swiss-style democracy supports the view that plebiscitary mechanisms often maintain the status quo, but they can also serve integrative purposes (Neidhart 1970). Furthermore, Switzerland's referendum democracy demonstrates that no automatic link exists between a plebiscitary democracy and the rise of a charismatically guided democracy, a 'Führerdemokratie', to quote Max Weber, who proposed a democratically elected charismatic leader as a counterweight to parliament in order to compensate for the loss of charismatic leadership caused by the abdication of the monarch in Germany in 1918 (Weber 1976: 156–7).

The view that full democracy generates potential gains has gradually replaced more pessimistic inspections of plebiscitary mechanisms. Sympathy for direct democracy has also marked the attitudes of Germany's political class to an increasing extent, in particular all those members of the political elite who were socialized after 1949 (Bürklin and Rebenstorf et al. 1997). Advocating plebiscitary mechanisms has also been a major effort mainly on the part of the Social Democratic Party and the Greens. Whether plans to establish plebiscitary institutions at the federal level in Germany will ever be realized remains questionable. Efforts to establish direct democracy at the federal level in 2002 did not win the requisite two-thirds majority in the lower house. And whether the expectation that direct democracy generates benign effects is compatible with German-style parliamentary government is also questionable. But in view of the powerful role of the political parties, it is not very likely that the addition of plebiscitary institutions to the German polity would restrain the party state. More likely is swift adaptation of the parties to the new participatory link between demos and government. It is also likely that, as in Switzerland, well-organized interests will be better at exploiting the possibilities of plebiscitary institutions than unorganized or disorganized groups

(Neidhart 1970). Furthermore, as long as direct democracy is subordinate to the supremacy of the Federal Constitutional Court, it is unlikely that adding plebiscitary institutions would fundamentally change the structures of Germany's constitutional democracy.

The enthusiasm which full democracy sometimes evokes should not conceal the considerable potential for ambivalent outcomes of direct democratic institutions. Depending upon the context and the preferences of the people, plebiscites may foster or inhibit integration or exclusion. Direct democracy may follow the status quo or deviate from traditional paths. It may respect or violate minority rights, and promote or restrict political innovations. In addition, the plebiscite can be a sharp majoritarian weapon, but it may also strengthen consociational practices, as the Swiss case of the legislative referendum shows. For example, if a powerful interest group credibly threatens to demand a referendum on a parliamentary bill, a rational lawmaker will strive to integrate that interest group into the process of consultation and bargaining on the bill in order to guard legislation against the undesirable outcomes of the referendum. But this effort to safeguard legislation against the referendum strengthens consociational structures and processes and turns direct democracy into a hybrid of referendum democracy and negotiation democracy (Neidhart 1970). Moreover, plebiscitary democracy may endanger political stability, if political leaders tend towards demagogy and if the people are badly informed and susceptible to propaganda. Furthermore, misuse of the plebiscitary mechanism has not been uncommon, above all in 'fragile democracies' (Casper 1995). But even in secure democracies, such as in the USA, plebiscitary institutions often prove to be liable to manipulation and capture by highly specialized interest groups (Stelzenmüller 1994). Capture of plebiscitary mechanisms, however, is also conceivable in other places, for example in a Swiss-style consociational democracy or a mixed majoritarian-consociational system, such as the Federal Republic of Germany.

Taking the various pieces of information together suggests that direct democratic structures may, viewed from the perspective of a best case scenario, improve the quantity and quality of political participation. But a worse outcome is conceivable, for example due to wildly fluctuating majorities or as a consequence of demagogy. Direct democracy is also not necessarily a recipe for improved policy making. It may significantly improve the problem-solving capacity, but it is more likely to result in status quo biased solutions or in prolonged reaction periods. Thus, there is not much which supports the view that adding plebiscitary elements to the political institutions at the federal level in Germany automatically improves the quality of problem solving. It may turn out this way, but it is at least as likely that it would not turn out this way.

5.6 Majoritarian and non-majoritarian structures in Germany's democracy

The Basic Law prescribes democratic government for the Federal Republic of Germany. Comparative measures of democracy, such as the Political Rights scale published by Freedom House (2001) and the democracy-autocracy-index (Jaggers and Gurr 1995), unequivocally show that this prescription has been fully implemented. According to these measures, the Federal Republic of Germany can pride itself as one of the well-established democracies—both in the pre- and the post-unification period (Lijphart 1999; Powell 2000). Rather than choosing presidentialism and semi-presidentialism, the architects of Germany's constitution have opted for a parliamentary form of government, with the executive accountable to parliament and dependent upon the support of the majority of the deputies. Furthermore, the founding fathers of Germany's constitutions have selected a predominantly representative democracy in contrast to a direct democracy.

Majoritarian and non-majoritarian structures of Germany's democracy

Regarding representative democracy and parliamentary government, Germany's democratic institutions are not particularly distinctive. Both forms of government are common in many modern democracies. But in contrast to many other democratic countries, Germany's democracy has been marked by an extraordinary combination of majoritarian and non-majoritarian structures.

Majoritarian structures play an important part in Germany's political process (Chapter 3). For example, the relative majority of the first vote in an election to the national parliament determines which candidates get the seats in the electoral districts. And the majority of the seats in the lower house of parliament determines whether a candidate for the office of

Chancellor wins or loses. It is also the majority of the deputies to the Bundestag that decides a constructive vote of no confidence against the Federal Chancellor. Furthermore, the majority in the Federal Convention, the Bundesversammlung, decides the election of the Federal President. And if the government controls the majority of the votes in the lower and the upper houses of parliament, it controls the potential for action. The structures of Germany's democracy are, thus, undoubtedly to a significant extent majoritarian in character.

However, Germany's democracy comprises not only majoritarian components, but also non-majoritarian ones. The dual structure of Germany's democracy is reflected in Lijphart's comparative study of modern democracies. According to Lijphart's measures, the Federal Republic is positioned in the middle between the two extreme poles marked by a Westminster-style majoritarian model of democracy and a 'consensus democracy' of the Swiss variety (Lijphart 1999: 312). Bargaining democracy and consociational practices do indeed play an important role in the political process, for reasons which were discussed in the preceding chapters of this book. The power-sharing functions of federalism, for example, belong to the major pillars upon which the non-majoritarian structures of democracy in Germany rest. Federalist power sharing adds a strong consociational element to the modes of conflict resolution through establishing unanimity or at least high consensus thresholds such as two-thirds majorities in legislation and, hence, requires extensive bargaining and compromise seeking. Similarly, cooperation between the states and federal government, or, alternatively, cooperation among the states only, also requires extended bargaining rather than majority rule or hierarchical decision making. In a similar vein, legislation liable to explicit agreement of the Bundesrat usually establishes a non-majoritarian mode of conflict resolution between Bundestag and Bundesrat as well as between government and opposition, as long as the latter controls the majority of the seats in the Bundesrat.

A democracy-friendly state and the input–output gap

Veto player theory is also consistent with the view that a strong non-majoritarian component characterizes Germany's democracy today. A large number of veto players and, thus, powerful constraints on policy making characterize Austria, Switzerland, and the USA, but also the Federal

Republic of Germany. In contrast to this, the total number and the political importance of veto players is much smaller in the Nordic countries and in Westminster-style democracies (Schmidt 2002c). Germany is a state full of veto players and other *de facto* co-governing forces. To overcome a veto ultimately requires unanimity and usually presupposes consensual practices rather than majority rule or hierarchical solutions. The high veto-player density in the Federal Republic thus adds a further non-majoritarian component to the prevailing modes of conflict resolution.

However, Germany is not only a state with a particularly wide variety of veto players, but also a country with a wide variety of participation opportunities—due to the high frequency of national and subnational elections, but also as a consequence of democratic self-administration in local government, universities, schools, and social insurance institutions, and also due to extended codetermination of labour representatives in plant-level decision making and in management boards of industrial enterprises (Schmidt 2000: 374–5). The political inputs in Germany are thus overproportionately friendly to democracy. The 'democracy friendly state' can be regarded as a comparative advantage when measured by normative-analytical theories of participatory democracy. But the advantage does not necessarily spill over to the quality of policy making, policy outputs and outcomes. The causes of the democracy friendly state, above all a wide variety of participation opportunities, numerous veto positions, and almost never-ending electoral campaigns, may turn out to be barriers to, and restrictions on, policy making in general and policies aiming at ambitious reforms in particular. For example, many veto players and frequent elections impede significant policy changes and extract high political costs in particular for cost containment or recalibration of major political programmes. The unintended effects of European integration also need to be considered in this context. Whatever the merits of European integration may be, it has so far been a process governed by a bureaucratic-consociationalist technocracy. The costs involved include a massive democratic deficit. The democratic deficit of the European Union is due to the lack of a European demos and a European public capable of debating the political choices in a common language, but it also reflects the nature of decision making in the European institutions, which is either predominantly bureaucratic or based on the narrowly constrained control capacities of the European Parliament. The European democratic deficit and the large number of veto players in Germany have been conducive to a major gap between the political input and output in the Federal Republic: the high democratic quality of the political input is narrowly constrained by the numerous domestic veto players and the European democratic deficit. The latter tend to slow down the policy-making capacity and can impair both the quality and quantity of the policy output; but they can also be conducive to political frustration on the part of the voters.

The input–output gap is a strain for Germany's polity. But it must be added that the input–output gap has so far not resulted in a paralysing crisis of the regime comparable to that which occurred during the last years of the Weimar Republic. Despite their importance, institutions do not dictate choices and do not determine outcomes. This applies also to the input–output gap. It is possible to reduce or bridge the input–output gap, for example by the cooperation of all the major actors in legislation. However, it is also possible to extend the input–output gap, for example through adversarial politics and the inclination of rival parties to dichotomize and sermonize issues and always to lay the blame at each other's door. But none of these outcomes is inevitable. Whether the one or the other occurs depends not only upon the restrictive and enabling conditions that institutions generate but also on the choices of the major political actors. This topic leads on to the next section of this chapter and to Chapter 6, which focus on Germany's political elite and on relationships between institutions and actors on the one hand and policy outputs and outcomes on the other.

5.7 Who governs? Germany's political elite before and after unification

Who governs Germany? The answers differ from one school of thought to another. If democracy is really 'government of the people, by the people (or by elected representatives) and for the people', to quote former US President Abraham Lincoln's famous definition, one would expect that it is the people who ultimately govern. Proponents of constitutional theory, however, point out that the centre of government resides not in the people, but rather in the elected representatives of the people and, above all, in the federal government, as well as in the cooperation of the federal government with the upper house, the representative chamber of the state governments. In contrast to this, analysts of the party state argue that modern Germany is chiefly governed by political parties, whereas supporters of veto-player theory mainly point to those collective actors who control the major veto positions. Advocates of systems theory locate the major determinants of governing Germany mainly in economic and social structures. Last but not least, promoters of elite surveys point to leadership positions when those who govern are to be identified. It is the latter approach and empirical studies on elites which guide the analysis in this chapter.

Leadership positions

According to the three major surveys on elites in the Federal Republic,[19] up to 4,600 top-level positions are to be found in the economy, society, and polity in today's Germany. In contrast to a tightly interconnected centralized power elite, the elites in the Federal Republic are positioned in a polycentric system in which power is geographically and functionally widely dispersed. The location of the major political institutions in Germany serves as a guide. There is a discernible trend towards centralization, but decentralization plays also a significant role. The federal government, the lower house and the upper house, the Federal President, and the headquarters of the political parties and major interest groups are based in Berlin—although a significant proportion of the government continues to be located in Bonn, the former capital. But the powerful Federal Constitutional Court resides in Karlsruhe; the German central bank and the European system of central banks are located in Frankfurt; and the sixteen heads of the state governments are based in sixteen different capitals at the state level, among them Munich, Hamburg, and Dresden.

Fragmentation also marks the political elite in Germany today. In contrast to France, Britain, or the USA, Germany 'lacks a clear establishment class' (Dalton 1989: 185) with shared values, beliefs, and attitudes as well as shared informal social relations. There is indeed no German equivalent to the *Grandes Écoles* of France, the elite Oxbridge campuses of Britain, or the Ivy League of the United States—neither in pre-1990 Germany nor in the post-unification period (Dalton 1989: 185). Furthermore, any effort that aims at altering this situation would clash with the interest of the sixteen states, which are concerned that their relative autonomy in culture and education should be preserved. This has significant implications for the structure and the position of the elite. Neither the German elite as a whole nor the political elite in the narrower sense constitutes a power elite or a distinct social class. It is rather the case that the German elite is post-totalitarian and pluralist in composition, character, and attitude.

The post-totalitarian elite

The political elite in the Federal Republic of Germany in the early twenty-first century differs markedly from Germany's political leaders before 1945 and from the leadership in East Germany's communism in 1949–90. The composition of the political elite has fundamentally changed. None of those who held political top-level positions after 1949 were in top positions in the National-Socialist regime.[20] Dominant after 1949 has been a post-totalitarian elite in West Germany (Edinger 1960). And in contrast to East Germany, elites with pro-democratic attitudes rather than anti-democratic beliefs held the reins of power in Western Germany. This marked a major break with the past in a country in which the majority of the elite had long been indifferent, if not hostile, to democracy (Zapf 1965). This also differed widely from the predominance of socialist and communist preferences in the political leaders in East Germany's socialism from 1945 to 1990.

The post-totalitarian composition and outlook of the West German political elite reflected the complete breakdown and the total discrediting of National-Socialist theory and practice, but it can also be attributed to the politics of 'dictatorial liberalisation' of the Western occupation forces in post-1945 Germany (Niethammer 1973: 178). These factors resulted in the exclusion of former National-Socialist leaders from top-level political positions, and were conducive to recruiting elite candidates mainly from non-National-Socialist groups. Most of the post-totalitarian leaders were recruited from younger age cohorts with few or no connections with the political leaders in the National-Socialist period and the Weimar Republic. The rise of the party state in the Federal Republic of Germany and the fact that parties increasingly provided virtually the only route to a political career added further momentum to recruiting elites from post-totalitarian groups. Almost complete substitution of a new elite for the old one distinguished only some of the elite sectors in West Germany's transition to democracy in the 1950s and 1960s. Almost complete substitution occurred in the political elite, the media, and the trade unions. In elite groups outside these sectors however, such as business, bureaucracy, or academia, continuity in top-level positions and stable recruitment patterns played a far greater role (Edinger 1960; Frei 2002).

In contrast to the West German transition from dictatorship to democracy, East Germany's transition after 1989–90 stands for the almost complete replacement of the communist elite by a new non-communist elite (Welzel 1997). That replacement included the transformation of top-level positions in politics, bureaucracy, the judiciary, education, research, media, military, and the economy, and resulted in recruitment for top-level positions mainly from the East German protest movements and the East German Protestant church as well as from West German elites.

Recruitment patterns

To what extent did the changing composition of the political elite in West Germany after 1949 and in East Germany after 1989–90 go together with changing recruitment patterns and the transformation of political attitudes and belief systems? The data from elite surveys point to both discontinuity and continuity. Continuity has long characterized the gender gap in top positions, that is, the disparity between the proportion of top positions filled by men and women. Over a longer period recruitment to positions in the political elite was almost exclusively a matter for male candidates only—both in West and East Germany. This pattern was in the mind's eye of those who invented the 'iron law of male dominance in elite positions' (Aberbach et al. 1981: 49) and classified the Federal Republic of Germany mainly as 'an *andrarchy*' (Dalton 1989: 1897), that is, 'a society ruled by males'. In 1981 only three per cent of all top-level political positions in West Germany were held by women. In this respect Communist East Germany was not very different from West Germany (Ludz 1970; Hübner 1999). But the 'iron law of male dominance' turned out to be a malleable tendency. According to the latest elite study in Germany, the Potsdam survey in 1995, the proportion of top-level positions held by women in 1995 (12 per cent) was four times as high as fourteen years earlier. Moreover, the female share in political top-level positions, such as cabinet seats, is relatively high when compared with top-level position outside politics. And compared with other nations at the beginning of the twenty-first century Germany, together with Sweden, Denmark, the Netherlands, and Argentina, is among a small group of countries with a female proportion of parliamentary seats above the 30 per cent mark (Siaroff 2000: 199; *The Economist*, 15 March 2002: 112). There has also been a large increase in the female proportion of cabinet seats in Germany in recent years (Siaroff 2000: 199) as the 46 percentage share in the second Schröder government in 2002 demonstrates. These data indicate a massive increase of gender equality in elite recruitment within a short period. This change has many causes, such as the impact of the educational revolution, the value change from materialistic goals to post-materialist and materialist/post-materialist mixed values, and the efforts of most political parties to upgrade the social position of women.

Despite these changes, social origin continues to matter in the career patterns leading to top-level positions. Germany is no different from other industrial countries in this respect. Recruitment from 'middle-aged, well-educated males from the higher social strata' (Edinger 1986: 127), still marks a major route to top-level positions, as more recent elite studies demonstrate (Bürklin and Rebenstorf et al. 1997). Particularly striking is the non-representation of the lowest social strata in Germany at the elite level, namely the migrant workers and their families. Among citizens of a higher level of educational attainment, however, upward mobility from lower status groups to top-level positions is easier than in pre-1949 Germany. This trend is exacerbated by the impact of trade unions and parties on elite recruitment—because both organizations *de facto* monopolize the access to top-level political positions. The major pathways are not difficult to identify: they reside largely in the Christian Democratic parties and the Social Democratic Party, in trade unions as well as in smaller leftist political parties, such as the Green Party and the PDS (Bürklin and Rebenstorf et al. 1997: 77–8; Rudzio 2000: 516). Because two large political parties compete with each other in Germany, the party-based upward mobility chances are particularly large when compared with other countries with less favourable party-based conditions for upward mobility (Aberbach et al. 1981: 64, 81). Thus, the party political segment of Germany's elite substitutes a more open recruitment pattern for the traditional upper-class-biased pattern of leadership recruitment. The rise of the party state in the post-1949 political system in Germany has therefore significantly contributed to transforming elite recruitment.

Recruitment to top-level positions has undergone major changes in the Federal Republic of Germany. Recruitment is no longer monopolized by people of middle-class or upper-class origin. Social origin matters, but education and party-based career patterns are also essential additional determinants of elite recruitment. Furthermore, former structurally privileged groups, such as the nobility and the landed property owners, no longer play a significant part in the recruitment to elite positions (von Beyme 1971; Hoffmann-Lange 1992). This is indicative of a broader tendency: property classes[21] no longer determine elite recruitment. What matters more for elite recruitment is affiliation to the labour force[22] together with education, party effects, and union effects.

The strong position held by the CDU-CSU in the party system has generated a further effect on elite recruitment, namely decreasing discrimination against Catholics. What would have been inconceivable in the German Empire is possible in today's Germany: political top-level positions, including those of the Federal Chancellor, are accessible not only to Protestants, as can be seen from Erhard, Schmidt, and Schröder, but also to Catholics—Adenauer, Kiesinger, and Kohl—and religiously non-affiliated persons (Brandt). But despite decreasing inequality along denominational lines, differences still exist between the Catholic and the Protestant shares in top-level positions (27 versus 45 per cent, whereas 28 per cent are not affiliated to any church) (Bürklin and Rebenstorf et al. 1997: 107). Under-representation of the Catholic population in elite positions has not been fully eliminated in modern Germany, but it has been significantly reduced.

A further change concerns the occupational background of the elite. Germany's elites have long been dominated by lawyers. Lawyers continue to hold an influential position in recruitment to top-level positions in modern Germany, above all in the political-administrative elite group. But the period of hegemony of the lawyers in the elite is over.

Major changes are also indicated by political beliefs and attitudes of the elites. The elite groups in the Federal Republic of Germany are pro-democratic rather than anti-democratic, secular rather than religious, and more liberal in their attitudes than the total population. Religious affiliation continues to be important in elite positions within the Christian Union parties, but it plays at best only a limited part in all other parties (Mayntz and Derlien 1989; Hoffmann-Lange and Bürklin 2001).

Recruitment to top-level positions of the elite and above all the political elite is more pluralistic than before. This reflects the impact of a wide variety of factors, including rising levels of educational attainment for a high proportion of the younger population, but it is also attributable to democratization and professionalization. Professionalization manifests itself in a rising share of career systems emphasizing professional expertise. That trend also concerns the political arenas as the rising share of 'politicos' demonstrates, that is, the increase in professional politicians who live on income from participating in government or opposition. The total share of 'politicos' had already climbed to 31.6 per cent in the third legislative period of the Bundestag (Loewenberg 1969: 162) and has meanwhile attained a significantly higher level (von Beyme 1999: 253, 259). A side effect has been the increasing structural dependence of the politicians on a successful career in politics and, hence, the increasing temptation to place priority on egoistic office-seeking motives rather than on policy pursuit for the people.

Social ascent to top-level positions in politics leads over numerous hurdles. The major pathways include climbing the career ladder within political parties, participation in parliamentary activities, and frequently also participation in local councils and local government. Due to the importance of federalism in Germany, success in the executive at the state level is often a stepping-stone to prominent national positions (Davis 1998: 107–8). For instance, Gerhard Schröder, the Federal Chancellor since 1998, previously held the position of minister-president in Lower Saxony. His predecessor, Helmut Kohl, was minister-president in Rhineland-Palatinate before he became opposition leader and later Chancellor. Willy Brandt, Federal Chancellor from 1969 to 1974, was earlier mayor in Berlin, the equivalent to a prime minister at the state level. And Kurt Georg Kiesinger, Chancellor in 1966–9, had served as minister-president in the state of Baden-Württemberg before he took over the chancellorship.

Moreover, membership in a political party is usually a major precondition of recruitment to top-level positions in politics. As in other advanced democracies (Davis 1998), most of those who come to office in the Federal Republic of Germany are experienced political figures, except for recruitment for the more unconventional smaller parties such as the Green Party and the Party of Democratic Socialism (PDS). The Greens and the PDS have recruited a larger proportion of their leaders from the rank and file of extra-parliamentary social movements of the 1980s and 1990s.[23] Apart from that recruitment of outsiders is rare; there remains little room for young turks and first-timers. Similarly, more attention is now being paid to opinion polling in the choice of political leaders in Germany as in many other democratic countries. And, like almost everywhere, television has come to play a major part in leadership campaigns and nominating conventions. In contrast to the United States of America, however, horizontal cross-sector mobility between the political elite and other elite groups, such as leadership positions in the economy, is rare in Germany. This may result in less collusion, but it can also contribute to a lack of experience and innovation in the political elite.

A relatively high level of educational attainment is usually a precondition for recruitment to top-level political positions. No less important, if not central, is its affinity to the roles of office-seeker, statesman, political entrepreneur, and a tough *Macher*, a fixer. In addition, climbing intra-party hierarchies presupposes highly ambitious characters who never tire of shaking hands. The list of requirements for top-level positions also includes the capacity to articulate well, the capability to present one's case in a way conducive to effective solicitation, the wisdom of a generalist, the ability to cope swiftly with a wide variety of issues, and the gift of presenting oneself as a credible person and an actor capable of integrating widely divergent interests. Moreover, recruitment to top-level positions in the political elite requires the willingness to sacrifice a very large proportion of the time budget to the public. Furthermore, a successful career for a professional politician requires the qualification of 'a generalist specialized in how to combat political opponents' (von Weizsäcker 1992: 150), but also expertise in a particular field. Last but not least, recruitment to elite positions often demands the capability to endure stormy changes in public opinion as well as ostracism-like accusations and condemnations in the public. Thus, politics as a profession and recruitment to top-level political positions in particular presuppose a multi-talented character and exceptionally strong nerves.

Duration in office

Occasionally the long pathways that lead to top-level positions are followed by only short periods in those positions. 'Ageing proceeds rapidly in top political positions', argued Rudolf Wildenmann, the head of the first large elite survey in Germany (Wildenmann 1982*a*, 1982*b*; Wildenmann et al. 1982). This was meant literally, because jobs in the political elite consume a lot of energy, and metaphorically, because holding top-level positions can be of short duration.

Of course, duration in office differs considerably in the various elite groups. The difference is largely due to manners and customs, but it also reflects political regulation. Short duration in top-level positions, for example, can reflect robust political calculation. The offices of the Federal Chancellor, the Federal President, and minister-president in a state are limited to a narrowly circumscribed period of four or five years. Of course, re-election can prolong the duration in office, but the Federal President may be re-elected only once. Army generals, to mention a further example, are candidates for early retirement for various reasons, including the prevention of a long-standing concentration of military power in a few hands. In contrast to this, longer duration in top-level positions is common in societal organizations, for example in mass media, trade unions, interest group associations, churches, and corporations.

Longer duration in office also occurs in government. Germany's first Federal Chancellor, Konrad Adenauer, held office for fourteen years—from September 1949 to October 1963. Helmut Kohl served as Chancellor even longer than Adenauer and all other German Chancellors—with the exception of von Bismarck who was in office from 1871 to 1890. Kohl stayed sixteen years in office (1982–98). Thus, he was longer in office than any other prime minister in the Western post-1945 democracies except for Australia's Prime Minister Sir Robert Gordon Menzies, who held the reins of power in 1939–41 and 1949–66.

Political attitudes and belief systems

In marked contrast to the pre-1945 period, the political elite and most of the extra-political elite groups in present-day Germany strongly support democracy. Politics of a National-Socialist complexion are discredited in all elite groups with a few exceptions among ultra-nationalists. Furthermore, the option of a communist system was no less thoroughly discredited by the rise and decline of East Germany's socialism in 1949–90—except for communist hard-liner factions in the PDS. The pro-democratic attitude of the large majority of Germany's elite has been a crucial determinant of the consolidation of democracy in post-1949 Germany.

While a pro-democratic consensus unites the various elite groups, party political preferences differ considerably. In the 1981 survey, the majority of the West German elite proved to be voters for the Christian Democrats and the Liberals. Only a minority opted for the SPD; above all these were labour union officials and, of course, Social Democratic deputies: while 51 per cent of the respondents in the 1981 elite survey voted for the Christian Democrats, 18 per cent selected the Liberals, and 29 per cent chose the Social Democrats. However, a wide range of variation marks the party vote in the various elite groups. Thus, for example, in the early 1980s, the Christian Democratic parties could count on 73 per cent of the votes from business leaders and 74 per cent from the military leaders. In contrast to this, a large majority of trade union leaders—84 per cent—unambiguously supported the SPD. Members of the media elites and academic elites revealed party preferences similar to those of the electorate.

The distribution of party preferences in the post-unification period has been more diverse, although the Christian Democratic parties remain the strongest party among members of the elites. But with 42.5 per cent of the party identifiers the CDU-CSU has lost the absolute majority. The vote falling to the SPD has increased to 31.9 per cent. In addition, the Green Party has gained 9.4 per cent and the PDS 1.7 per cent of the votes from elite groups.[24]

The difference between the party preferences of the elite and the mass public has decreased. The ideological distance between the elite and the masses is smaller in 1995 than in 1981. But marked differences persist in attitudes and belief systems. The 1981 and the 1995 elite surveys demonstrate that Germany's leaders are, on average, more liberal,[25] more secular and more post-materialist than the electorate as a whole. According to the 1995 study, for example, the share of post-materialists in Germany's elite is surprisingly large—49 per cent in West Germany and thus twice as much as the post-materialists' share in the total population and even 55 per cent in the East German elite compared to 7 per cent post-materialist in the total East German population. Conversely, pure materialists are a small majority in the elite groups—5 per cent in West Germany (compared to 17 per cent in the population) and 1 per cent in East Germany compared to 25 per cent in the total population. Finally, mixed values, that is respondents with significant materialist and post-materialistic values, characterize 46 per cent of the West German elite and 44 per cent of the East German leaders (Bürklin and Rebenstorf et al. 1997: 372).

East–west differences

Major east–west differences exist in the elites' attitudes on the role of government and distribution of labour between state and market. In general, the East German elite favours a much stronger role of the state, while the West German elite (except for the left-wing sections) prefers a more reduced role of the state. The East German elite also advocates a far more active role of the state in social policy and in combating unemployment. Furthermore, when faced with the equality-efficiency trade-off, a larger proportion of the East German elites raise their voices far louder than their West German counterparts in favour of priority for social policy over economic policy (Bürklin and Rebenstorf et al. 1997: 327–44). This mirrors a broader pattern. Influenced by the legacies of East Germany's state socialism, the elite in the eastern part of the country continues to advocate big government rather than minimal government and rejects efforts geared towards reducing the role of the state (Bürklin and Rebenstorf et al. 1997: 343–4). Thus, the consensus on the right distribution of labour between government and market is clearly weaker in Germany's post-1990 elite than before unification.

Moreover, the preferred model of democracy differs remarkably in the elite groups in unified Germany. Following the 1995 elite survey, the difference concerns the preference for representative democracy (including the approval of strong leadership as well as the rejection of direct democracy and unconventional political participation) on the one hand and the advocacy of a plebiscitary model of democracy on the other, emphasizing the new politics and increasing the participation and promotion of direct democratic arrangements (Bürklin and Rebenstorf et al. 1997: 400–3). Closer inspection of the data reveals however a somewhat less dramatic, though still significant, change. The change does not comprise increased advocacy of a purely plebiscitary democracy. What is advocated to a far greater measure than before 1990 is to supplement representative democracy with more competition and a higher level of political participation.

This marks a significant change in political beliefs and attitudes. The underlying causes of that change comprise mainly five factors: position, office experience, political generation, elite group, and party preferences. More political participation and more political competition is advocated above all by elite groups which have not yet attained top-level positions; have been in office for a limited period; belong to the political generation born after 1945; have gained elite positions in one of the political parties or in the media; and prefer the Social Democratic Party or the Green Party.

Changing political generations

Advocacy of extended political participation and intensified competition is also influenced by changes in the political generations (Bürklin and Rebenstorf et al. 1997: 396). In contrast to the pre-1990 period, the political generation of the Republic's founding fathers no longer participate in governing post-1990 Germany. Thus, the generation which was politically socialized in the German Empire, the Weimar Republic and the National-Socialist era is no longer participating in politics and policy making. The institutional preferences of that group were mainly shaped by the traumatic experience of the Weimar Republic's decline in the 1930s, the experience of two World Wars, the deep economic crisis of the early 1930s, and mass unemployment. The founding fathers' generation identified institutional defects as major causes of the decline of the Weimar Republic, among them the plebiscitary elements of the Weimar constitution and the structural weakness of the Chancellor and his cabinet in a semi-presidential system. In the view of this generation, a viable institutional design for the Second Republic required a representative democracy with a strong Chancellor, a weak President, and the absence of plebiscitary components at least at the level of the federation.

In contrast to this, the younger members of the Federal Republic of Germany's elite were exposed to a different type of political socialization. They found themselves confronted with peace and prosperity rather than economic crisis and war. Moreover, the new elite no longer mistrusted increasing levels of participation, plebiscitary institutions, and extending the scope of democracy to society at large. The 'successor generation' (Szabo 1983) of the founding fathers' generation has indeed cared more about new politics issues, such as environmental quality, the democratization of society, women's rights, and more recently migrants' rights. Furthermore, the successor generation has been 'more prone to protests and other forms of direct citizen action' (Dalton 1989: 201). In addition, this generation has been more inclined to turn to ideological principles in interpreting and explaining political problems. Last but not least the successor generation tends to be more competitive in political struggle. While the pre-1990 elite in Germany has been marked 'by an unprecedented degree of mutual trust and cooperation' (Edinger 1986: 132), the successor generation emphasizes competition and conflict more than cooperation and consensus seeking.

The West German successor generation is mainly recruited from the ranks of the 'protest and wealth generation' (Bürklin and Rebenstorf et al. 1997: 415). This tendency is particularly pronounced in the left-wing factions of the Social Democratic Party and, above all, in the Green Party. One-third of the Green Party's delegates in parliament in the 1980–7 period, for example, were recruited from communist and other extreme leftist tendencies. Hardly less pronounced has been the recruitment of the new East German political elite from protest movements against the communist regime of the German Democratic Republic (Derlien 1997; Welzel 1997).

The coexistence of two diverging models of democracy in Germany's elites is indicative of a broader pattern in unified Germany: the differences within the elite groups are larger than before 1990; and the social, economic, and political differences in Germany as a whole are wider and deeper than in the two or three decades before unification. Furthermore, dissent and open or latent conflict play a more important role than in pre-unification Germany. Germany as a whole has become more heterogeneous and more conflict prone. Other things being equal, this inhibits consensus-oriented solutions. Particularly serious tensions exist in post-unification Germany between the two political camps of parties and political generations: between the elites with party preferences for the CDU-CSU on the one hand and the elites which favour the SPD, the Green Party and partly also the PDS on the other. Even more dramatic is the difference between elite groups of different political generations, particularly between elites born after 1945 and those born before the mid-1930s.

The general conclusion that these observations suggest is that the institutional and cultural conditions required for consensus-oriented politics and policy have been significantly weakened in post-1990 Germany. Conversely, the odds are that conflict-oriented politics in Germany has gained a more important role than in the pre-unification period. However, Germany's formal political institutions continue to require in most cases cooperation and consensus as a precondition for conflict resolution and sustainable problem solving. Thus, the conflict between institutional requirements and actor constellations has become more intense in unified Germany than before.

5.8 Conclusion

In this chapter, attention has been mainly centred on the electoral system, voting behaviour, parties and the party system, organized interest groups, networks between the state and the interest associations, the political elites both prior to and after unification, and the role played by the various forms of democracy which coexist in Germany—representative and direct, and majoritarian and non-majoritarian. The analysis of the links between people and institutions points altogether to vital political inputs in the Federal Republic of Germany. This lends further support to the view that a vital democracy has emerged in the post-1949 period and has been maintained both prior to and after the unification of the country in 1990. But the analysis also points to a significant amount of stress in the political process. Germany's formal political institutions continue to require a large degree of cooperation and consensus as a precondition for conflict resolution and sustainable problem solving. However, the cultural conditions required for consensus-oriented politics and policy have been significantly weakened in post-1990 Germany. Due to a variety of reasons, among them value change, unification, and dealignment, conflict-oriented non-cooperative politics has gained a more important role than in most of the pre-unification period. Thus, the conflict between institutional requirements, which require cooperation, and actor constellations, which emphasize non-cooperative politics, has become more intense in unified Germany than before. This is part of a substantial input–output gap in Germany. The vital democratic quality of the political input is constrained by a large number of veto players in Germany and restrictions such as the European democratic deficit. This may slow down the policy-making capacity and impair both the elasticity and adjustment capabilities of policy making; but it may also be conducive to voter frustration.

KEY TERMS

- Alliance/Green Party '90
- associational man
- capture
- CDU-CSU
- cleavage
- coalition
- corporatism
- democracy-friendly state
- direct democracy
- FDP
- ideological spectrum of party system
- input-output gap
- interest groups
- issue competence

- majority rule
- non-majoritarian structures
- number of parties
- party identification
- party system
- PDS
- pluralism
- polarized pluralism
- policy position
- proportional representation
- pro-welfare state parties
- representative government
- secular-conservative party
- SPD
- 'The Big Four'

QUESTIONS FOR CHAPTER 5

1 What are the major political consequences of the electoral formula in the Federal Republic of Germany?

2 Why has the Federal Republic of Germany come to be regarded as a case in which two pro-welfare state parties compete?

3 What are the political consequences of the higher degree of volatility on the part of the voters in present day Germany?

4 What are the pros and cons of the predominance of representative government over direct democracy in the Federal Republic of Germany?

5 What are the principal virtues and the major drawbacks of the mixture of majoritarian and non-majoritarian democracy in the Federal Republic of Germany?

NOTES

1 For deviations due to excess seats see further below.

2 With one or two seats through relative majority in the first vote and less than 5 per cent of the second vote, as with the PDS in the national election in 2000, a party keeps these seats, but cannot use its second vote.

3 Measured by Lijphart's index of electoral disproportionality, a measure of the vote-seat-share deviation of the political parties in national elections (see Lijphart 1999: 158, 1962, 313).

4 On the limits of the 'catch-all-parties' hypothesis see Schmidt 1985 and Padgett 2001.

5 Major differences concern, for example, the choice between permissive and non-permissive social policy, such as abortion, pro-public or pro-private ownership, clericalism vs. anticlericalism, the pros and cons of decentralization and democratization, and conflicts over priority for the environment over growth versus growth over the environment. See Laver and Hunt 1992: 196–201.

6 See, for example Mintzel 1977; Pridham 1977; Haungs 1983; Paterson 1985; Schmid 1990; Hanley 1994; Gehler, Kaiser, and Wohnout 2001.

7 Oskar Lafontaine (SPD), at that time Chairman of the SPD and Federal Minister for Finance in an interview in *BILD-Zeitung* 12 Feb. 1999.

8 'Greens grow up' (1999), *The Economist*, 7 Aug., 21.

9 Ibid.

10 At that time the CDU-CSU placed major emphasis on a pro-market economic policy, rearmament, and the rapid integration of West Germany into the international and supranational organization of the West, while the Social Democratic Party opted for a nationalistic reunification policy and a democratic-socialist economic policy.

11 Calculation from the author's data archive on elections in OECD democracies (poolwahl_1_MB 2001). N = 319.

12 The data were taken from a survey conducted by V&M Services, Konstanz (Germany) (see FAZ No. 228, 1 Oct. 2001: 11). Data are for 2001.

13 Registration of the central associations is a precondition for the allocation of subsidies from the state.

14 Theodor Eschenburg cited in Reutter (2001*b*: 87).

15 Schmidt's and Lehmbruch's scales of corporatism classified West Germany as a case of medium corporatism in contradistinction to strong corporatism in Austria, the Netherlands, Sweden, and Norway, and in further contrast to weak corporatism in Italy, pluralism in the United States, Canada, Australia, and New Zealand, as well as corporatism without labour in Japan and France (Schmidt 1982*c*; Lehmbruch 1984; Siaroff 1999; see also Crouch 1994).

16 German employers and employees have the right to negotiate collective agreements without interference from the government. The general conditions of industrial relations are set by legislation. But legislation does not cover the wages and salaries to be paid to the employees of the market economy. In contrast to this, the wages for the employed in the public sector are based on legislative acts which

usually take over the wage agreement of the social partners.

17 According to Article 29 Basic Law, a referendum is held in the states from whose territories or partial territories a new state or a state with redefined boundaries is to be formed.

18 While direct democracy also plays an important role in local government and in various states of the USA, such as California (Butler and Ranney 1994).

19 These are the 1968 survey and the 1981 survey conducted by Rudolf Wildenmann and the 1995 survey headed by Willy Bürklin. See Wildenmann 1982*a*, 1982*b*; Hoffmann-Lange 1992; Bürklin and Rebenstorf et al. 1997: 64. For an analysis of the first elite survey see von Beyme 1971.

20 Hans Globke, Adenauer's chief of staff, and Kurt Georg Kiesinger, the Federal Chancellor in 1966 to 1969, are no exceptions to this rule; both of them were members of the NSDAP, but not members of the elite in Nazi Germany.

21 Defined in terms of Max Weber's 'Besitzklasse', that is a social class defined by property rights and income from property rights.

22 Defined in terms of Weber's 'Erwerbsklasse'. Within this class, the income derived from manual or non-manual labour and from input such as human capital counts most. See, for a masterful application of Weber's sociology of class to the Federal Republic, Lepsius 1990*b*; see also Lepsius 1990*a*, 1993.

23 Examples include Joschka Fischer (Green Party), the Minister of Foreign Affairs, and Jürgen Trittin, Federal Minister for Environment, Protection of Nature and Nuclear Power Station Safety in the first and second Schröder government. See Krause-Burger (1999) and 'Fischer, a sterner shade of Green', in *The Economist*, 15 May 1999: 32.

24 Calculated from Bürklin and Rebenstorf et al. 1997: 347 (as a percentage of the total number of party identifiers).

25 A remarkable contrast to the view advanced in Dahrendorf 1967. Dahrendorf argued that Germany's elite is mainly non-liberal.

GUIDE TO FURTHER READING

Bürklin, W., and Rebenstorf, H., et al. (1997), *Eliten in Deutschland* (Opladen: Leske & Budrich). Comprehensive analysis of the most recent elite survey in Germany.

Dalton, R. J. (1993), *Politics in Germany*, 2nd edn. (New York: HarperCollins). Overview of political institutions and political process in Germany.

Klingemann, H.-D., and Kaase, M. (eds.) (2001), *Wahlen und Wähler: Analysen aus Anlass der Bundestagswahl 1998* (Wiesbaden: Westdeutscher Verlag). Instructive collaborative volume on voting behaviour in Germany.

Lehmbruch, G. (2000), *Parteienwettbewerb im Bundesstaat*, 3rd edn. (Wiesbaden: Westdeutscher Verlag). Major historical-institutionalist contribution on party competition and federalism in Germany.

Padgett, S., and Pogunkte, T. (eds.), (2001), *Continuity and Change in German Politics: Beyond the Politics of Centrality?*

Festschrift for Gordon Smith (London: Frank Cass). Important collaborative volume on continuity and discontinuity in Germany after 1990.

——and SAALFELD, T. (eds.) (1999), *Bundestagswahl '98: End of an Era? German Politics*, 8/2 (London: Frank Cass). Useful collaborative volume on voting behaviour in Germany.

REUTTER, W. and RÜTTERS, P. (eds.) (2001), *Verbände und Verbandssysteme in Westeuropa* (Opladen: Leske & Budrich). Instructive volume on interest groups and interest group systems in democratic nations.

ROBERTS, G. K. (1997), *Party Politics in the New Germany* (London: Pinter). Succinct overview of parties and the party system in post- and pre-1990 Germany.

6

Continuity and Discontinuity in the Federal Republic of Germany

This chapter explores some of the policy consequences of the political institutions portrayed in Chapters 1 to 5. The topics covered in this chapter include the major institutional constraints on public policy in Germany and the possibilities of circumventing veto positions and veto players. In a discussion of the 'policy of the middle way', the present chapter also focuses on the distinctiveness of the public policy profile in pre- and post-unification Germany. In addition, it examines the extent to which European integration has shaped public policy in Germany. Finally, this chapter investigates the extent to which both continuity and discontinuity have marked the political institutions, the political process, and the substance of public policy in reunified Germany.

6.1 Semi-sovereignty, grand coalition state, and the policy of the middle way

A high degree of political–institutional fragmentation and power sharing rather than a concentration of political power distinguishes the Federal Republic of Germany from unitary states and majoritarian democracies, such as Britain, France, and Sweden. Moreover, a mix of 'majoritarian' and 'consensus democracy' typifies the Second German Republic, to borrow from Arend Lijphart's studies on different types of the democratic government (Lijphart 1999). Furthermore, the claim of the supremacy of the law narrowly circumscribes the room for manoeuvre for policy makers. In these circumstances, the federal government's scope for policy making (and also the scope for action on the part of the state governments) is

confined by a wide variety of institutional constraints, among them powerful co-governing institutions, such as the opposition party, and numerous
veto players, such as the upper house of parliament in most legislative
processes. These circumstances also constrain the political parties, a group
of major players in Germany's party state. It is largely due to these constraints that policy change in domestic politics in Germany usually
requires a longer planning period, is often incremental in nature, and
borders occasionally on a degree of institutional inertia which critics
describe as 'policy immobilization' or '*Reformstau*'.[1]

The institutional restrictions in Germany's polity, the theory goes, may
also inhibit the preferences for, and the possibilities of, radical policy
change for the government, regardless of the partisan complexion. Radical
party-induced policy changes, it is argued, have therefore been rarer in
Germany than partisan cycles in policy making in a majoritarian democracy such as Britain. And radical policy changes have been less likely
than policy shifts in a unitary state with dominant or hegemonic social
democratic governments, such as Sweden (Schmidt 1982*b*, 1992*a*; Huber
and Stephens 2001). Moreover, the institutional restrictions on policy
making in Germany may also inhibit the adjustment potential to major
challenges, such as the adaptation to reform demand accumulated in
Germany's highly regulated labour market (Eichhorst et al. 2001). Furthermore, the large number of veto points and veto players tends to reduce
the short-term elasticity of the political institutions (Zohlnhöfer 2001). But
reduced elasticity together with the consensus requirement inherent in the
structures of Germany's democracy are particularly delicate because most
voters expect their preferred party to adopt competitive strategies of the
winner-takes-all type rather than cooperative moves. Furthermore, most
voters premiss their expectations largely on a majoritarian model of democracy. But the Federal Republic of Germany is not a majoritarian democracy. Germany's democracy is a hybrid, a blend of majoritarian and
negotiation democracy. This type of democracy, however, produces policy
outputs and outcomes which often resemble the outputs and outcomes of
a consociational democracy (Steiner and Ertman 2002).

The government in the Federal Republic of Germany is in many aspects,
as this book has shown, 'semi-sovereign' (Katzenstein 1987). And Germany's democracy is also in many aspects semi-sovereign, not least due to
the wide variety of veto players with which each elected governments finds

itself confronted. Moreover, grand coalition state requirements exist for most major policy processes. These requirements include in the case of constitutional amendments two-thirds majorities in the Bundestag and the Bundesrat, and in legislation subject to approval of the Bundesrat co-governance of the Bundesrat. The cooperation requirement is particularly strong in periods of divergent party political majorities in the Bundestag and Bundesrat. In these circumstances, legislation requires the formation of a formal or informal grand coalition between the majorities in the Bundestag and the Bundesrat and a coalition between the incumbent parties and the parliamentary opposition party, other things being equal. Due to these constraints and because most major legislation directly or indirectly touches the powers of the states and, hence, is liable to the approval of the Bundesrat, it is almost impossible in the Federal Republic not to be governed by a formal or informal grand coalition of the major established parties and a coalition of the federal government and a majority of state governments, as long as the parties involved aim at avoiding a blocked decision-making process. In view of the high consensus requirements of Germany's political institutions, solo runs of the federal government are possible only in matters within the exclusive legislative power of the federation.

In periods of convergent party political majorities in the lower and upper houses of parliament, the federal government can of course count on greater room for manoeuvre. In these circumstances, the partisan complexion of government, as predicted by the partisan theory of public policy (Hibbs 1977, 1992), can make a particularly large difference (Schmidt 1995, 2002c). But even in these cases, solo runs of the federal government are rare, because most legislation touches upon the interest of the states and requires therefore the consent of the Bundesrat.

Manoeuvrability despite numerous hurdles

Although 'semi-sovereignity' and the grand coalition state place priority on incremental policy change, they exclude neither incremental change nor minor or major political innovation. The capability to achieve minor innovations is demonstrated by the coexistence of continuity in national institutions and widespread flexibility and experimentation in less visible arenas of politics, such as the parapublic institutions and in the networks of cooperative federalism. This was a major message of Katzenstein's insightful study on the Federal Republic in the pre-unification period (1987). But Katzenstein's book also pointed out that major political innovations were launched despite semi-sovereignty. Examples include the numerous major policy changes in the 'Adenauer era' (Schwarz 1981), such as the decision to rearm Germany, join NATO and the European Community, and the reconstruction and expansion of the welfare state (Hartwich 1970; Schwarz 1981, 1983, 1993). Major policy changes also occurred in the 1966–9 experiment of a grand coalition of the CDU-CSU and the SPD (Hildebrand 1984), in the SPD-FDP coalition 1969–82 (Schmidt 1978), in the 'Kohl era' (Wewer 1998), including the policy on German unification in 1989–90 (Grosser 1998; Jäger 1998; Korte 1994; Hancock and Welsh 1994), and in the red-Green coalition in the period from 1998 to 2002 (Lees 2000). As these cases show, there have been two routes to major policy changes in the Federal Republic—despite numerous veto players and co-governing forces. One route is based on a formal or informal grand coalition composed of CDU-CSU and SPD, such as from 1966 to 1969, and in legislation on German unification. In contrast to this, the second route is based on a CDU- or SPD-led coalition and a majority in the Bundesrat which results from convergent party political majorities in the upper and lower houses of parliament or, alternatively, from the mobilization of a temporary inter-party majority in the Bundesrat.

Although Germany's political institutions constrain policy makers, they do not dictate policy choices, nor do they determine policy outcomes. There have been examples of ambitious policy change, including strategies that are targeted towards widening the room for manoeuvre of the federal government. Among these, the following should be mentioned first: circumventing veto players is one possible way out of the confining restrictions. For example, a government which renounces legislative changes which require two-thirds majorities in the Bundestag and the Bundesrat, such as constitutional amendments, outmanoeuvres potential veto players. *Divide et impera* strategies are a further promising avenue out of the restrictions which semi-sovereignty imposes. *Divide et impera* strategies were employed by various governments. The Schröder government has been particularly skilful in the reform of taxation in 2000 and pension reform in 2001, which added a capital-funded component to old age pensions. In both cases, the red-Green government needed the consent of the Bundesrat and depended thus on the approval of at least some of the

CDU-led governments, which commanded a veto position in the Bundestag. In both cases, the federal government succeeded in mobilizing a sufficiently large number of votes from CDU-led states to pass the majority threshold.

Alternative strategies aimed to widen the otherwise narrow room for manoeuvre comprise the delegation of political will formation and decision making to informal institutions outside the arrangements prescribed by the constitution or statute law. Examples include compromise seeking in coalition round tables, for example in the Alliance for Jobs and the National Council on Ethical Questions of the Schröder government, but they also involve bargaining between the Chancellor and the Chancellor's Office on the one hand and interest groups on the other, such as in the case of the old age pension reform in 2001 and in cost containment in health care in 2001.[2]

Further ways out of narrowly constrained choices include the mobilization of consensus in favour of projects widely perceived to be of national importance. The reform of the old age pensions systems in 1989, jointly carried by the Kohl government and the Social Democratic opposition party, is a major example. Functional equivalents include participation in international projects of major importance, such as peacekeeping missions in Afghanistan after the fall of the Taliban regime in 2001.

Last but not least, skilful mixing of clientele-oriented policy and 'catch-all' strategies (Kirchheimer 1965) aimed at the general public and crossing demarcations between political parties proved to be conducive to overcoming some of the confining conditions in Germany's policy making process. Clientelism in public policy involves patronage in favour of members and voters of the incumbent parties. In contrast to this, 'catch-all' policies focus on topics and target groups both within and outside the traditional domain of a mass integration party. A catch-all policy aims at gaining the support of all major sectors within society. It does so typically through political communication with potentially attractive signals to most voters, including the emphasis on general valence issues and on the leadership qualities of candidates. The catch-all methods comprise also the takeover of topics, issues, and problem-solving techniques of the major opposition party and culminate in generalized coalition building, that is formation of coalitions with a wide variety of parties of a wide variety of political-ideological positions. An example of the latter is the SPD's coalition strategy since the late 1990s which emphasizes openness not only for classical social-liberal SPD-FDP coalitions or red-Green alliances but also for open or tacit coalitions with the PDS.

Output and outcome

The political institutions and the choices of the major political actors have been conducive to a distinctive pattern of public policy in Germany.

The Federal Republic of Germany is a state in which numerous veto players participate in politics, but there has been leeway for expanding the scope of government, measured by government revenue, or general government expenditure as a percentage of gross domestic product (GDP). The percentage share of gross domestic product allocated to government climbed from 31.5 per cent in 1950 to 46.8 in 2000. While the increase may be regarded as modest when compared with the North-European nations—Sweden reported an all-time high government outlay–GDP ratio of 67.9 per cent in 1993, more than 35 percentage points above the level of 1960—German government grew and became bigger than before (OECD 2001). Big government in Germany manifested itself in the expansion of a wide variety of policy sectors. In the 1950s, increasing levels of public expenditure mainly resulted from spending on economic reconstruction, housing, social policy, and rearmament. After 1960 fiscal resources were shifted chiefly to social policy and health and for a more limited period also to education. Since unification in 1990 massive public transfers to Eastern Germany, further expansion of the welfare state in both East and West Germany, and the increasing costs involved in managing the public debt have been the major beneficiaries of public expenditure, while the share of non-social expenditure in gross domestic product is lower than in most other member countries of the OECD.

A distinctive pattern of public policy emerges also from the impact of federalism. German-style federalism may hinder swift and radical policy changes but it functions smoothly as an efficient device of power sharing and integrating the opposition party (Schmidt 2001*d*). It also enables incremental problem solving, although the delay in policy responses may be considerable and externalization of the cost involved cannot be excluded, such as shifting costs from federal and state governments to local government (Wachendorfer-Schmidt 1999). The German party system, to mention a further determinant of public policy, is biased in favour of an advanced welfare state (Schmidt 1998; Huber and Stephens 2001). It is the existence of two major pro-welfare state parties rather than one pro-social policy party, such as in Britain, which makes the difference: the centre-leftist SPD and the centre-right CDU-CSU are parties in favour of a strong welfare state. Similarly, the partisan complexion of federal government in Germany—centre-left or centre-right coalitions bordering on a quasi catch-all party—is inherently favourable to welfare largesse, particularly so in periods of rapid economic growth. But even in periods of reduced economic growth rates, the will and skill needed to cut welfare state expenditures decisively remains limited. This is largely due to the broad and deep popular support for the welfare state, but it also mirrors the temptation of the opposition party to adopt the role of a defender of the welfare state against potential cuts, cost containment, and structural reforms on the part of the government (Pierson 2001; Siegel 2002).

The federalist structure of the state and the important role that state governments, local government, and social insurance funds play in public spending account for a further characteristic of public policy in Germany. Although Germany as a whole is a case of big government, the size of the central government budgets is relatively small. The budget of the federal government as a percentage of gross domestic product has rarely exceeded the 15 per cent mark, while the states, local government, and social insurances consume a share of gross domestic product which is almost three times as large.[3] The relatively small central state budget constrains ambitious fiscal policy, such as Keynesian economic policy or any type of determined fiscal policy (Scharpf 1988). But together with the central bank's preference for controlling inflation the small size of the central state budget—too small for vigorous employment promotion—weakens the effort to combat unemployment and strengthens the 'politics of price stability' (Busch 1993).

The policy of the middle way

This discussion of the impact of Germany's political institutions on social and economic policy outputs and outcomes leads to the distinctiveness of the political economy in present day Germany. The aggregate outcome of Germany's political institutions and the choices of its political leaders comprise a distinctive public policy profile, the 'policy of the middle way' (Schmidt 1987, 2001c). The policy of the middle way comprises a middle route between Swedish welfare state capitalism, which is politically based upon the powerful position of a social democratic party and a social democratic labour movement, and North American market-driven capitalism, which rests politically mainly on democratic market-oriented parties of rightist or centrist complexions. In contrast to this, Germany's policy of the middle way resides mainly on the coexistence of two encompassing welfare state-oriented parties, the Social Democrats and the Christian Democrats.

The policy of the middle way has four constituent components. Its first element is the priority of price stability over all other economic policy goals, including full employment goals, if no other choice exists. The second part of the middle way policy is a response to the 'equality–efficiency trade-off' (Okun 1975) which aims simultaneously at economic efficiency and ambitious social policy. The keystone of both regimes consists of a 'Social Market Economy' based on private ownership and competition policy on the one hand, and an advanced welfare state, free collective bargaining of labour and employers' associations over wages and work regulation, and far-reaching employment protection and codetermination of labour representatives on the other. A relatively high share of public spending (as a percentage of gross domestic product) and a moderate share of public employment in total employment have been the third constituent of the middle way policy. This reflects the quantitatively significant role of government, and more emphasis on public transfers, such as old age pensions, than on public services, such as the National Health Service. Finally, the fourth component of Germany's middle-way policy is the tradition of delegating major public policy functions to half-autonomous, half-parapublic institutions supervised by the state. Examples include the social insurance institutions, corporatist administration of labour market policy, private–public arrangements in health care, welfare services of the charitable organizations, as well as the free collective bargaining of labour and employers' associations.

The policy of the middle way is deeply rooted in Germany's political institutions and practice. The first root lies in Germany's long-standing tradition of state-led social amelioration and control of the economy. Part of that tradition is the German Empire's role as a pioneer in social policy in the 1880s. That tradition has been conducive to the rise of an ambitious welfare state based mainly on social insurances, transfers, health care, and social assistance for all in need on the one hand and labour protection on the other.

The second root of the middle way rests upon Germany's deep-seated tradition of corporatist relations between the state and societal associations (Armingeon 1994). The corporatist tradition manifested itself after 1949 most visibly in social partnership-based labour relations, free collective bargaining of labour and capital, and cooperation of unions and employers' associations in the administration and implementation of social security and labour market policy.

The third origin of the middle way policy resides in the rise of the welfare state in the Weimar Republic until the late 1920s, the reconstruction of social policy after 1949, and the rapid expansion of the social policy mainly from the second half of the 1950s until the first oil price shock in 1973–4. The rise of the welfare state in the Weimar Republic was based on a coalition mainly between the Catholic Centre Party, the Social Democratic Party, and non-communist trade unions. In contrast to this, the support for social policy in the Federal Republic came chiefly from two pro-welfare state parties, the Social Democratic Party and the Christian Democratic parties, as well as from the trade unions and the support of an electorally increasingly influential welfare state clientele.

The fourth core of the middle way consists of institutional products of learning from the political catastrophes in Germany's history. Central to this process of learning were the hyperinflation of 1923, the agony of the Weimar Republic, and the structure and practice of the National-Socialist state. Learning from Germany's catastrophes has shaped the architecture of West Germany's political institutions and has resulted in a high degree of semi-sovereignty in the Katzensteinian sense (Katzenstein 1987), a large number of institutional 'veto players', proportional representation, and a centrist party system. Regarding economic institutions, the outcome has been a 'coordinated market economy' (Soskice 1999)—in contrast to an 'uncoordinated market economy' and a state-led economy (Hall and Soskice 2001). But the lessons learnt from the catastrophes produced a widely shared concern not only for rigorous control of inflationary pressure and the promotion of economic activity but also for an ambitious social policy.

The new institutions which emerged from these policy learning processes have profoundly shaped the origin and the reproduction of the middle way. The relative success in price stability politics, for example, would have been inconceivable without the autonomy of the central bank, the firm commitment of the central bank community to monetary discipline, and the strong demand for 'stable money'. Furthermore, free collective bargaining and federal legislation on the constitutional framework of labour relations have promoted self-governance and corporatist relations between the state and the social partners. Moreover, social security measures, the promotion of employment protection, codetermination laws and labour market policy have not only improved the lot of the welfare state's clientele; they have also shielded labour and the unions against the ups and downs of the business cycle. The preference for ambitious social policy in the CDU-CSU and the SPD, not least due to programmatic commitments as well as expected electoral returns, reinforces the emphasis on social protection.

Why Germany's federalism has been compatible with an advanced welfare state

Germany's federalism has been a further determinant of the middle-way policy. In contrast to classical theories of federalism as a barrier against big government, Germany's federalism has not confined the growth of the welfare state. The causes have been manifold.

A first major cause has been historical. The power of legislation with respect to the core branches of the welfare state has resided in Germany almost from the beginning of modern social policy with the central government—a marked contrast to all other federalist states, where regional governments retained considerable autonomous power in legislation on social policy, except Austria. Because the competence for social policy was allocated largely to central government (although with codetermination rights of the states as long as their jurisdiction was concerned) and because all subsequent legislation followed a more or less pragmatic path-dependent course of action, the route for future expansionary social policy legislation was largely fixed.

The second major cause resides in the power of political ideas which emphasize state-led social amelioration and political control of the economy. Part of this tradition is also the constitutional prescription that the Federal Republic shall be a 'social federalist state', to quote Article 20 of the constitution. The commitment to a social federal state thus adds a strong social protection motive to policy making.

The third major reason for the coexistence of federalism and an advanced welfare state lies with party competition. The Federal Republic of Germany is one of those rare cases in which the two largest parties are determined pro-welfare state parties, namely the Social Democrats and the Christian Democrats. Moreover, the Federal Republic is together with Austria one of the few countries in which the strongest incumbent party in the federal government has always been a strong supporter of the welfare state. Furthermore, the political complexion of the powerful state governments in Germany has also been dominated by the pro-welfare state parties, with Social Democratic strongholds mainly in the western and northern parts of the country and the Christian Democrats as the major parties in the South, above all in Bavaria and Baden-Württemberg. If further proof of the pro-welfare state configuration of the party system in Germany were needed, it could be found in the party affiliation of the Federal Minister of Work and Social Affairs and in the Ministers for Social Affairs in the states. All Federal Ministers of Work and Social Affairs and almost all ministers of social policy in the states have been Social Democrats or Christian Democrats. The hegemony of two large pro-welfare state parties in the German party system both at the federal and the state level has a major impact on social policy choice. Within these circumstances, ambitious social policy efforts can count upon almost optimal conditions, while unfavourable conditions exist for major cuts in social policy, cost containment, and recalibration of the welfare state, other things being equal.

The fourth central cause of the coexistence of federalism and an advanced welfare state is to be found in the incentives and disincentives for federal government and the states. The federal government's interest in social policy is obvious: the federal government finances broadly one-fifth of the total social budget (BMA 2002: 526), but it participates to a large extent in most of the political benefits of the welfare state, such as policy satisfaction, industrial peace, and crisis prevention as well as electoral returns. The state governments' calculation is similar, although the states cannot count on a potential electoral benefit of social policy as large as the benefit for the federal government. But as long as they perceive social policy as not harmful to their fiscal interests, the state governments have reason to tolerate the reconstruction, expansion, and maintenance of the welfare state even in economically hard times. This can be regarded as a natural response to the financial sources of the social budget: social security contributions of employers and employees finance broadly 60 per cent of Germany's social budget, while the states do not contribute more than about 10 per cent of the total social budget.

A fifth factor accounts for the compliance of the states with the welfare state, regardless of the political party in power. A majority of the states, and hence the politically decisive actor in the Bundesrat, capitalizes on a secondary redistribution effect of the welfare state. Through the nationwide uniform regulation of social transfer and services, the welfare state shifts resources from richer to poorer regions and also from richer to poorer states, mainly from the west and south to the east and the north of Germany. This concerns especially old age pensions, sickness insurance, and unemployment insurance, while the effects from social assistance, which is financed by local governments and the states, works in the opposite direction. However, the regional redistribution which social policy has generated is further enhanced by massive distributive effects of the compulsory Structural Risk Compensation Fund which redistributes money from wealthier health insurance organizations to poorer ones, many of which are located in economically less wealthy states.

A sixth factor has been conducive to the coexistence of federalism and welfare largesse. The states are likely to oppose decisive cuts in social policy and major deregulation of the welfare state because they fear that a larger part of the bill involved would fall on their shoulders. Spending cuts at the federal level, for example, would inevitably increase the demand for social assistance. But that demand would have to be satisfied by the states and the local governments, because local government and the states are responsible for financing social assistance.

How social protection and the 'politics of price stability' reinforce each other

German federalism, thus, has proved to be fully compatible with an advanced welfare state. At the same time, the fragmentation of the budgets of general government in a federalist system has impeded Keynesian fiscal policy or any other sort of ambitious demand management and taxation policy. Moreover, budgetary fragmentation, most of which is federalism-based, has impeded both the design and the implementation of an ambitious employment policy.[4] One implication has been a comparative institutional advantage for the central bank and the policy of price stability: the non-existence of a powerful Keynesian policy and the weakness of employment policy cleared the way for ambitious monetary policy goals. German federalism thus proved itself to be compatible both with the priority of relative price stability and an advanced welfare state, two of the four constituent parts of the policy of the middle way.

The size of Germany's welfare state and the cost involved in financing the social budget—32.1 per cent of GDP in 2001 (BMA 2002: 500)—which is financed mainly from social security contributions, has major effects on employment, job holders, and the unions. First of all, welfare state institutions such as unemployment insurance and sickness pay shelter both job holders and unions against the ups and downs of the business cycle. Secondly, the welfare state's protection and the rising social security contributions tempt trade unions to pursue a more ambitious wage policy aimed mainly at higher wage rates and less wage dispersion. At the same time the welfare state creates the option for trade unions and employers' association to externalize the costs of high wage rates, such as deepening the division between job holders and the unemployed, to the social budget. For the low productivity level of the East German economy the high wage policy proved to be particularly detrimental, because the high wage rate raised labour cost far above a critical level (Sinn and Sinn 1993). Moreover, the high wage rates reinforced the central bank's preference for tight monetary policy. But tight monetary policy affected investment and employment in both East and West Germany negatively and exacerbated the problem of chronically insufficient revenue of the tax state and the social insurance funds. At the same time the insider–outsider division in Germany's labour market between job holders and the unemployed strengthened the demand for additional welfare state provisions for the unemployed and the economically inactive population. Thus, the joint impact of strict control of inflationary pressure on the part of the central bank, high wage policy of the social partners, and ambitious social protection on the government's part reproduced the unique mixture of social protection and priority of price stability over ambitious employment goals, if necessary, which characterizes the middle-way policy.

The policy of the middle way can thus largely be attributed to distinctive features of Germany's political history, learning from catastrophes when it comes to policy-making, and the political institutions which emerged from these learning processes in the Federal Republic of Germany.

6.2 The 'trading state' and pro-European foreign policy

West Germany's political history has been described as the 'growth of a semisovereign state' (Katzenstein 1987). Katzenstein's notion of semi-sovereignty referred mainly to domestic affairs. Semi-sovereignty in foreign affairs is even more obvious in the Federal Republic.

The Federal Republic of Germany entered world politics as a penetrated system, that is, as a nation state exposed to control from outside. This meant above all the direct or indirect rule of the Western Allies. A large degree of international and supranational integration since then has characterized the fate of the country, as the membership of NATO and the European Community demonstrate. A leitmotif of the Federal Republic's foreign policy stance has been political and economic integration into the West in exchange for sovereignty transfer to international and supranational organizations. To that policy stance belongs the choice of the 'trading state' approach in contrast to the 'big power' approach, that is, priority for civilian foreign policy, including free trade, not priority for the use of military power (Rosecrance 1986).

Within this context, membership of the European Community has played a major role. To tame the power of the German state was one major motive for the foundation of the community of European states in the 1950s and for Germany's membership. Another motive was to create a sound environment for economic growth, social progress, and peace through economic and political European integration. And a third motive derived from the expectation that membership in the European Community might eventually bridge the division of Europe into a Western and an Eastern part.

Germany's participation in the European Community involved the transfer of a considerable proportion of national sovereignty to the supranational European level. Initially, this transfer was largely confined to a few selected policy areas, particularly agricultural policy, tariff and trade regulation, as well as the regulation of atomic energy. Owing to the acceleration of European integration in the 1980s and, subsequent to German unification, in the 1990s, sovereignty transfers began to involve to an increasing extent selected areas of economic policy, monetary policy, environmental policy, transport, employment, and social affairs (Schmitter 1996).

The political leaders of all major parties in Germany and also the leaders of the unions and the employers' associations have been among the most energetic advocates of European integration. The reasons for the pro-European policy stance were manifold. They include the belief that European integration itself is a valuable good. Part of the enthusiasm for Europe resides also in the conviction that any alternative would foster potentially explosive conflicts between today's EU member states. Furthermore, advocating an integrated Europe fills a gap in the otherwise ideologically monotonous policy programme of most politicians. Finally, pro-Europeanism has been fuelled by a rational calculation of the national interest. Being in favour of Europe promised political benefits for German diplomacy, such as the integration of the country to the world of the Western nations, and economic benefits, such as advantage for export-oriented sectors of the economy.

While almost all major collective political actors in Germany and a large majority of its political elite have supported the pro-European integration stance in policy, the mass public has been less enthusiastic. The partial exception from the pro-European policy stance in the political elite is the half-hearted support for the European Community among the governments and parliaments in the German states. While the states support the case of European economic integration in principle, they draw the line at further expanding the level of political integration. This reflects the apprehension of the state governments and most politicians at the state level that unconstrained political integration in Europe undermines federalism through Brussels-led centralization and, thus, destroys the *raison d'être* of the German states. In the parliamentary debate and legislation on the Maastricht Treaty the states, however, gained substantial concessions from the federal government. The major instrument for safeguarding the interests of the states has been the new Article 23 of the Basic Law of 1992 which allocates a variety of access points and veto points to the states on practically all issues of sovereignty transfer to the European Union of concern to the states.[5] The Maastricht Treaty has not downgraded the states, as many feared, it has rather upgraded the position of the states in German politics and in the networks of Community decision making in Europe.

The extent to which the European Union has altered politics and policy in Germany has been controversially debated. One school of thought holds that German politics and policy is mainly framed by the requirements of European integration as well as by legislative and executive acts of the European Union. The proponents of this view point out that the scope of European Union, measured for example by the extent to which the policy process is governed by European legislation, has continuously increased over the last four decades (Héritier, Knill, and Mingers 1996; Wallace and Wallace 2000). According to the opposite view, politics and policy making in the nation states largely continue to shape the timing and substance of the EU policy makers and circumscribe the extent to which European legislation and EU policy are implemented in the EU member states. A third school of thought points to a wide range of sectoral variation in governance structures at the national and the EU level. According to the proponents of this view, some policy areas are indeed governed by the European Union, such as policy on trade and tariffs, monetary policy, and agricultural policy, whereas others are mainly controlled at the national level, such as the core institutions of the welfare state (Scharpf 1999).

A considerable range of variation marks the extent to which the EU interferes with policy making at the level of the nation state. The evidence accumulated so far suggests that the bulk of policy making and legislation up to the present has been largely determined by nation-state-based institutions and actors. However, monetary policy and agricultural policy are almost completely part of the EU policy process. Furthermore, the overall empirical trend in the division of labour between autonomous policy making in the nation state and policy making within EU jurisdiction seems to run in favour of the European Community (Schmitter 1996).

6.3 Continuity and discontinuity—before and after unification

Compared with countries in which governments have plenty of room for manoeuvre, such as Britain and Sweden, the Federal Republic of Germany is often regarded as a country in which major policy changes have been rare or untypical (Dahrendorf 1967; Katzenstein 1987). Germany's federalism and its social policy in particular, so the theory goes, have been notorious for a high degree of path dependence if not immobilized policy making (Scharpf 1994; von Arnim 1998; Scharpf and Schmidt 2000). That most of the political institutions of the Federal Republic have weathered the storms of globalization, European integration and German unification, the 'seven-point upheaval on history's Richter scale',[6] is commonly regarded as lending further support for the view that a large degree of continuity, including policy continuity, characterizes the German polity.

Path dependence versus discontinuous development

Continuity has indeed played a major role in the political history of the Federal Republic of Germany. But discontinuous development has hardly been less remarkable. Major examples include the massive changes in domestic politics and in foreign affairs in both West and East Germany not only after 1989, that is the year in which the Berlin Wall and the Iron Curtain between West and East Europe collapsed, but also before 1989. The restoration and consolidation of a democracy and the rise of a state governed by law in West Germany have been part of a successful trajectory away from an authoritarian past. The reconstruction and expansion of social policy have also been of great consequence. Without the ambitious social policy effort, political and social life in Germany would have been far more conflict prone and politically probably less stable. In addition, foreign policy mattered a great deal: the economic, political, and military integration of the Federal Republic into the community of the Western nations was of major relevance, and so, too, was the policy of détente vis-à-vis the Socialist countries in the post-1969 period.

These were the outcomes of truly important policy changes before 1989. But major changes have also characterized politics in post-1989 Germany, such as German unification. That the pro-unification policy of the West German government profoundly shaped Germany and Europe as a whole is obvious. But political change in the post-1989 period was driven not only by unification, but also by European integration and the challenges generated by globalization on the one hand and social change, such as the ageing of society, on the other (see Table 10).

One of the most obvious changes in the post-1989 Federal Republic concerns territorial expansion and population increase due to the unification of East and West Germany on 3 October 1990. Since that time the Federal Republic of Germany has comprised the areas of the 'Ancient Federal Republic' (Blanke and Wollmann 1991) and the former communist German Democratic Republic. Regarding population size, the accession of the East German states turned the Federal Republic into the most populous country in Western Europe. Concerning the social fabric of the nation, Germany in the post-1990 period is more heterogeneous, more Protestant, and more northern in character. Economically, the accession of the East German territory brought as a dowry a non-competitive economy with a productivity level of broadly 35 per cent of West German productivity, reducing Germany's gross domestic product per capita in 1990 to 96 per cent of the 1989 level. It took Germany's economy five years to surpass the level of gross domestic product per capita attained prior to unification (calculated from Maddison 2001: 276).

The transfer of West German legal, political, and economic institutions to the East German states is a further dramatic change resulting from unification. The institutional transfer involved redistribution from West to East of an unprecedented magnitude. Both the transfer of the 'ready-made' institutions and the redistribution were highly welcome in the East and cushioned the transition of the new states to a far greater measure than the transition to a democratic market economy in Central and Eastern Europe. But the institutional transfer from West to East Germany undoubtedly exposed East Germany to its fourth fundamental regime change since the changes in 1918–19, 1933, and 1945–9.

Continuity and discontinuity in constitutional structures

The constitutional structures of the Federal Republic, however, were initially largely unaffected by the process of unification of the divided country. The Basic Law has changed relatively little in the process of unification and its aftermath—to the disappointment of those who demanded a new constitutional contract between West and East Germany. The constitutional change that can be attributed to unification was relatively minor, although the addition of policy goals to the constitution must not be belittled, such as effective realization of the equality of women and men, protection of the environment, and the establishment of higher thresholds for interventions of the federal government into the jurisdiction of the *Länder* (Batt 2001). But more important than unification was the impact of European integration on the German constitution. Two changes deserve particular mention. First, the new Article 23 added to the Basic Law in 1992 upgraded the role of the states in European affairs to a very large extent. According to Article 23, the federation may delegate sovereign powers to the EU, provided that the Bundesrat consents, and must cooperate with the Bundesrat in practically all matters of European legislation. Moreover, Article 23 protects the federalist structure of the Federal Republic of Germany against potential encroachment of the EU. Secondly, the amendment of Article 88 opened the route towards transferring the powers of the Deutsche Bundesbank, Germany's central bank, to the European Central Bank. Moreover, Article 88 explicitly states that the European Central Bank must be independent and is primarily bound by the purpose of securing stability of prices—a marked contrast to the pre-1992 state of affairs, in which the commitment to price stability was not constitutionally enshrined but was part of a statute law which the majority in parliament could change if it wished to do so.

Continuity and discontinuity in the executive

The executive in Germany's political system has also been characterized by but continuity and discontinuity. Continuity marked the constitutional foundation of the Chancellor Democracy. What did change, however, was the type of governance and the relative weight of the various modes of governing Germany. At the federal level, governance in the 1980s and 1990s was anchored in greater measure than before in informal interest aggregation and decision making mostly in party political arenas, such as coalition round tables or coalition committees and an informal club of advisers to the Chancellor, while the political institutions prescribed by the constitution and statute law were often largely confined to ratifying compromises that were hammered out in extra-parliamentary arenas (Manow 1996). Informalization of the political process played also a major role in the red-Green Schröder government, which followed the Kohl government after the 1998 Bundestag election. But in contrast to the emphasis on informalization and the party state in the Kohl governments, the core of the 'Kohl system' (Hennis 1998), Schröder's preference for a presidential chancellorship (Helms 2001) was conducive to the establishment of various formal or informal advisory boards for the Chancellor on the one hand and solo runs of the Chancellor in interest intermediation in a wider variety of popular issues on the other, for example interventions in firms threatened by bankruptcy and informal deals with major interest groups. Moreover, the existence of traditional links between the Social Democratic Party and the labour unions resulted in the increased importance of corporatist modes of interest intermediation, with the Alliance for Jobs, an informal tripartite arrangement in which representatives of federal government, unions, and employers associations participated, as an example.

Continuity and discontinuity have also characterized the office of the Federal President. The Federal President has been predominantly the guardian of ceremonial functions before and since 1990. And none of the Federal Presidents before or since 1990 has found himself confronted with the challenge of managing a constitutional crisis. However, noteworthy changes have marked the party affiliation of the Federal President. With the election of Johannes Rau (SPD) in 1999 a long era of presidents with Christian Democratic party affiliation came to an end and opened the route towards a presidency with clearly recognizable preferences for genuinely Social Democratic projects.

The party state and veto players

Throughout the pre- and post-1989 period, Germany has been a party state. But at the same time Germany has also been a state full of veto players and a state which delegates major public policy functions to societal associations. But continuity should not belittle discontinuity in the state structures after 1989. The increase in big government from 1990 until the mid-1990s is one of the remarkable changes. Even more remarkable is that big government grew under the Kohl government, which had explicitly taken over the reigns of power in 1982 in order to reduce the role of the state and to upgrade the market economy and self-help (Schmidt 2001c). The increase of big government after 1989–90 can be attributed to the effects of unification, but it also reflected the impact of the institutionalization of care for the elderly as a fifth pillar of social security in 1995.

The increasing role of government until the mid-1990s expanded the potential scope for partisan determination of public policy. But there has also been an increase in the total number of veto players in the post-1989 period—mainly due to the effects of unification and intensified European integration, most notably the larger number of states, the increasing importance of the states in legislation on European affairs, and the establishment of the European Central Bank as a new powerful player in European economic policy. The increasing number of veto players has tended to reinforce the limits on party influences on policy. Other changes have concerned the division of labour between government and autono-

mous or parapublic institutions: notwithstanding the continuing delegation of state functions to societal associations, the integrative capacity of
some of the interest associations, among them trade unions and employers' associations, has clearly decreased (Bertelsmann Stiftung and Hans-
Böckler-Stiftung 1998; Wiesenthal 2001).

Changes in the structure of federalism

The accession of the former German Democratic Republic to the Federal
Republic of Germany in 1990 and the restitution of the five East German
Länder have changed the structure of federalism profoundly. The following
are the important changes. (1) The total number of states increased from
eleven to sixteen. From this resulted a more complicated process of consensus formation and conflict resolution and a higher probability of prolonged policy formation and stalemate outcomes. (2) What had been an
economically relatively homogeneous federalism composed of ten states
and West Berlin turned after 3 October 1990 into a more complex, heterogeneous federalist system burdened by large economic disparities and massive political-cultural differences mainly between West and East Germany.
Within the context of Germany's 'unitarian federalism' (Hesse 1962) and
the network of an elaborate version of highly redistributive fiscal federalism, the economic disparities resulted in a major shift of fiscal resources
from wealthier to poorer states, that is from West Germany mainly to East
Germany and to the heavily indebted states of Bremen, Saarland, and later
also Berlin. (3) The accession of the five new eastern states in 1990
strengthened the leftist, Protestant, and religiously non-affiliated components of the political culture in today's Germany. (4) There has been a
significant change in the distribution of seats in the Bundesrat, representing the state governments: the formation of five new eastern states adds
with the PDS a further influential partisan actor to the political process. (5)
The five new states in eastern Germany altered the distribution of Bundesrat seats between the rich and the poor states. The poor ones in the east
and that group of western German Länder which is commonly regarded as
economically weak and relatively poor now have a majority of 43 to 26 over
the rich Länder.[7]

This is unprecedented for German federalism. The precarious balance of
power between rich and less wealthy states impedes consensus formation
among the states and weakens their position as a whole relative to the

federal government. Moreover, the distribution of power in Germany's new federalism widens the room to move for the federal government. Particularly strong is the incentive for the federal government to adopt a *divide et impera* strategy against the *Länder*. That may involve the formation of a coalition of the federal government and the poor states against the rich *Länder*, or an alliance between the federal government together with the states of the same partisan complexion and the East German states, regardless of their political complexion. Federalism in reunified Germany thus provides the federal government and the incumbent parties with greater room for manoeuvre, but it also poses new demands on the federal government, such as costly fiscal transfers to the poor states in the east and the political and fiscal costs involved in designing and applying *divide et impera* strategies. These strategies usually generate heated controversies between the states and the federal government, between the incumbent and the opposition parties, and also among the states, as the three major manifestations of that strategy in the Schröder government from 1998 to 2002 demonstrate, that is, the taxation reform in 2000, the old age pension reform in 2001, and the constitutional row generated by the passing of the immigration law in 2002.

Unification has not been the only determinant of Germany's changing federalism in the post-1990 period. European integration has also had a significant impact. The greater role of European politics has narrowed the room for manoeuvre available to the federal government and state governments, other things being equal. But at the same time the new Article 23 of the Basic Law from 1992 has upgraded the position of the states in European politics.

Continuity and change in the legislature and the judiciary

Regarding legislation, two of the most visible changes concerned the increasing number of basic mandates in the lower house of parliament and the increase in the number of seats in the Bundesrat due to the accession of the East German states to the Federal Republic of Germany. Other noteworthy changes in the legislature were mainly due to the European Union, such as the increasing number of EU submissions for the national parliaments and the shrinking degree of autonomy of the national parliaments vis-à-vis the European Community. Furthermore, the increase in legislative activity of the Bundestag in the first half of the 1990s can largely be attributed to unification and European integration. However, there were also changes which reflected neither unification nor Europe, such as the continuing trend towards professionalization and the increasing proportion of female deputies to the Bundestag in the 1990s.

Compared with the Federal Republic in the pre-1990 period, the structure of the judiciary and its claim of supremacy over the political has been left basically untouched in the post-1990 period—a major indicator of institutional continuity before and after unification. The major discontinuity in the post-1990 era again concerns East Germany. Within a very short period, the West German legal system was transferred to the new states in East Germany and substituted civil rights and political rights of the Western tradition for 'socialist jurisprudence' of the former German Democratic Republic.

Linkages between the people and the government: stability and change

The linkages between the people and the government, the topic of Chapter 5 of this book, have also been marked by continuity and discontinuity. With the exception of a soft 5 per cent clause in the 1990 Bundestag election, Germany's electoral formula has been maintained since 1990. A personalized version of proportional representation with a 5 per cent hurdle against smaller parties thus governs the transformation of votes into parliamentary seats. In contrast to the relatively homogeneous party system before 1990, two party systems coexist in unified Germany—an East German three-party system comprising CDU, PDS, and SPD as the major players, and a West German party system, in which two large parties, the Christian Democrats and the Social Democrats, and two small parties, the Liberals and Greens, compete with each other, while the PDS is almost non-existent in the western part of the country.

The underlying trends in voting behaviour comprise the dealignment of a significant proportion of voters and, as a consequence, the emergence of a more flexible electoral market. Both trends make life for all political parties more difficult. But due to different coalition options, the position on the electoral market differs from one party to the other. Due to a wider range of coalition options, which include the Greens, the Liberals, and (at least in the states) the PDS and the CDU, the SPD finds itself in principle in a more advantageous position than the CDU-CSU as long as the Christian Democrats' coalition options are confined to the Liberals and possibly

TABLE 10	Continuity and change in the Federal Republic of Germany before and after 1990

Book chapter	Area	Continuity and discontinuity (post-1990 versus pre-1990)
1	The anti-totalitarian constitution of the Federal Republic of Germany	Continuity of anti-totalitarian constitution; relatively few unification-based constitutional changes; major changes in EU-oriented articles (Articles 23 and 88, Basic Law)
2	Governing the semi-sovereign state: Germany's executive	Continuity and discontinuity (see 2.1–2.6)
2.1	Chancellor Democracy	Continuity of formal structure; informal modes of governance gain more importance; change in power 1998
2.2	The roles of the Federal President	Continuity in formal rules; change in the party-political affiliation
2.3	The rise of the party state and partisan composition of the executive	Continuity of party state; changes in the political composition of government at the federal and the state level
2.4	A state full of veto players	Continuity and discontinuity; states acquire veto position in European politics; European Central Bank as a new player
2.5	Germany's federalism	16 states instead of 11, large increase in economic disparities and in redistribution from wealthier to poorer states; majority of less wealthy states in Bundesrat
2.6	The delegating state: transfer of public policy functions to civil society	Largely continuity, but organizational capacity and steering capacity of organized labour and capital decreases
3	The role of the legislature, parliamentary government, and the party state	Increase in number of basic mandates due to accession of East German deputies; increase in number of Bundesrat seats; EU feedback to parliamentary agenda; decreasing autonomy of parliament, but higher legislative activity; professionalization; increasing proportion of female deputies since 1990s

Book chapter	Area	Continuity and discontinuity (post-1990 versus pre-1990)
TABLE 10	*Continued*	
4	The judiciary, the court system, and judicial review or the supremacy of the law	Transfer of West German legal system to East Germany; continuous structure and continuous predominant role of the judiciary
5	Linking the people and political institutions	Discontinuity and continuity (see 5.1.–5.8)
5.1	Electoral system	Continuity—except for 'soft' 5 per cent clause in Bundestag election in 1990
5.2	Parties and party system	Significant discontinuity; unified nation— divided party system; rise of PDS in the East
5.3	Electoral behaviour	Dealignment, higher flexibility in electoral markets; increase in coalition options for SPD in 1998; left vote exceeds non-left vote
5.4	Interest associations	Partial erosion of integrative capacity of major producer group associations; potentially weaker capacity of interest groups in collective problem solving
5.5	Representative government and less frequent use of referenda	Increased importance of plebiscitary mechanisms in the states and in local government
5.5	Structures of democracy	Largely continuity at national level, but increasing role of EU and increase in negotiated democracy component; upgrading of direct democratic institutions at state level
5.6	Who governs? Germany's political elite before and after unification	Change in generational structure of political elite: post-1945 socialization, exposure to post-materialism and GDR experience; increasing intra-elite diversity on plebiscites and role of the state vis-à-vis the market
6	Policy consequences	Continuity and discontinuity (see 6.1–6.2)

TABLE 10	*Continued*	
Book chapter	Area	Continuity and discontinuity (post-1990 versus pre-1990)
6.1	Policy of the middle way	Major changes after 1990: middle-way policy more costly and conflict-ridden; price stability associated with higher costs; loss of Germany's lead in controlling inflationary pressure; decreasing steering capacity of social partners in implementation of public policy functions
6.2	The 'trading state' and the pro-European stance in foreign policy	Continuity of the 'trading state', but increasing role of participation in joint military policy

also to new centre-right or rightist parties, such as the *Partei Rechtstaat-licher Offensive* in Hamburg. A further significant change marked the 1990s: measured by the ratio of the vote for the centre-left and leftist parties and the vote for centre-right or rightist parties, the left surpassed the non-leftist parties in 1998 and in 2002.

Compared with the party system and voter alignments, the system of interest groups has been marked by significantly less discontinuity. Interest groups remain an important part of the political system as a whole. Furthermore, the coexistence of pluralist and corporatist modes of interest intermediation has survived the unification in 1990. Nevertheless, the remaining changes are non-trivial. Regarding interest groups, one of the noteworthy changes since 1990 concerns the gradual decrease of the integrative capacity of most major producer group associations, most notably trade unions and employers associations. This is not to argue the case of full erosion of the associations' power; it is rather an argument which emphasizes a process of partial erosion. Whether this results in a dramatically declining capacity for problem solving in bilateral or tripartite arrangements between interest groups and government is an open question.

Notwithstanding remarkable continuity at the level of the federation, the interplay of representative democracy and plebiscitary structures has undergone a couple of significant changes chiefly in the states but also in local government. The main trend has been to upgrade the role of plebiscitary mechanisms—above all in the East German states, but also, albeit more muted, in the West German states. The new emphasis on direct democracy may at least partly be attributable to the greater preference in the East German elite for adding plebiscitary components to the constitutional structures. This inclination varies with the preference of East German political leaders for a stronger role of the state and more emphasis on the market on the part of the West German elites. Common to both the East German and West German elites is a fundamental change in the generational composition. While the political elite in Germany up to the late 1980s was dominated by age groups which grew up in National Socialism, in the period of the Weimar Republic, or in the German Empire before 1918, the generational composition of the political elite since 1989 has changed profoundly. Almost all members of Germany's political elite of today were politically socialized after 1945. Many of them had their formative political experience in 1968 and the post-1968 period.

The policy of the middle way: trends in the post-1990 period

Public policy in Germany has also been marked by both continuity and discontinuity. Four major trends have shaped the policy of the middle way in the post-1990 period.

First, ambitious social protection goals and economic efficiency are more difficult to achieve and more costly than before 1990. While most politicians have so far regarded ambitious social protection as untouchable, the promotion of economic growth and macroeconomic outcomes has been less successful than before unification. Germany's average rate of economic growth in the post-1990 era is not only lower than in the 1980s, not to mention the 1970s, 1960s, and 1950s, it is at the beginning of the twenty-first century also one of the lowest in the OECD area. This is at least partly due to the imbalance between advanced social policy and employment protection on the one hand and economic policy on the other. Furthermore, the conflict between social policy and employment policy goals is more intense than before. This also reflects a wide variety of factors, but these include disincentives for job search and job creation resulting from relatively high social income and high labour costs, including the high costs of social security for employers. The dominant mode of funding Germany's social budget aggravates the conflict: roughly 60 per cent of the social budget in 2001 is financed by the social security contributions of employers and employees. This raises non-wage-labour costs for employers to a very high level and reduces the take-home pay of workers (BMA 2002: 524). Trade unions respond to this normally by demanding high wage increases in order to safeguard or increase take-home pay. But that wage policy exacerbates incentives for labour saving and capital intensive investment, if not export of capital to an economically more attractive location outside Germany. Labour saving and capital intensive investment, however, result in fewer workers or fewer working hours, and capital export reinforces this trend. These processes will increase both the jobless rate and the demand for social security on the one hand and a downturn in employment as well as the volume of social security contributions on the other. The price to be paid for the policy of the middle way is in this respect clearly higher in the post-1990 period than before 1990.

The second component of the policy of the middle way consists of the combination of big government (measured by public expenditure as a percentage of gross domestic product) and the relatively moderate share of employment in general government (as a percentage of total employment). That combination has not been fundamentally altered in the post-1990 period. But the proportions have changed in a discernible way: the share of public expenditure as a percentage of gross domestic product in the post-1990 period is higher than before 1990—and the share of employment in general government as a percentage of total employment is lower than in the preceding decades, not least due to the effects of privatization of the postal services, telecommunications, and German rail (OECD 2001). Even more dramatic changes have occurred in East Germany's transition from a planned economy to a market economy. East Germany's former socialist economy was almost completely privatized, and the high ratio of employment in general government to total employment was reduced to a lower level.

The delegation of public functions to interest organizations in civil society, the third component of the middle way, continues to play an important part since 1990. But there have also been relevant changes, such as the decreasing steering capacity of the unions and employers' associations in Germany's labour relations. Their capacity to manage conflict and to adjust social partnership to external economic and social change is lower in the post-1990 period than before 1990 (Bertelsmann-Stiftung and Hans Böckler-Stiftung 1998; Streeck 1999). The reasons for this are manifold. They include the exit of enterprises from costly regulation and the exit of employees to the shadow economy. Both are mainly responses to what is widely perceived as an oversized level of total taxation and a large tax wedge, that is, a gap between employees' gross and take-home income. The consequences for the policy of the middle way are sizeable: one of the constituents of the middle way, namely the delegation of public functions to civil society, is more fragile in the post-1990 era than it was before 1990.

Fourth, continuity and discontinuity also characterize the preference for price stability, the fourth component of the middle way. Monetary policy has been heading for relative price stability in the pre- and post-1990 periods. However, the degree to which it has succeeded has differed. The outcome of the 'politics of price stability' (Busch 1993) since 1990 has been the relatively costly restitution of a low inflation rate in the second half of the 1990s after a unification-induced rise in the inflation rate. The restitution of monetary stability in the post-1990 period has been associated with a significantly higher unemployment rate than in the pre-1990 period. Moreover, most other industrial nations, in particular most EU member states, have caught up with Germany's successful control of inflationary pressure. And some of the EU member countries have achieved lower inflation rates than Germany, such as Belgium, Denmark, Finland, France, and the Netherlands in the period from 1990 to 2000 (OECD *Economic Outlook*, various issues 1990–2001). Thus, in the post-1990 era, the Federal Republic of Germany has lost its superior position in inflation control. This has been largely due to the diffusion of the German model of inflation control throughout the European Union. Success breeds success, but the one from whom the formula for successful problem-solving is copied loses his or her comparative advantage. This belongs to the cost involved in Germany's successful control of inflationary pressure in a period of 'Europeanised politics' (Goetz and Hix 2000).

Continuity and discontinuity in foreign policy

A further critical issue in the debate on political continuity and discontinuity in unified Germany has been foreign policy. The core question of that debate is this: will German unification result in a fundamental change in foreign policy, and will it in particular result in a change from a 'trading state' to a 'big power state'?

There are five relevant indicators that deserve discussion in this context.

1. Measured by classical indicators of the power of nation states, the post-1990 Federal Republic carries more weight than the West German Republic or East Germany's Socialism. In terms of international law the Federal Republic of Germany regained full sovereignty in 1990, transfer of sovereignty rights to supranational organizations deducted. Moreover, the population has increased from 64 million to 80 million, and the volume of its gross domestic product (GDP), though not GDP per capita, is, due to unification, 8–10 per cent above the pre-unification level. Furthermore, the political representatives of the new Federal Republic are likely to speak with louder voices and act with more self-confidence than the representatives of the divided German states in the period from 1949 to 1990.

2. However, these changes should not be overestimated. Empirically, these changes are moderate, and some of them are associated with higher burdens for the new Republic, such as the costs involved in reconstructing the East German economy.

3. Some of the indicators point to decreasing power potential rather than increasing power. A relevant case is the size of the German army. As a result of an agreement reached between the Soviet Union and the West German government in summer 1990, the size of Germany's army was reduced to 370,000 soldiers in 1994, and thus will be roughly equivalent to 50 per cent of the West German Bundeswehr and the East German Nationale Volksarmee combined. Expenditure cuts have further reduced the size of Germany's army since 1994.

4. Moreover, a variety of classical power indicators point to continuity, for example the institutional stability of the German Foreign Office. The Foreign Office of unified Germany is identical with West Germany's Foreign Office—there has been no transfer from the East German diplomatic body to the West German Auswärtige Amt. Continuity also typifies Germany's membership in international and transnational organizations, in particular the European Community and NATO.

5. The fifth aspect worth mentioning in this context concerns continuity in foreign economic policy. The Federal Republic of Germany has long pursued a 'trading state' policy rather than a 'big power'

approach. A 'trading state' places priority on peaceful exchange of goods and services; it emphasizes trade rather than military gambles, economic expansion on world markets rather than military expansion, and prefers an open economy to autarchy. Precisely that kind of trading state policy has been—coupled with the policy of the middle way—a major pillar of West Germany's economic success story after 1949. The 'trading state' approach has also been part of the foreign policy consensus between the major parties in unified Germany.

These observations lend further support to the view that most of the distinctive traits of pre-1990 German foreign policy are still clearly discernible in the foreign policy of the so-called 'Berlin Republic', that is the foreign policy since Berlin was substituted for Bonn as the capital of the Federal Republic (Staack 2000). The Berlin Republic's policy 'is still strongly Western-oriented, strongly "multilateralist" and Euro-centric' (Webber 2001b: 15). The principal change in foreign policy however 'consists in the curtailment, if not erosion, of the civilian character of pre-1990 policy' (Webber 2001b: 15), insofar as Germany in the post-1990 period reluctantly shares the burden of military intervention in international crises, such as in the Balkan wars and in the military response to the terrorist attacks on the United States on 11 September 2001. But that change resulted from external pressure from Western partners and allies, who wanted Germany to share the burden. That change therefore does not support the apprehension that foreign policy in the unified Federal Republic would be 'alarmingly ambitious'.[8]

6.4 Conclusion

Chapter 6 has explored in more detail the policy consequences of the political institutions portrayed in Chapters 1 to 5 and the policy choices of the major political actors. Regarding distinctive policy consequences and policy choices, Germany has been marked by a policy of the middle way. This has been in a sense a 'third way' between the two extreme poles marked by market-driven capitalism on the one hand and welfare state capitalism along Swedish lines on other. To a significant extent, the policy of the middle way reflects also the impact of the political institutions, such as the grand coalition state requirement for major policy changes, and the large number of co-governing forces and veto players, including federalism and party competition between two large pro-welfare state parties. However, grand coalition state requirements, powerful co-governing forces, and veto players must be interpreted with care. Although all of these factors can turn policy making into a difficult and often time-consuming enterprise, the outcome does not consist of a blocked decision-making process. And despite many co-governors or explicit veto players, the Federal Republic of Germany has in principle been capable of reform and adjustment to external or internal challenges. But a central precondition of reform and elastic adjustment is a relatively large degree of cooperation between the major political parties. Without the latter, the high barriers to policy formation in the lower and the upper houses of parliament, to mention only two of the hurdles, cannot be overcome.

Chapter 6 has also investigated the extent to which the political institutions, the political process, and the substance of public policy have been marked by continuity and discontinuity in reunited Germany. The overall results again point to major changes. While political continuity has played a major role in the history of the Federal Republic of Germany, discontinuous development has hardly been less remarkable. Major examples of discontinuity include the massive changes in domestic politics and in foreign affairs not only after 1989 and 1990, but also before unification. The restoration and consolidation of a democracy and the rise of a state governed by law in West Germany have been part of a successful trajectory away from an authoritarian past. Of great consequence have also been the reconstruction and expansion of social policy. In addition, economic, political, and military integration of the Federal Republic into the community of the Western nations was of major relevance, and so, too, was the policy of détente vis-à-vis the Socialist countries in the post-1969 period.

These were the outcomes of truly important policy changes. But major changes have also characterized politics and political institutions in post-1989 Germany, such as the emergence of an east–west division of the electorate and the rise of two party systems, one in the West German states and the other in the eastern part of the country. German unification plays of course a major role as a trigger of political change. But political change in the post-1989 period was also driven by European integration and challenges generated by globalization on the one hand and social change, such as the ageing of society, on the other (see Table 6).

The overall pattern has been a mixture of relatively successful adaption on the one hand and insufficient elasticity on the other. Particularly grave are the increasing costs involved in maintaining the policy of the middle way. No less burdensome are the east–west divisions in economic productivity and political attitudes, with a significantly higher demand for increasing roles of government in the east despite a massive transfer of fiscal resources from west to east as a major problem.

KEY TERMS

- Berlin Republic
- bureaucratic consociationalism
- constitutional structures
- continuity
- convergent and divergent majorities in the Bundestag and Bundesrat
- discontinuity
- *divide et impera* strategies
- European structural democratic deficit
- European Union
- federalism
- fragmentation

- German unification
- grand coalition state
- majoritarian democracy
- path dependence
- policy immobilization (*Reformstau*)
- policy of the middle way
- politics of price stability
- power sharing
- power state
- semi-sovereignty
- trading state
- veto players
- veto positions
- welfare state

QUESTIONS FOR CHAPTER 6

1 To what extent have continuity and discontinuity characterized the political history of the Federal Republic of Germany before and since unification in 1990?

2 Why has Germany come to be regarded as the 'trading state'?

3 What are the pros and cons of the pro-European policy stance in the Federal Republic of Germany?

4 What are the major virtues and the major drawbacks of the unification of East and West Germany in 1990?

5 To what extent is the policy of the middle way an attractive formula, and why?

....

NOTES

1 Literally translated 'reform congestion'.

2 For a deal between Schröder and pharmaceutical enterprises see Hoffmann 2001; for a deal between the Chancellor's office and the Metalworkers Union on the eve of the parliamentary vote on the reform of the old age pension in 2001 see Fleischhauer, Reiermann, and Sauga 2001.

3 Calculated from Sachverständigenrat zur Begutachtung der gesamtwirtschaftlichen Entwicklung 2002: 408–12.

4 The labour market policy under the jurisdiction of the Federal Office of Labour cannot fill the gap which the weakness of macroeconomic employment policy leaves behind.

5 'Gesetz zur Änderung des Grundgesetzes vom 21.12.1992' (*Bundesgesetzblatt* I: 2086).

6 'Model Vision: A Survey of Germany', *The Economist*, 21 May 1994: 30.

7 The club of the rich states includes Bavaria, Baden-Württemberg, Hesse, North Rhine-Westphalia, and Hamburg. All other states are less wealthy, or poor, or find themselves confronted with massive home-made debt such as Bremen, Saarland, and Berlin. Without the East German *Länder*, the rich states would have been the majority in the Bundesrat.

8 *The Economist*, 16 June 2001: 34. The quote refers to the hopes and fears of EU countries and on what others say on Germany.

....

GUIDE TO FURTHER READING

VON BEYME, K. (1999), *Das politische System der Bundesrepublik Deutschland*, 9th edn. (Wiesbaden-Opladen: Westdeutscher Verlag). Important overview of politics and political institutions in Germany at the end of the twentieth century.

CZADA, R., and WOLLMANN, H. (eds.) (2000), *Von der Bonner zur Berliner Republik*, (Wiesbaden: Westdeutscher Verlag). Collaborative volume on politics and policy in unified Germany.

EDINGER, L. J., and NACOS, B. L. (1998), *From Bonn to Berlin: German Politics in Transition* (New York: Columbia University Press). Study in German politics in the 1990s emphasizing unification-related developments.

ELLWEIN, T., and HOLTMANN, E. (eds.) (1999), *Fünfzig Jahre Bundesrepublik Deutschland: Rahmenbedingungen— Entwicklungen—Perspektiven* (PVS Sonderheft 30/1999) (Wiesbaden: Westdeutscher Verlag). Important collection of articles on five decades of political institutions, political processes, and policy making in Germany.

HELMS, L. (ed.) (2000), *Institutions and Institutional Change in the Federal Republic of Germany* (Houndmills: Macmillan). Instructive collection of articles on political institutions and institutional change.

MERKL, P. H. (ed.) (1999), *The Federal Republic of Germany at Fifty: The End of a Century of Turmoil* (Houndmills: Macmillan) Collaborative volume on five decades of political institutions and the political process in the Federal Republic of Germany.

RITTBERGER, V. (ed.) (2001), *German Foreign Policy since Unification: Theories and Case Studies* (Manchester: Manchester University Press). Important analysis of foreign policy in unified Germany.

SCHARPF, F. W. (1999), *Governing Europe: Efficient and Democratic?* (Oxford: Oxford University Press). Study on institutions and policy-making capacity of the European Union and the multi-level politics between member states and EU institutions.

SMITH, G., PATERSON, W. E., MERKL, P. H., and PADGETT, S. (eds.) (1996), *Developments in German Politics 2* (Houndmills: Macmillan). Important overview of political change in unified Germany up to the mid-1990s.

STURM, R., and PEHLE, H. (2001), *Das neue deutsche Regierungssystem: Die Europäisierung von Institutionen, Entscheidungsprozessen und Politikfeldern in der Bundesrepublik Deutschland* (Opladen: Leske & Budrich). Systematic overview of the European Union's impact on political institutions and policy making in the Federal Republic of Germany.

WEBBER, D. (ed.) (2001), '*New Europe, New Germany, Old Foreign Policy?*' *German Politics*, 10/1 (London: Frank Cass). Instructive volume on continuity and discontinuity in German foreign policy since unification.

7

....

Conclusion

Taking the various pieces of information together, the overview of the continuous and discontinuous developments in Germany's pre- and post-unification institutions and their impact on public policy suggests several conclusions.

A successful route to a constitutional democracy

From a broader historical perspective, one of the most important findings of this book concerns the truly dramatic difference between the Federal Republic of Germany and the structure and practice of Germany's most extreme political regimes, that is, National Socialism in the period from 1933 to 1945 and the rise and decline of East German communism from 1945 to 1990 (Ash 1993; Ritter 1998). Germany's second republic is light years away from the National-Socialist state. It is neither a 'Behemoth', to borrow from Franz Neumann's account of the National-Socialist state in 1933–45 (Neumann 1977), nor a 'Leviathan' of the Hobbesian tradition, nor a state under the tutelage of a one state party, such as the Socialist Unity Party-led state of East Germany in 1949–90 (Mayer 1997; Schroeder 1998). In sharp contradistinction to all authoritarian and totalitarian regimes, the Federal Republic is a secure constitutional democracy which follows the basic traditions of West European and North American constitutional thought. The difference between the period from 1933 to 1945 and East German socialism from 1949 to 1990 on the one hand and the Federal Republic of Germany on the other is fundamental and concerns both macro- and microstructures in politics, economics, and society (Ritter 1998). The Federal Republic of Germany has turned into a firmly rooted constitutional democracy based on a pluralistic society with a social structure broadly similar to that of other West European states (Winkler 2000). And in contrast to the National-Socialist era and the East German socialist experiment, the Federal Republic has a highly developed competitive economy, specializing mainly in products and services of a civilian rather than a military character (Smith-Owen 1994; Dyson 1996, 2001).

Continuity and discontinuity

The review of the literature and the available data points out that a remarkable degree of continuity and a no less remarkable degree of change have characterized Germany's political institutions and public policy in the post-1990 period. Regarding the continuity of the political institutions, the Federal Republic after 1990 did not turn into a 'Third Reich', but remained firmly on the path chosen in the pre-1990 period, namely the path of a constitutional state with a democratic republic, rule of law, federalism, strong social policy, a powerful party state, and a pro-European integration policy. The Federal Republic also continued the policy of the middle way after 1990, although at higher costs. But there has also been noteworthy discontinuity in reunified Germany, such as a more populous state with a far higher degree of economic, political, and cultural heterogeneity than before 1990. Moreover, the analysis also suggests that a large part of the change can be attributed to three major processes: German unification was one of them. The impact of Europeanized politics on the nation state has also been important. And a third major process has been driven by social and economic change, with the ageing of society, lower rates of economic growth, and high unemployment as the major challenges.

A democratic, fragmented, and constrained party state

A further conclusion to be derived from the preceding chapters of this book concerns the nature of the party state. The Federal Republic of Germany in the post-1949 era is a party state. But in contrast to the totalitarian party state of National-Socialist origin, and also in contrast to the communist party state in socialist East Germany, in which the Marxist-Leninist Socialist Unity Party played the hegemonic role, the party state of the Federal Republic is democratic in character, and it is also fragmented and constrained. It is fragmented by the federal organization of the state, and it is constrained by the rule of law and a wide variety of co-governing forces and veto players. The implications are grave. Unconstrained policy making of political parties is inconceivable within this context. From this follow major restrictions on the degree to which parties can influence public policy (Schmidt 1995, 1996). There are policy areas in which the role of the political parties is very limited, such as areas under the control of experts. The German Bundesbank and the European Central Bank are examples. Due to the principle of delegating a considerable number of public policy functions to societal organizations, a wide range of economic and social policy sovereignty resides not in government, in parliament, or in the parties but rather in the jurisdiction of organized labour and capital. *Tarifautonomie* is the keyword in this context, that is, free collective bargaining among the representatives of labour and capital on the wage rate, working conditions, and other aspects of individual and collective labour law. In other policy areas the political parties have gained a more important role, such as in the welfare state, in immigration, in control of atomic energy, and in education. But even in these areas, the constraints are non-trivial. The German welfare state is famous for its relatively high degree of path dependence. But precisely this path dependence may narrowly circumscribe the social policy choices of the parties.

Dahrendorf's cartelization hypothesis and Katzenstein's semi-sovereignty revisited

This leads to the fourth conclusion. The wide variety of co-governing forces and veto players can turn politics and policy making in the Federal Republic of Germany into a sometimes extraordinarily difficult and frustrating enterprise. Within this context, a blocked decision-making process cannot be excluded, although that has been the exception rather than the rule. Moreover, detailed analysis also reveals major political change, including successful policy adaptation, in the decades before and after unification in 1990. This underlines the validity of a more general view: it is the view that the political institutions in present day Germany allow for a moderately high level of elasticity and adaptiveness in the policy making process, despite the indisputable existence of numerous veto players and co-governing forces. The analysis presented here thus also sheds new light on influential views of governing the Federal Republic. One of these views, the hypothesis of total policy immobilization, echoes earlier critical accounts of an alleged inferior capacity of the Federal Republic to adjust and to reform, such as the cartelization hypothesis advanced by Ralf Dahrendorf in his famous book on society and democracy in post-1949 Germany (Dahrendorf 1965). According to Dahrendorf, a cartel among politicians against major policy change together with deep-seated preferences for conflict avoidance, and, thus, the lack of truly 'open society' of the Anglo-American variety, were the major restrictions on what he regarded as a more liberal, more open Federal Republic. Twenty-two years later Katzenstein's diagnosis of a 'semisovereign state' constrained by numerous checks and balances and powerful parapublic institutions focused attention more closely than Dahrendorf's on the political institutional barriers to large policy changes. Katzenstein attributed the priority for incremental policy making and deliberate experimentation mainly to the constraints on central government that were caused by a wide variety of co-governing institutions and actors, such as federalism, coalitions, and parapublic institutions, as well as to consensus requirement inherent in an open economy and to the existence of ideologically moderate parties (Katzenstein 1987: 367).

But neither Dahrendorf nor Katzenstein offered a complete story of politics and policy in Germany. One year after the publication of Dahrendorf's book the formation of a grand coalition made up of Christian Democrats and Social Democrats (1966) and three years later the change in power from a CDU-CSU-SDP coalition to the SPD-FDP coalition started a period of major reforms in domestic politics and foreign affairs. And barely three years after Katzenstein's book on West Germany was published in 1987, Germany's policy makers opted for a truly dramatic policy change, namely a 'big bang' policy of unification actively supported or at least tolerated by the former Allies of the Second World War, and an almost complete transfer of West German institutions to the eastern part of the country together with the most massive redistribution of fiscal resources the country has ever seen, namely redistribution from West Germany to East Germany of a magnitude equivalent to broadly 5 per cent of gross domestic product annually for a period longer than one decade. This has been no mean achievement, but rather a major policy change with massive long-term consequences. Moreover, in the post-1990 period Germany turned into a country with a particularly wide variety of minor and major policy changes, by joining the club of the Euro-member countries, opting for a deeper and a larger European Union, as well as by joining in military 'out of area'-missions of NATO as the major examples, not to mention the introduction of care for the elderly in 1994 and the privatization of telecommunications, postal services, and German rail.

These policy changes are incompatible with the view that Germany's polity is immobile and incapable of solving impending problems of social integration and system integration. Germany's political system may well be 'beautiful in its complexity, but difficult to change'.[1] Much can be said in favour of the view that Germany's 'elaborate system of checks and balances [. . .] restricts the power of the government'.[2] Furthermore, the Federal Republic is indeed a polity with a very large number of veto points and veto players (Scharpf 1994, 2002; Schmidt 2000: 352–4). However, these factors do not necessarily obstruct or totally block the capacity to design and implement major policy change. The view 'that the whole system is based on consensus politics'[3] and that German governments abstain from unpopular decisions also needs to be revised. Consensus requirements in the Federal Republic are indeed strong, as may be seen in the grand coalition state requirements discussed in this book (see sections 3.3 and 6.1 above). But consensus politics coexists in today's Germany with adversarial politics, deep conflicts, and bitter struggles between political actors. Furthermore, the major decisions made by the German governments include measures that were taken against the wishes of the majority of the people: rearming Germany in the 1950s and joining NATO as well as substituting the Euro for the beloved Deutsche Mark are examples. These observations and a wide variety of studies in German politics rather point towards a political system which, despite its complex architecture and the numerous veto players and co-governing forces, is endowed with a reasonable level of elasticity and adaptiveness, provided that the challenge is large enough and the major political actors broadly agree in their perception of the issues at stake and are willing and capable to cooperate. However, these preconditions are, it must be conceded, often not fulfilled.

Dispersal of power as a comparative institutional advantage

A fifth conclusion concerns the dispersal of power resources in present day Germany. Politics and policy in the Federal Republic cannot be well understood with concepts derived from a state with highly concentrated power resources, such as Britain, France, or Sweden, not to mention centralized authoritarian regimes. It is not the concentration of power resources which marks politics and policy in modern Germany, it is an exceptionally high degree of dispersal of power resources on the one hand and power sharing on the other which matter. The division of powers of the executive, the legislature, and the judiciary makes a difference, and when that division is blurred, such as in parliamentary government, additional checks and balances constrain the public powers, such as federalism, judicial review, and coalition politics. Furthermore, the division of labour between government and societal associations, to which a significant proportion of public policy functions have been transferred, also provides for the fragmentation of power resources. Within this context the policy process is more complicated and often reduces accountability to a large measure. It is also the case that the exceptionally high degree of dispersal of public power in present day Germany constrains the manoeuvrability of the policy-making process (Lehmbruch 1989; Scharpf 1973, 2002). But this outcome is in a sense precisely what the architects of Germany's constitution hoped to achieve, namely to effectively tame state power and to tie down as thoroughly as possible the government Goliath by numerous checks and balances, veto points, and veto players, in order to prevent the restoration of unlimited public powers. That achievement deserves to be called historic.

The integration of the opposition party as a further comparative advantage

The complex structure of Germany's political system and, above all, the existence of a federalism composed of the federation and sixteen states has generated a further important institutional advantage which is often overlooked by observers from countries with unitary state structures: a high potential for integrating the opposition party. A political party which loses an election for the Bundestag or a longer series of elections to the lower house of parliament, such as the SPD in 1949–65 and from 1982 to 1994 and the Christian Democratic parties from 1969 to 1980, and in 1998 and 2000, remains a potentially powerful opposition party. Through success in elections to state parliaments and the formation of a majority in the Bundesrat, the upper house of parliament, the opposition party in the Bundestag can compensate for its subordinate role and turn into a highly influential co-governing actor, such as the CDU-CSU from 1972 to 1982 and from 1999 until the time of writing (October 2002) or the SPD from June to October 1990 and between 1991 and 1998. This possibility has major effects: it reduces the intensity of political struggles, eases the acceptance of electoral defeats, allows for integrating the opposition party and their followers rather than alienating them from the polity, and is thus conducive to a higher level of social cohesion.

Semi-sovereignty

The seventh conclusion concerns the international and transnational foundation of Germany's polity and economy. Germany is 'semi-sovereign' not only in domestic affairs but also in foreign policy and international relations. Most political tendencies in post-1949 Germany have been firmly pro-NATO and pro-European. In fact, they have been pro-European to an astonishing degree, because participation in the process of European state building involved considerable loss of sovereignty for the nation state and posed a challenge to democracy, which has a more limited room for manoeuvre than before. But the international and transnational foundation of Germany may indicate more clearly than all other indicators how different the Federal Republic of Germany has been when compared to all other political regimes in Germany in the nineteenth and twentieth century. A new state has emerged in Germany, one which need no longer be feared by its neighbours.

Deficiences and strengths of the Federal Republic of Germany

The remaining weaknesses of the political institutions and policy making in Germany should not be decried. The list of deficiences is long (see for example Eichhorst et al. 2001; Miegel 2002; Schmidt 2002a). It includes a climate of perennial electoral campaigns, an often slow policy response, an imbalance between advanced social security and underdeveloped provision for future-oriented policy areas (such as education, science, and family- and children-friendly environments), rigid labour markets with extensive job-holder protection on the one hand and high unemployment on the other, the continuity of a 'wall in the mind' that separates many westerners (*Wessis*) and easterners (*Ossis*), continuous major economic divisions between the western and the eastern regions despite massive redistribution from west to east, and a remarkable increase in decision-making costs after unification and as a result of unification (Sturm 1996). However, compared with pre-1949 Germany and the socialist East German state in 1949–90, the Federal Republic of Germany has performed well. Compared with countries of similar economic wealth and political structure, the political performance of the Federal Republic of Germany is neither brilliant nor bad, when measured with indicators of political productivity. Political stability is assured.[4] And measured by most performance indicators, Germany is positioned in the middle or above the middle (Lijphart 1999; Schmidt 1992b; Roller 2001).[5] Germany's policy of the middle way thus seems to be a key indicator of a more general middle of the road performance.

For highly ambitious players, the position in the middle is unsatisfactory. But for players who have long been behind, the middle is a relative success. The latter regard the glass as half-full, the former as half-empty. In view of the political history of Germany before 1949, above all in 1933–45, and in view of the legacy of the communist dictatorship in East Germany from 1949 to 1989–90, it is fair to argue that the glass is half-full.

....

KEY TERMS

- adaptiveness
- ageing of society
- cartelization hypothesis
- consensus politics
- continuity
- democratization
- discontinuity
- dispersal of power
- elasticity
- Europeanization
- fiscal stress
- free collective bargaining
- incremental policy making
- party state
- perennial electoral campaign
- policy immobilization
- policy of the middle way
- position in the middle
- regime change
- semi-sovereignty
- transnational foundation
- *Wessis* and *Ossis*

....

QUESTION FOR CHAPTER 7

1 The Federal Republic of Germany was regarded in 1989 as 'a success story' (Dalton 1989). What are the pros and cons of this view today?

....

NOTES

1 Thomas R. Cusack in a presentation at the Science Center Berlin for Social Research on 7 March, 2002.

2 'Model Vision: A Survey of Germany', *The Economist*, 21 May 1994: 3.

3 Ibid. 3.

4 'Political productivity' is a concept for the measurement of political performance which comprises mainly the following dimensions: system maintenance, adaptation to changes in the socio-economic environment, participation, compliance and support, procedural justice, the level of welfare, security for the citizens, and the degree of liberty (Almond and Powell 1996: 144).

5 See also Bark and Gress 1993; von Beyme 1999; Conradt 2001; Czada and Wollmann 2000; Edinger and Nacos 1998; Ellwein and Holtmann 1999; Hancock 1995, Hancock et al. 2002; Helms 2000a; Kielmansegg 2000; Larres 2000; Löwenthal and Schwarz 1974; Merkl 1999; Paterson and Southern 1991; Pulzer 1995; Schmidt 1992a; Schoenbaum and Pond 1996; Smith et al. 1992, 1996.

....

GUIDE TO FURTHER READING

CZADA, R., and WOLLMANN, H. (eds.) (2000), *Von der Bonner zur Berliner Republik* (Wiesbaden: Westdeutscher Verlag). Collaborative volume on politics and policy in unified Germany.

DAHRENDORF, R. (1967), *Society and Democracy in Germany* (Garden City, NY: Doubleday; first German edn. in 1965). Stimulating political-sociological account of West Germany in the 1960s.

KATZENSTEIN, P. J. (1987), *Policy and Politics in West Germany: The Growth of a Semisovereign State* (Philadelphia: Temple University Press). Important contribution to the study of political constraints on the policy process in western Germany.

KIELMANSEGG, P. Graf (2000), *Nach der Katastrophe—die Deutschen und ihre Nation: Eine Geschichte des geteilten Deutschlands* (Berlin: Siedler). Important study of politics in West and East Germany until the collapse of the Berlin Wall.

LEPSIUS, M. R. (1990b [1979]), 'Soziale Ungleichheit und Klassenstrukturen in der Bundesrepublik Deutschland', in M. R. Lepsius (ed.), *Interessen, Ideen und Institutionen* (Opladen: Westdeutscher Verlag), 117–52. Important political-sociological analysis of the class structure and the order of political interest intermediation in the Federal Republic in the late 1970s.

SCHROEDER, K. (1998), *Der SED-Staat: Partei, Staat und Gesellschaft, 1949–1990* (Munich: Hanser). Comprehensive overview of political institutions and policy outputs in the communist German Democratic Republic (1949–90).

WINKLER, H. A. (2000), *Der lange Wege nach Westen*, 2 vols. (Munich: C. H. Beck). Important historical overview of Germany's road from the nineteenth to the late twentieth century.

REFERENCES

ABERBACH, J. D., PUTNAM, R. D., and ROCKMAN, B. A. (1981), *Bureaucrats & Politicians in Western Democracies* (Cambridge, Mass.: Harvard University Press).

ABROMEIT, H. (1993), *Interessenvermittlung zwischen Konkurrenz und Konkordanz* (Opladen: Leske & Budrich).

—— (1998), *Democracy in Europe: Legitimizing Politics in a Non-State Polity* (New York: Oxford University Press).

—— (2000), 'Unternehmerverbände', in Andersen and Woyke 2000: 612–16.

AGNOLI, J. (1968), 'Die Transformation der Demokratie', in J. Agnoli and P. Brückner (eds.), *Die Transformation der Demokratie* (Frankfurt a. M.: EVA), 7–41.

ALBER, J. (1987), *Der Sozialstaat der Bundesrepublik Deutschland 1950–1983* (Frankfurt a. M.: Campus).

ALEMANN, U. von (1987), *Organisierte Interessen in der Bundesrepublik* (Opladen: Leske & Budrich).

—— (2000), *Das Parteiensystem der Bundesrepublik Deutschland* (Opladen: Leske & Budrich).

—— and WESSELS, B. (eds.) (1997), *Verbände in vergleichender Perspektive* (Berlin: Edition Sigma).

ALMOND, G. A., and POWELL, G. B., Jr. (1996), *Comparative Politics Today*, 6th edn. (New York: Longman).

—— STROM, K., and DALTON, R. J. (2000), *Comparative Politics Today*, 7th edn. (New York: Longman).

ANDERSEN, U., and WOYKE, W. (eds.) (2000), *Handwörterbuch des politischen Systems der Bundesrepublik Deutschland,* 4th edn. (Opladen: Leske & Budrich).

ARMINGEON, K. (1988), *Die Entwicklung der westdeutschen Gewerkschaften 1950–1985* (Frankfurt a. M.: Campus).

—— (1994), *Staat und Arbeitsbeziehungen: Ein internationaler Vergleich* (Opladen: Westdeutscher Verlag).

—— (2002), 'Verbändesystem und Föderalismus: Eine vergleichende Analyse', in Benz and Lehmbruch 2002: 213–33.

ARNIM, H.-H. von (1997), *Fetter Bauch regiert nicht gern: Die politische Klasse—selbstbezogen und abgehoben* (Munich: Kindler).

—— (1998), 'Reformblockade der Politik?', *Zeitschrift für Rechtspolitik,* 31/4: 138–47.

—— (2001a), *Politik macht Geld: Das Schwarzgeld der Politiker—weißgewaschen* (Munich: Droemersche Verlagsanstalt Th. Knaur Nachf.).

—— (2001b), *Das System: Die Machenschaften der Macht* (Munich: Droemersche Verlagsanstalt Th. Knaur Nachf.).

ASH, T. G. (1993), *In Europe's Name: Germany in a Divided Continent* (New York: Random House).

AVENARIUS, H. (2001), *Die Rechtsordnung der Bundesrepublik Deutschland,* 3rd edn. (Bonn: Bundeszentrale für Politische Bildung).

BACH, M. (1999), *Die Bürokratisierung Europas: Verwaltungseliten, Experten und politische Legitimation in Europa* (Frankfurt a. M.: Campus).

—— (ed.) (2001), *Die Europäisierung*

nationaler Gesellschaften (Wiesbaden: Westdeutscher Verlag).

BACHRACH, P., and BARATZ, M. S. (1979), *Power and Poverty: Theory and Practice* (New York: Oxford University Press).

BADURA, P., and DREIER, H. (eds.) (2001), *Festschrift 50 Jahre Bundesverfassungsgericht* (Tübingen: Mohr (Paul Siebeck)).

BAGEHOT, W. (1963 [1867]), *The English Constitution* (Harmondsworth: Penguin).

BARK, D., and GRESS, D. (eds.) (1993), *The History of West-Germany*, 2 vols. (London: Blackwell).

BATT, H. (2001), *Verfassungsrecht und Verfassungswirklichkeit im vereinigten Deutschland* (Heidelberg: Ph.D.).

BAUER, T. (1998), *Der Vermittlungsausschuss: Politik zwischen Konkurrenz und Konsens* (Bremen: Ph.D.).

BENDA, E. (2001), 'Ein mächtiges Reich der Stille: Das Bundesverfassungsgericht zwischen Recht und Politik—eine persönliche Geburtstagsbetrachtung seines früheren Präsidenten', *Süddeutsche Zeitung,* 27 Sept.

BENZ, A. (1999), 'From Unitary to Asymmetric Federalism in Germany: Taking Stock after 50 Years', *Publius: The Journal of Federalism,* 29/4: 55–78.

——(2002), 'Lehren aus entwicklungsgeschichtlichen und vergleichenden Analysen', in Benz and Lehmbruch 2002: 391–403.

——and LEHMBRUCH, G. (eds.) (2002), *Föderalismus* (PVS Sonderheft 32/2001) (Wiesbaden: Westdeutscher Verlag),

BERNDT, U. (1998), 'Germany', in R. Wuthnow (ed.), *The Encyclopedia of Politics and Religion* (London: Routledge), 299–302.

BERTELSMANN STIFTUNG and HANS

BÖCKLER-STIFTUNG (eds.) (1998), *Mitbestimmung und neue Unternehmenskulturen: Bilanz und Perspektive* (Gütersloh, Düsseldorf: Bertelsmann Stiftung and Hans-Böckler-Stiftung).

BETZ, H.-G., and IMMERFALL, S. (eds.) (1998), *The New Politics of the Right: Neo-Populist Parties and Movements in Established Democracies* (Houndmills: Macmillan).

BEYME, K. VON (1971), *Die politische Elite in der Bundesrepublik Deutschland* (Munich: Piper).

——(1984), *Parteien in den westlichen Demokratien* (Munich: Piper).

——(1989), 'Wirtschafts- und Sozialpolitik im Deutschen Bundestag', in Thaysen, Davidson, and Livingstone 1989: 342–65.

——(1993), *Die politische Klasse im Parteienstaat* (Frankfurt a. M.: Suhrkamp).

——(1997), *Der Gesetzgeber: Der Bundestag als Entscheidungszentrum* (Opladen: Westdeutscher Verlag).

——(1999), *Das politische System der Bundesrepublik Deutschland,* 9th edn. (Wiesbaden-Opladen: Westdeutscher Verlag).

——(2000a), 'The Bundestag: Still the Centre of Decision-Making?', in Helms 2000b: 32–47.

——(2000b), *Parteien im Wandel: Von den Volksparteien zu den professionalisierten Wählerparteien* (Wiesbaden: Westdeutscher Verlag).

——(2001a), 'Das Bundesverfassungsgericht aus der Sicht der Politik- und Gesellschaftswissenschaften', in Badura and Dreier 2001: 493–505.

——(2001b), 'Elite Relations in Germany', in Padgett and Poguntke 2001: 19–37.

BLANKE, B., and WOLLMANN, H. (eds.) (1991), *Die alte Bundesrepublik: Kontinuität und Wandel*, Leviathan Special Edition 12 (Opladen: Westdeutscher Verlag).

BLANKENBURG, E. (1996), 'Changes in Political Regimes and Continuity of the Rule of Law in Germany', in H. Jacob (ed.), *Courts, Law, and Politics in Comparative Perspective* (New Haven: Yale University Press), 249–314.

BLASIUS, R. (2002), 'Feuertaufe für Verfassungsrichter', *Frankfurter Allgemeine Zeitung*, 31 Jan.

Blickpunkt, *Bundestag*, No. 4 (1998).

BRACHER, K. D., JÄGER, W., and LINK, W. (1986), *Republik im Wandel. 1969–1974: Die Ära Brandt* (Stuttgart: Deutsche Verlags-Anstalt and F. A. Brockhaus).

BRETTSCHNEIDER, F. (2002), *Spitzenkandidaten und Wahlerfolg: Personalisierung—Kompetenz—Parteien. Ein internationaler Vergleich* (Wiesbaden: Westdeutscher Verlag).

BUDGE, I. et al. (1997), *The Politics of the New Europe: Atlantic to Urals* (London: Longman).

—— and KEMAN, H. (1990), *Parties and Democracies: Coalition Formation and Government Functioning in 20 States* (Oxford: Oxford University Press).

BÜHRER, W., and GRANDE, E. (eds.) (2000), *Unternehmerverbände und Staat in Deutschland* (Baden-Baden: Nomos Verlag).

Bundesarbeitsblatt No. 1 (2000).

Bundesminister für Arbeit und Sozialordnung (BMA) (ed.) (1998), *Übersicht über das Arbeitsrecht*, 7th edn. (Bonn: BMA).

—— (ed.) (2000), *Übersicht über das Sozialrecht*, 6th edn. (Bonn: BMA).

—— (ed.) (2002), *Sozialbericht 2001* (Bonn: BMA).

BÜRKLIN, W., and REBENSTORF, H. et al.

(1997), *Eliten in Deutschland* (Opladen: Leske & Budrich).

BUSCH, A. (1993), 'The Politics of Price Stability: Why the German-Speaking Nations are Different', in Castles 1993: 35–92.

—— (1999), 'Das oft geänderte Grundgesetz', in W. Merkel and A. Busch (eds.), *Demokratie in Ost und West: Für Klaus von Beyme* (Frankfurt a. M.: Suhrkamp), 549–74.

BUTLER, D., and RANNEY, A. (eds.) (1994), *Referendums around the World: The Growing Use of Direct Democracy* (Washington DC: AEI Press).

CAMERON, D. R. (1978), 'The Expansion of the Public Economy', *American Political Science Review*, 72/4: 1243–61.

—— (1984), 'Social Democracy, Corporatism, Labor Quiescence and the Representation of Economic Interest in Advanced Capitalist Society', in J. Goldthorpe (ed.), *Order and Conflict in Contemporary Capitalism* (New York: Oxford University Press), 143–78.

CAPOCCIA, G. (2002), 'The German Electoral System at Fifty', *West European Politics*, 25/3: 171–202.

CASPER, G. (1995), *Fragile Democracies: The Legacies of Authoritarian Rule* (Pittsburgh: University of Pittsburgh Press).

CASPER, G. (2001), 'Laudatio auf die Karlsruher Republik', *Süddeutsche Zeitung*, 29 Sept.

CASTLES, F. G. (1982), 'The Impact of Parties on Public Expenditure', in F. G. Castles (ed.), *The Impact of Parties: Politics and Policies in Democratic Capitalist States* (London: Sage Publications), 21–96.

—— (ed.) (1989), *The Comparative History of Public Policy* (Cambridge: Polity Press).

—— (ed.) (1993), *Families of Nations:*

Patterns of Public Policy in Western Democracies (Aldershot: Dartmouth).

CASTLES, F.G. (1998), *Comparative Public Policy: Patterns of Post-war Transformation* (Cheltenham: Edward Elgar).

CONRADT, D. P. (2001), *The German Polity*, 7th edn. (New York: Longman).

CROUCH, C. (1994), *Industrial Relations and European State Traditions* (Oxford: Clarendon Press).

CURRIE, D. P. (1997), 'Foreword to the Second Edition', in D. P. Kommers, *The Constitutional Jurisprudence of the Federal Republic of Germany*, 2nd edn. (Durham, NC: Duke University Press), pp. ix–x.

CZADA, R., and WOLLMANN, H. (eds.) (2000), *Von der Bonner zur Berliner Republik* (Leviathan Sonderheft) (Wiesbaden: Westdeutscher Verlag).

DAHRENDORF, R. (1965), *Gesellschaft und Demokratie in Deutschland* (Munich: Piper).

—— (1967), *Society and Democracy in Germany* (Garden City, NY: Doubleday).

DALTON, R. J. (1993), *Politics in Germany* 2nd edn. (New York: HarperCollins).

—— (1996a), 'A Divided Electorate?', in Smith et al. (eds.) 1996: 35–54.

—— (ed.) (1996b), *Germans Divided: The 1984 Bundestag Elections and the Evolution of the German Party System* (Oxford: Berg).

—— (2000), 'Politics in Germany', in Almond et al. 2000: 271–326.

—— (2002), *Citizen Politics: Public Opinion and Political Parties in Advanced Industrial Democracies*, 3rd edn. (New York: Chatham House).

—— and WATTENBERG, M. P. (2000), *Parties without Partisans: Political Change in Advanced Industrial Democracies* (Oxford: Oxford University Press).

DÄSTNER, C. (2001), 'Zur Entwicklung der Zustimmungsbedürftigkeit von Bundesgesetzen seit 1949', *Zeitschrift für Parlamentsfragen*, 32/2: 290–308.

DAVIS, J. W. (1998), *Leadership Selection in Six Western Democracies* (Westport, Conn.: Greenwood).

Der Fischer Weltalmanach 2000 (1999), (Frankfurt a. M.: Fischer).

Der Fischer Weltalmanach 2001 (2000), (Frankfurt a. M.: Fischer).

DERLIEN, H.-U. (1997), 'Elitenzirkulation zwischen Implosion and Integration: Abgang, Rekrutierung und Zusammensetzung ostdeutscher Funktionseliten 1989–1994', in H. Wollmann et al. (eds.), *Transformation der politisch-administrativen Strukturen in Ostdeutschland* (Opladen: Leske & Budrich).

Deutscher Bundestag & Bundesarchiv (eds.) (1974–1977), *Der Parlamentarische Rat 1948–1949: Akten und Protokolle*, vols. i–xi (Boppard: Boldt; Munich: Oldenbourg).

DI FABIO, U. (1998), *Das Recht offener Staaten* (Tübingen: Mohr (Paul Siebeck)).

DYSON, K. (1996), 'The Economic Order: Still Modell Deutschland?', in Smith et al. 1996: 194–210.

—— (2001), 'The German Model Revisited: From Schmidt to Schröder', in Padgett and Pogunkte 2001: 135–54.

EDINGER, L. J. (1960), 'Post-totalitarian Leadership: Elites in the German Federal Republic', *American Political Science Review*, 54/1: 58–82.

—— (1986), *West German Politics*, 3rd edn. (New York: Columbia University Press).

—— and NACOS, B. L. (1998), *From Bonn to Berlin: German Politics in Transition* (New York: Columbia University Press).

EHMKE, H. (2001), 'Und wenn ich Karlsruhe einschalten muss. Ein Leben für den befriedeten Streit: Weshalb Adolf Arndt gegen das Wachstum der Verfassungsbeschwerden noch keine Beschwerde einlegte', *Frankfurter Allgemeine Zeitung*, 14 Aug.

EICHHORST, W., PROFIT, S., and THODE, E. in Zusammenarbeit mit der Arbeitsgruppe 'Benchmarking' des Bündnisses für Arbeit, Ausbildungs- und Wettbewerbsfähigkeit: Fels, G., Heinze, R. G., Pfarr, H., Schmid, G., & Streeck, W. (2001), *Benchmarking Deutschland: Arbeitsmarkt und Beschäftigung* (Berlin: Springer-Verlag).

ELLWEIN, T., and HOLTMANN, E. (eds.) (1999), *Fünfzig Jahre Bundesrepublik Deutschland: Rahmenbedingungen— Entwicklungen—Perspektiven* (PVS Sonderheft 30) (Wiesbaden: Westdeutscher Verlag).

'Empty vessels?' (1999), *The Economist*, 24 July, 33–4.

Enquetekommission Verfassungsreform des Deutschen Bundestages (1976), *Beratungen und Empfehlungen zur Verfassungsreform: Schlußbericht der Enquetekommission Verfassungsreform des Deutschen Bundestages*, vol. i: Parlament und Regierung (Bonn: Presse- und Informationszentrum des Deutschen Bundestages).

ESCHENBURG, T. (1955), *Herrschaft der Verbände?* (Stuttgart: DVA).

ESPING-ANDERSEN, G. (1990), *The Three Worlds of Welfare Capitalism* (Cambridge: Cambridge University Press).

——(1999), *Social Foundations of Post-Industrial Economies* (Oxford: Oxford University Press).

ESSER, H. (ed.) (2000), *Der Wandel nach der Wende: Gesellschaft, Wirtschaft, Politik in Ostdeutschland* (Wiesbaden: Westdeutscher Verlag).

FALTER, J., and SCHOEN, H. (1999), 'Wahlen und Wählerverhalten', in Ellwein and Holtmann 1999: 454–70.

——and SCHUMANN, S. (1994), 'Politische Konflikte, Wählerverhalten und die Struktur des Parteienwettbewerbs', in Gabriel and Brettschneider 1994: 192–219.

FLEISCHHAUER, J., REIERMANN, C., and SAUGA, M. (2001), 'Anruf genügt', *Der Spiegel*, 29 Jan.

Forschungsgruppe Wahlen e. V. (ed.) (1977–2002), *Politbarometer* (Mannheim: Forschungsgruppe Wahlen).

——(1994), *Bundestagswahl (1994): Eine Analyse der Wahl zum 13. Deutschen Bundestag am 16. Oktober 1994* (Mannheim: FG Wahlen).

——(1998), *Bundestagswahl (1998): Eine Analyse der Wahl zum 14. Deutschen Bundestag am 27. Oktober 1998* (Mannheim: FG Wahlen).

——(2002), *Bundestagswahl. Eine Analyse der Wahl vom 22. September 2002* (Mannheim: FG Wahlen).

FORSTHOFF, E. (1971), *Der Staat der Industriegesellschaft* (Munich: C. H. Beck).

FRANZ, W. (2002), *Die SPD: Vom Proletariat zur Neuen Mitte* (Berlin: Alexander Fest Verlag).

Freedom House (2001), *Freedom in the World: 2000–2001. The Annual Survey of Political Rights & Civil Liberties* (New York: Freedom House).

FREI, N. (ed.) (2002), *Die schwere Hypothek der jungen Bundesrepublik: Hitlers Eliten nach 1945* (Frankfurt a. M.: Campus).

FRIEDRICH, C. J. (1949), 'Rebuilding the German Constitution, II', *American Political Science Review*, 43/4: 704–20.

——(1953), 'The Constitution of the

German Federal Republic', in Litchfield 1953: 117–51.

FRIEDRICH, C. J. (1968), *Constitutional Government and Democracy*, 4th edn. (Waltham, Mass.: Blaisdell).

FROMME, F. K. (1962), *Von der Weimarer Verfassung zum Bonner Grundgesetz: Die verfassungspolitischen Folgerungen des Parlamentarischen Rates aus Weimarer Republik und nationalsozialistischer Diktatur*, 2nd edn. (Tübingen: Mohr (Paul Siebeck)).

FUCHS, D. (1999), 'The Democratic Culture of Unified Germany', in N. Pippa (ed.), *Critical Citizens: Global Support for Democratic Government* (Oxford: Oxford University Press), 123–45.

FULBROOK, M. (1995), *Anatomy of a Dictatorship: Inside the GDR, 1949–1989* (New York: Oxford University Press).

GABRIEL, O. W., and BRETTSCHNEIDER, F. (eds.) (1994), *Die EU-Staaten im Vergleich: Strukturen, Prozesse, Politikinhalte*, 2nd edn. (Opladen: Westdeutscher Verlag).

——and NELLER, K. (2000), 'Stabilität und Wandel politischer Unterstützung im vereinigten Deutschland', in Esser 2000: 67–90.

——NIEDERMAYER, O., and STÖSS, R. (eds.) (2001), *Parteiendemokratie in Deutschland* (Bonn: Bundeszentrale für politische Bildung).

GALLAGHER, M., LAVER, M., and MAIR, P. (2001), *Representative Government in Western Europe* (New York: McGraw Hill).

GEHLER, M., KAISER, W., and WOHNOUT, H. (eds.), (2001), *Christdemokratie in Europa im 20. Jahrhundert* (Cologne: Böhlau).

GOETZ, K. H. (1996), 'The Federal Constitutional Court', in Smith et al. 1996: 96–116.

——and CULLEN, P. J. (eds.) (1994), *Constitutional Policy in Unified Germany*, German Politics, 3/3 (London: Frank Cass).

——and HIX, S. (eds.) (2000), *Europeanised Politics? European Integration and National Political Systems*, West European Politics, 23/4.

GOHR, A. (2001), 'Was tun, wenn man die Regierungsmacht verloren hat? Die Sozialpolitik der SPD-Opposition in den 80er Jahren', University of Bremen: PhD.

GRIMM, D. (2001), 'Die bundesstaatliche Verfassung: Eine Politikblockade?', in D. Grimm, *Die Verfassung und die Politik: Einsprüche in Störfallen* (Munich: C. H. Beck), 139–50.

GROSSER, D. (1998), *Das Wagnis der Währungs-, Wirtschafts- und Sozialunion: Politische Zwänge im Konflikt mit ökonomischen Regeln* (Stuttgart: DVA).

——LANGE, T., MÜLLER-ARMACK, A., and NEUSS, B. (1988), *Soziale Marktwirtschaft. Geschichte.—Konzept—Leistung* (Stuttgart: Kohlhammer).

GUNLICKS, A. B. (2000), 'Föderative Systeme im Vergleich: Die USA und Deutschland', in H.-H. von Arnim, G. Färber, and S. Fisch, (eds.), *Föderalismus: Hält er noch, was er verspricht?* (Berlin: Duncker & Humblot), 41–62.

HALL, P. A., and SOSKICE, D. (eds.) (2001), *Varieties of Capitalism: The Institutional Foundations of Comparative Advantage* (Oxford: Oxford University Press).

HANCOCK, M. D. (1995), 'Germany', in S. M. Lipset (ed.), *The Encyclopedia of Democracy*, vol. ii (Washington DC: Congressional Quarterly Inc.), 522–9.

——and WELSH, H. A. (eds.) (1994),

German Unification: Process and Outcomes (Boulder, Colo.: Westview Press).

HANCOCK, M. D. et al. (2002), *Politics in Europe*, 3rd edn. (New York: Chatham House).

HANLEY, D. (ed.) (1994), *Christian Democracy in Europe* (London: Pinter Publishers).

Hanns Seidel Stiftung (ed.) (1995), *Geschichte einer Volkspartei: 50 Jahre CSU* (Munich: Hanns Seidel Stiftung).

HANRIEDER, W. (1995), *Deutschland, Europa, Amerika: Die Außenpolitik der Bundesrepublik Deutschland 1949–1994*, 2nd edn. (Paderborn: Ferdinand Schöningh).

HARTWICH, H.-H. (1970), *Sozialstaatspostulat und gesellschaftlicher Status quo* (Opladen: Westdeutscher Verlag).

HAUNGS, P. (1983), 'Die Christlich Demokratische Union Deutschlands (CDU) und die Christlich Soziale Union in Bayern (CSU)', in Veen 1983: 9–194.

HELMS, L. (1996a), 'Das Amt des deutschen Bundeskanzlers in historisch und international vergleichender Perspektive', *Zeitschrift für Parlamentsfragen*, 27/4: 697–711.

——(1996b), 'Executive Leadership and Parliamentary Democracies: The British Prime Minister and the German Chancellor Compared', *German Politics*, 5/1: 101–20.

——(1998), 'Keeping Weimar at Bay: The German Federal Presidency since 1949', *German Politics and Society*, 16/2: 50–68.

——(ed.) (2000a), *Institutions and Institutional Change in the Federal Republic of Germany* (Houndmills: Macmillan).

——(2000b), 'The Federal Constitutional Court: Institutionalizing Judicial Review in a Semi-Sovereign

Democracy', in Helms 2000a: 84–104.

——(2001), 'The Changing Chancellorship: Resources and Constraints Revisited', *German Politics*, 10/2, 155–68.

——(2002), 'Executive Leadership in Western Democracies: A Comparative Study of the United States, Britain and Germany' (Berlin: Humboldt University, unpubl. manuscript).

HENKEL, H.-O. (1998), *Jetzt oder nie: Ein Bündnis für Nachhaltigkeit in der Politik* (Berlin: Siedler).

HENNIS, W. (1964), *Richtlinienkompetenz und Regierungstechnik* (Tübingen: Mohr (Paul Siebeck)).

——(1998), *Auf dem Weg in den Parteienstaat: Aufsätze aus vier Jahrzehnten* (Stuttgart: Reclam).

—— and KIELMANSEGG, P. Graf (eds.) (1977), *Regierbarkeit* (Stuttgart: Klett-Cotta).

HÉRITIER, A., KNILL, C., and MINGERS, S. (1996), *Ringing the Changes in Europe: Regulatory Competition and Redefinition of the State. Britain, France, Germany* (Berlin: DeGruyter).

HESSE, J. J., and ELLWEIN, T. (1992), *Das Regierungssystem der Bundesrepublik Deutschland*, 7th edn. (Opladen: Westdeutscher Verlag).

HESSE, K. (1962), *Der unitarische Bundesstaat* (Karlsruhe: C. F. Müller).

HIBBS, D. A., Jr. (1977), 'Political Parties and Macroeconomic Policy', *American Political Science Review*, 71/4: 1467–87.

——(1992), 'Partisan theory after fifteen years', *European Journal of Political Economy*, 8/3: 361–73.

HILDEBRAND, K. (1984), *Von Erhard zur Großen Koalition 1963 bis 1969* (Wiesbaden: Deutsche Verlags-Anstalt and F. A. Brockhaus).

HOBBES, T. (1985 [1651]), *Leviathan* (London: Penguin Books).

HOBBES, T. (1682), *Behemoth* (London: Crooke).

HOFFMANN, A. (2001), 'Willkommen in Schröders Basar. Der Kanzler protegiert die Pharmakonzerne—und blamiert seine Ministerin', *Süddeutsche Zeitung*, 10 Nov.

HOFFMANN-LANGE, U. (1992), *Eliten, Macht und Konflikt in der Bundesrepublik* (Opladen: Leske & Budrich).

——and BÜRKLIN, W. (2001), 'Eliten, Führungsgruppen', in Schäfers and Zapf 2001: 170–82.

HOFMANN, G., and PERGER, W. A. (eds.) (1992), *Die Kontroverse: Weizsäckers Parteienkritik in der Diskussion* (Frankfurt a. M.: Eichborn).

HUBER, E., RAGIN, C., and STEPHENS, J. D. (1993), 'Social Democracy, Christian Democracy, Constitutional Structure, and the Welfare State', *American Journal of Sociology*, 99/3: 711–49.

——and STEPHENS, J. D. (2001), *Development and Crisis of the Welfare State: Parties and Policies in Global Markets* (Chicago: The University of Chicago Press).

HUBER, P. M. (1994), 'Der Parteienstaat als Kern des politischen Systems. Wie tragfähig ist das Grundgesetz?', *Juristen Zeitung*, 49: 689–96.

HÜBNER, P. (ed.) (1999), *Eliten im Sozialismus: Beiträge zur Sozialgeschichte der DDR* (Cologne: Böhlau).

HUELSHOFF, M. G., MARKOVITS, A., and REICH, S. (eds.) (1993), *From Bundesrepublik to Deutschland: German Politics after Unification* (Ann Arbor: University of Michigan Press).

IMMERGUT, E. (1992), *Health Politics: Interests and Institutions in Western Europe* (Cambridge, Mass.: Cambridge University Press).

ISENSEE, J., and KIRCHHOF, P (eds.) (1987–2000), *Handbuch des Staatsrechts der Bundesrepublik Deutschland*, 10 vols. (Heidelberg: Müller).

ISMAYR, W. (2000), *Der Deutsche Bundestag im politischen System der Bundesrepublik Deutschland* (Opladen: Leske & Budrich).

JACHTENFUCHS, M., and KOHLER-KOCH, B. (eds.) (1996), *Europäische Integration* (Opladen: Leske & Budrich).

JÄGER, W. (1988), 'Von der Kanzlerdemokratie zur Koordinationsdemokratie', *Zeitschrift für Politik*, 35/2: 15–32.

——(1998), *Die Überwindung der Teilung: Der innerdeutsche Prozeß der Vereinigung 1989/90* (Stuttgart: DVA).

——and LINK, W. (1987), *Republik im Wandel: 1974–1982. Die Ära Schmidt* (Stuttgart: Deutsche Verlags-Anstalt and F. A. Brockhaus).

JAGGERS, K., and GURR, T. R. (1995), 'Transitions to Democracy: Tracking the Third Wave with Polity III Indicators of Democracy and Autocracy', *Journal of Peace Research*, 32/4: 469–82.

JARAUSCH, K. H., and SIGRIST, H. (eds.) (1997), *Amerikanisierung und Sowjetisierung in Deutschland 1945–1970* (Frankfurt a. M., New York: Campus).

JEFFERY, C. (ed.) (1999a), *Recasting German Federalism: The Legacies of Unification* (London: Pinter).

——(1999b), 'From cooperative federalism to a "Sinatra doctrine" of the Länder', in Jeffery 1999a: 329–42.

JESSE, E. (1990), *Elections: The Federal Republic of Germany in Comparison* (London: Berg Publishers).

JONES, G. W. (ed.) (1991), *West European Prime Ministers*, West European Politics, 14/2 (London: Frank Cass).

KAACK, H. (1976), *Zur Geschichte und Programmatik der Freien*

Demokratischen Partei (Meisenheim am Glan: Verlag Anton Hain).

KAASE, M., EISEN, A., GABRIEL, O., NIEDERMAYER, O., and WOLLMANN, H. (1996), *Politisches System* (Opladen: Leske & Budrich).

——and SCHMID, G. (eds.) (1999), *Eine lernende Demokratie: 50 Jahre Bundesrepublik Deutschland* (Berlin: Edition Sigma).

KATZ, R. S., and MAIR, P. (eds.) (1992), *Party Organisations: A Data Handbook on Party Organisations in Western Democracies, 1960–90* (London: Sage).

KATZENSTEIN, P. J. (1987), *Policy and Politics in West Germany: The Growth of a Semisovereign State* (Philadelphia: Temple University Press).

KELLER, B. (1999), *Einführung in die Arbeitspolitik: Arbeitsbeziehungen und Arbeitsmarkt in sozialwissenschaftlicher Perspektive*, 6th edn. (Munich: Oldenbourg).

KEMAN, H. (ed.) (1997), *The Politics of Problem-Solving in Postwar Democracies* (Houndmills: Macmillan).

——(ed.) (2002), *Comparative Democratic Politics* (London: Sage Publications).

KERSBERGEN, K. van (1995), *Social Capitalism: A Study of Christian Democracy and the Welfare State* (London: Routledge).

KERSCHER, H. (2001), 'Das Gericht der Republik', *Süddeutsche Zeitung*, 28 Sept.

KERSHAW, I. (1998), *Hitler 1889–1936: Hybris* (London: Penguin Press).

——(2000), *Hitler 1936–1945: Nemesis* (London: Penguin Press).

KIELMANSEGG, P. Graf (1989), *Lange Schatten: Vom Umgang der Deutschen mit der nationalsozialistischen Vergangenheit* (Berlin: Siedler).

——(1996), Parlamentarisches System

und Direkte Demokratie', *Akademie-Journal* 2/1996, 2–5.

——(2000), *Nach der Katastrophe—die Deutschen und ihre Nation: Eine Geschichte des geteilten Deutschlands* (Berlin: Siedler).

——(2002), 'Mehrheiten sind nicht mehr garantiert', *Frankfurter Allgemeine Zeitung*, 23 Aug: 9.

KING, A. (1994), 'Chief Executives in Western Europe', in I. Budge and D. McKay (eds.), *Developing Democracy: Comparative Research in Honour of J. F. P. Blondel* (London: Sage), 9–24.

KIRCHHEIMER, O. (1965), 'Der Wandel des westeuropäischen Parteiensystems', *Politische Vierteljahresschrift*, 6/1: 20–41.

——(1966), 'Germany: The Vanishing Opposition', in R. A. Dahl (ed.), *Political Opposition in Western Democracies* (Princeton: Princeton University Press), 237–59.

KLEIN, H.-J. (2001), 'Vereine', in Schäfers and Zapf 2001: 705–15.

KLINGEMANN, H.-D. (1987), 'Election Programmes in West Germany: 1949–1980, Explorations in the Nature of Political Controversy', in I. Budge, D. Robertson, and D. Hearl (eds.), *Ideology, Strategy and Party Change: Spatial Analyses of Post-War Election Programmes in 19 Democracies* (Cambridge: Cambridge University Press), 294–323.

——and KAASE, M. (eds.) (2001), *Wahlen und Wähler: Analysen aus Anlass der Bundestagswahl 1998* (Wiesbaden: Westdeutscher Verlag).

——and VOLKENS, A. (2001), 'Struktur und Entwicklung von Wahlprogrammen in der Bundesrepublik Deutschland 1949–1998', in Gabriel, Niedermayer, and Stöss 2001: 507–27.

KOGON, E. (1978 [1945]), *Der SS-Staat: Das System der deutschen Konzentrationslager* (Munich: Heyne).

KOLINSKY, E. (2001), 'Party Governance, Political Culture and the Transformation of East Germany since 1990', in Padgett and Pogunkte 2001: 169–83.

KOMMERS, D. P. (1975), *Judicial Politics in West Germany* (Beverly Hills, Calif.: Sage).

——(1997a), 'The Government of Germany', in M. Curtis and G. Ammendola (eds.), *West European Government and Politics* (New York: Longman), 153–221.

——(1997b), *The Constitutional Jurisprudence of the Federal Republic of Germany*, 2nd edn. (Durham, NC: Duke University Press).

KORTE, K.-R. (1994), *Die Chance genutzt? Die Politik zur Einheit Deutschlands* (Frankfurt a. M.: Campus Verlag).

——(2000), *Wahlen in der Bundesrepublik Deutschland*, 3rd edn. (Bonn: Bundeszentrale für politische Bildung), 74–8.

KRAUSE-BURGER, S. (ed.) (1999), *Joschka Fischer: Der Marsch durch die Illusionen* (Stuttgart: Deutsche Verlagsanstalt).

KROUWEL, A. (1999), *The Catch-All Party in Western Europe 1945–1990: A Study in Arrested Development* (Academisch Proefschrift, Vrije Universiteit Amsterdam).

LANDFRIED, C. (1984), *Bundesverfassungsgericht und Gesetzgeber* (Baden-Baden: Nomos).

——(1994), 'The Judicialization of Politics in Germany', *International Political Science Review*, 15/2: 113–24.

——(ed.) (1988), *Constitutional Review and Legislation: An International Comparison* (Baden-Baden: Nomos).

LARRES, K. (2000), *Germany since Unification: The Development of the Berlin Republic* (Basingstoke: Palgrave).

LAVER, M., and HUNT, W. B. (1992), *Policy and Party Competition* (New York: Routledge).

——and SCHOFIELD, N. (1990), *Multiparty Government: The Politics of Coalition in Europe* (Oxford: Oxford University Press).

LEES, C. (2000), *The Red-Green Coalition in Germany: Politics, Personality and Power* (Manchester: Manchester University Press).

LEHMBRUCH, G. (1984), 'Concertation and the Structure of Corporatist Networks', in J. H. Goldthorpe (ed.), *Order and Conflict in Contemporary Capitalism. Studies in the Political Economy of Western European Nations* (Oxford: Oxford University Press), 60–80.

——(1987), 'Administrative Interessenvermittlung', in A. Windhoff-Héritier (ed.), *Verwaltung und ihre Umwelt* (Opladen: Westdeutscher Verlag), 14–45.

——(1989), 'Marktreformstrategien bei alternierender Parteiregierung: Eine vergleichende institutionelle Analyse—Theodor Eschenburg zum 85.

——(1993), Geburtstag gewidmet', in T. Ellwein et al. (eds.), *Jahrbuch zur Staats- und Verwaltungswissenschaft*, vol. iii (Baden-Baden: Nomos), 15–45.

——(1990), 'Die improvisierte Vereinigung: Die Dritte Deutsche Republik', *Leviathan*, 18/3: 462–86.

——(1999), 'The Intermediation of Interests in Agricultural Policy: Organized Interests and Policy Networks', in K. Frohberg and P. Weingarten (eds.), *The Significance of Politics and Institutions for the Design and Formation of Agricultural Policies*

(Kiel: Wissenschaftsverlag Vauk), 92–104.

—— (2000a), *Parteienwettbewerb im Bundesstaat: Regelsysteme und Spannungslagen im politischen System der Bundesrepublik Deutschland*, 3rd edn. (Wiesbaden: Westdeutscher Verlag).

—— (2000b), 'German Federalism and the Challenge of Unification', in J. J. Hesse and V. Wright (eds.), *Federalizing Europe? The Costs, Benefits, and Preconditions of Federal Political Systems* (Oxford: Oxford University Press), 169–203.

—— (2002), 'Der unitarische Bundesstaat in Deutschland: Pfadabhängigkeit und Wandel', in Benz and Lehmbruch 2002: 53–110.

—— and SCHMITTER, P. C. (eds.) (1982), *Patterns of Corporatist Policy Making* (London: Sage Publications).

LEIBFRIED, S., and PIERSON, P. (2000), 'Social Policy: Left to Courts and Markets?' in Wallace and Wallace 2000: 167–292.

LEIBHOLZ, G. (1951), 'Der Parteienstaat des Bonner Grundgesetzes', *Recht, Staat, Wirtschaft*, 3: 99–125.

—— (1966), *Das Wesen der Repräsentation und der Gestaltwandel der Demokratie im 20. Jahrhundert*, 3rd edn. (Berlin: DeGruyter).

LEPSIUS, M. R. (1990a), 'Die Prägung der politischen Kultur der Bundesrepublik durch institutionelle Ordnungen', in M. R. Lepsius (ed.), *Interessen, Ideen und Institutionen* (Opladen: Westdeutscher Verlag), 63–84.

—— (1990b, [1979]), 'Soziale Ungleichheit und Klassenstrukturen in der Bundesrepublik Deutschland', in M. R. Lepsius (ed.), *Interessen, Ideen und Institutionen* (Opladen: Westdeutscher Verlag), 117–52.

—— (1993), *Demokratie in Deutschland: Soziologisch-historische Konstellationsanalysen* (Göttingen: Vandenhoek & Ruprecht).

LIJPHART, A. (1999), *Patterns of Democracy: Government Forms and Performance in Thirty-Six Countries* (New Haven: Yale University Press).

LITCHFIELD, E. H. (ed.) (1953), *Governing Postwar Germany* (Ithaca, NY: Cornell University Press).

LOEWENBERG, G. (1967), *Parliament in the German Political System* (Ithaca, NY: Cornell University Press).

LOEWENSTEIN, K. (1959), *Verfassungslehre* (Tübingen: Mohr (Paul Siebeck)).

LÖSCHE, P., and WALTER, F. (1992), *Die SPD: Klassenpartei—Volkspartei— Quotenpartei* (Darmstadt: Wissenschaftliche Buchgesellschaft).

—— (1996), *Die FDP: Richtungsstreit und Zukunftszweifel* (Darmstadt: Wissenschaftliche Buchgesellschaft).

LÖWENTHAL, R., and SCHWARZ, H.-P. (eds.) (1974), *Die zweite Republik: 25 Jahre Bundesrepublik Deutschland— Eine Bilanz* (Stuttgart: Deutsche Verlags-Anstalt and F. A. Brockhaus).

LUDZ, P. C. (1970), *Parteielite im Wandel: Funktionsaufbau, Sozialstruktur und Ideologie der SED-Führung*, 3rd edn. (Cologne: Westdeutscher Verlag).

MADDISON, A. (2001), *The World Economy: A Millenial Perspective* (Paris: OECD).

MAIER, H. (1999), 'Die Herrschaft des Rechts über die Politik', *Frankfurter Allgemeine Zeitung*, 7 May.

MAIR, P. (ed.) (2001), 'The Green Challenge and Political Competition: How Typical is the German Experience?', *German Politics*, 10/2: 99–116.

—— and VAN BIEZEN (2001), 'Party Membership in Twenty European

Democracies, 1980–2000', *Party Politics*, 7/4, 5–22.

MANN, S. (1994), *Macht und Ohnmacht der Verbände: Das Beispiel des Bundesverbandes der Deutschen Industrie e.V. (BDI) aus empirisch-analytischer Sicht* (Baden-Baden: Nomos).

MANOW, P. (1996), 'Informalisierung und Parteipolitisierung—Zum Wandel exekutiver Entscheidungsprozesse in der Bundesrepublik', *Zeitschrift für Parlamentsfragen*, 27/1: 96–107.

MAYER, C. (1997), *Dissolution: The Crisis of Communism and the End of East Germany* (Princeton: Princeton University Press).

MAYNTZ, R., and DERLIEN, H. U. (1989), 'Party Patronage and Politicization of the West German Administrative Elite 1970–1987—Toward Hybridization?', *Governance* 2/4: 384–404.

MERKEL, W. (1993), *Ende der Sozialdemokratie?* (Frankfurt a. M.: Campus).

MERKL, P. H. (ed.) (1999), *The Federal Republic of Germany at Fifty: The End of a Century of Turmoil* (Houndmills: Macmillan).

MEZEY, M. L. (1979), *Comparative Legislatures* (Durham, NC: Duke University Press).

MICHALOWSKI, S., and WOODS, L. (1999), *German Constitutional Law: The Protection of Civil Liberties* (Aldershot: Ashgate Dartmouth).

MIEGEL, M. (2002), *Die deformierte Gesellschaft: Wie die Deutschen ihre Wirklichkeit verdrängen* (Munich: Propyläen).

MINTZEL, A. (1977), *Geschichte der CSU* (Opladen: Westdeutscher Verlag).

'Model Vision: A Survey of Germany' (1994), *The Economist*, 21 May: 29–31.

MÜLLER-ROMMEL, F. (1988), 'The Centre of Government in West Germany: Changing Patterns under 14 Legislatures (1949–1987)', *European Journal of Political Research*, 16: 171–90.

——(1993), *Grüne Parteien in Westeuropa: Entwicklungsphasen und Erfolgsbedingungen* (Opladen: Westdeutscher Verlag).

——and POGUNTKE, THOMAS (eds.) (2002), *Green Parties in National Government* (London: Frank Cass).

NEIDHART, L. (1970), *Plebiszit und pluralitäre Demokratie: Eine Analyse der Funktion des schweizerischen Gesetzesreferendums* (Bern: Francke).

NEUMANN, F. (1950), 'German Democracy 1950', *International Conciliation* (New York: Carnegie Endowment for International Peace), 251–96.

——(1977 [1944]), *Behemoth: Struktur und Praxis des Nationalsozialismus 1933–1944* (Frankfurt a. M.: EVA).

NICLAUSS, K. (1988), *Kanzlerdemokratie* (Stuttgart: Kohlhammer).

——(2000), 'The Federal Government: Variations and Chancellor Dominance', in Helms: 2000a: 65–83.

NIETHAMMER, L. (1973), 'Zum Verhältnis von Reform und Rekonstruktion in der US-Zone am Beispiel der Neuordnung des öffentlichen Dienstes', *Vierteljahrshefte für Zeitgeschichte*, 21/2: 177–88.

NOHLEN, D. (2000), *Wahlrecht und Parteiensystem*, 3rd edn. (Opladen: Westdeutscher Verlag).

NORTON, P. (ed.) (1990), *Parliaments in Western Europe, West European Politics*, 13/3 (London: Frank Cass).

OBERREUTER, H. (2000), 'Bundestag', in Andersen and Woyke 2000: 87–99.

OECD (1990–2001), *Economic Outlook* (Paris: OECD).

—— (1997), *Employment Outlook 1997* (Paris: OECD).

—— (2001), *Historical Statistics 1960–1999* (Paris: OECD).

OKUN, A. M. (1975), *Equality and Efficiency: The Big Tradeoff* (Washington, DC: Brookings Institution).

OLSON, MANCUR (1965), *The Logic of Collective Action: Public Goods and the Theory of Groups* (Cambridge, Mass.: Harvard University Press).

PADGETT, S. (1999), 'The Boundaries of Stability: The Party System before and after the 1998 Bundestagswahl', in Padgett and Saalfeld 1999: 88–107.

—— (2001), 'The German *Volkspartei* and the Career of the Catch-All-Concept', *German Politics*, 10/2: 51–72.

—— and Poguntke, Thomas (eds.) (2001), *Continuity and Change in German Politics: Beyond the Politics of Centrality? Festschrift for Gordon Smith* (London: Frank Cass).

—— and SAALFELD, THOMAS (eds.) (1999), *Bundestagswahl '98: End of an Era? German Politics*, 8/2 (London: Frank Cass).

PAPIER, H.-J. (2000), 'Teilhabe an der Staatsleitung: Verfassungsgerichtsbarkeit und Politik', *Frankfurter Allgemeine Zeitung*, 23 May.

PATERSON, W. E. (1985), 'The Christian Union Parties', in H. G. P. Wallach and G. K. Rohrmoser (eds.), *West German Politics in the Mid-Eighties* (New York: Praeger), 60–80.

—— and SOUTHERN, DAVID (1991), *Governing Germany* (Oxford: Basil Blackwell).

PEMPEL, T. J. (ed.) (1990), *Uncommon Democracies: The One-Party Dominant Regimes*, (Ithaca, NY: Cornell University Press).

PIERSON, P. (ed.) (2001), *The New Politics of the Welfare State* (Oxford: Oxford University Press).

POGUNTKE, T. (2001), 'The German Party-System: Eternal Crisis?', *German Politics*, 10/2: 37–50.

POWELL, G. B., Jr. (2000), *Elections as Instruments of Democracy: Majoritarian and Proportional Visions* (New Haven: Yale University Press).

PRIDHAM, G. (1977), *Christian Democracy in Western Germany* (London: Croom Helm).

PULZER, P. (1995), *German Politics 1945–1995* (Oxford: Oxford University Press).

—— (1999), 'Luck and Good Management: Helmut Kohl as Parliamentary and Electoral Strategist', in Padgett and Saalfeld 1999: 126–140.

RASCHKA, J. (2000), *Justizpolitik im SED-Staat: Anpassung und Wandel des Strafrechts während der Amtszeit Honeckers* (Cologne: Böhlau).

RASCHKE, J. (2000), *Die Zukunft der Grünen: 'So kann man nicht regieren'* (Frankfurt a. M.: Campus).

REUTTER, W. (2001*a*), 'Einleitung', in Reutter and Rütters 2001: 9–30.

—— (2001*b*), 'Deutschland', in Reutter and Rütters 2001: 75–102.

—— and RÜTTERS, P. (eds.) (2001), *Verbände und Verbandssysteme in Westeuropa* (Opladen: Leske & Budrich).

RITTBERGER, V. (ed.) (2001), *German Foreign Policy since Unification: Theories and Case Studies* (Manchester: Manchester University Press).

RITTER, G. A. (1998), *Über Deutschland* (Munich: C. H. BECK).

ROBERTS, G. K. (1997), *Party Politics in the New Germany* (London: Pinter).

ROLLER, E. (1999), 'Shrinking the Welfare State: Citizen Attitudes towards Cuts in Social Spending in Germany in the 1990s', *German Politics*, 8/1: 21–39.

—— (2001), *Die Leistungsfähigkeit von Demokratien: Eine Analyse des Einflusses politischer Institutionen auf die Effektivität von Politiken und Politikmustern in westlichen Demokratien 1974–1995*, Freie Universität Berlin: Habilitationsschrift.

ROSECRANCE, R. (1986), *The Rise of the Trading State* (New York: Basic Books).

ROTH, D. (1998), *Empirische Wahlforschung* (Opladen: Leske & Budrich).

RUDZIO, W. (2000), *Das politische System der Bundesrepublik Deutschland*, 5th edn. (Opladen: Leske & Budrich).

SAALFELD, T. (1990), 'The West German *Bundestag* after 40 Years: The Role of Parliament in a "Party Democracy"', *West European Politics*, 13/3: 86–9.

—— (1995), *Parteisoldaten und Rebellen: Eine Untersuchung zur Geschlossenheit der Fraktionen im Deutschen Bundestag (1949–1990)* (Opladen: Leske & Budrich).

—— (1998), 'Coalition Politics and Management in the Kohl Era', *German Politics*, 8/2: 141–73.

Sachverständigenrat zur Begutachtung der Gesamtwirtschaftlichen Entwicklung (2001a), *Neuregelung des Länderfinanzausgleichs in Deutschland: Konzeptionelle Überlegungen und finanzielle Auswirkungen*, Wiesbaden, 20 June 2001.

—— (2001b), *Jahresgutachten 2000/01 des Sachverständigenrates zur Begutachtung der gesamtwirtschaftlichen Entwicklung* (Deutscher Bundestag Drucksache 14/4792).

—— (2002), *Jahresgutachten 2001/02 des Sachverständigenrates zur Begutachtung der gesamtwirtschaftlichen Entwicklung* (Deutscher Bundestag Drucksache 14/7569).

SAMPLES, G. (1998), *Bürgerpartizipation in den neuen Länderverfassungen: Eine verfassungshistorische und verfassungsrechtliche Analyse* (Berlin: Spitz).

SARTORI, G. (1976), *Parties and Party Systems* (Cambridge: Cambridge University Press).

SCARROW, S. E. (1997), 'Party Competition and Institutional Change: The Expansion of Direct Democracy in Germany', *Party Politics*, 3/4: 451–72.

SCHÄFERS, B., and ZAPF, W. (eds.) (2001), *Handwörterbuch zur Gesellschaft Deutschlands*, 2nd edn. (Opladen: Leske & Budrich).

SCHARPF, F. W. (1973), *Planung als politischer Prozeß* (Frankfurt a. M.: Suhrkamp).

—— (1988), *Crisis and Choice in European Social Democracy* (Ithaca, NY: Cornell University Press).

—— (1994), *Optionen des Föderalismus in Deutschland* (Frankfurt a. M.: Campus).

—— (1999), *Governing in Europe: Effective and Democratic?* (Oxford: Oxford University Press).

—— (2002), 'Die gefesselte Republik', *Die Zeit*, 35; 22 Aug: 9.

—— REISSERT, B., and SCHNABEL, F. (1976), *Politikverflechtung: Theorie und Empirie des kooperativen Föderalismus in der Bundesrepublik* (Kronberg/Ts.: Scriptor).

—— and SCHMIDT, V. (eds.) (2000), *Welfare and Work in the Open Economy*, 2 vols. (Oxford: Oxford University Press).

SCHINDLER, P. (1999), *Datenhandbuch zur Geschichte des Deutschen Bundestages 1949 bis 1999*, 3 vols. (Baden-Baden: Nomos).

SCHMID, J. (1990), *Die CDU* (Opladen: Leske & Budrich).

—— (1996), *Wohlfahrtsverbände in*

modernen Wohlfahrtsstaaten: Soziale Dienste in historisch-vergleichender Perspektive (Opladen: Leske & Budrich).

SCHMIDT, M. G. (1978), 'The "Politics of Domestic Reform" in the Federal Republic of Germany', *Politics & Society*, 8/2: 165–200.

—— (1980), *CDU und SPD an der Regierung: Ein Vergleich ihrer Politik in den Ländern* (Frankfurt a. M.: Campus).

—— (1982a), *Wohlfahrtsstaatliche Politik unter bürgerlichen und sozialdemokratischen Regierungen: Ein internationaler Vergleich* (Frankfurt a. M.: Campus).

—— (1982b), 'The Role of the Parties in Shaping Macroeconomic Policy', in F. G. Castles (ed.), *The Impact of Political Parties: Politics and Policies in Democratic Capitalist States* (London: Sage Publications), 97–176.

—— (1982c), 'Does Corporatism Matter? Economic Crisis, Politics and Rates of Unemployment in Capitalist Democracies in the 1970s', in Lehmbruch and Schmitter 1982: 237–58.

—— (1985), 'Allerweltsparteien in Westeuropa? Ein Beitrag zu Kirchheimers These vom Wandel des westeuropäischen Parteiensystems', *Leviathan*, 13/3: 376–97.

—— (1987), 'West Germany: The Policy of the Middle Way', *Journal of Public Policy*, 7/2: 135–77.

—— (1989), 'Learning from Catastrophes: West Germany's Public Policy', in Castles 1989: 56–99.

—— (1992a), *Regieren in der Bundesrepublik Deutschland* (Opladen: Leske & Budrich).

—— (ed.) (1992b), *Die westlichen Länder* (Munich: C. H. Beck).

—— (1993), 'Gendered Labour Force Participation', in Castles 1993: 179–238.

—— (1995), 'The Parties-Do-Matter-Hypothesis and the Case of the Federal Republic of Germany', *German Politics*, 4/3: 1–21.

—— (1996), 'When Parties Matter: A Review of the Possibilities and Limits of Partisan Influence on Public Policy', *European Journal of Political Research* 30/2: 155–83.

—— (1998), *Sozialpolitik in Deutschland: Historische Entwicklung und internationaler Vergleich*, 2nd edn. (Opladen: Leske & Budrich).

—— (2000), *Demokratietheorien*, 3rd edn. (Opladen: Leske & Budrich).

—— (2001a), 'Still on the Middle Way? Germany's Political Economy at the Beginning of the Twenty-First Century', *German Politics*, 10/3: 1–12.

—— (2001b), 'Grundlagen der Sozialpolitik in der Deutschen Demokratischen Republik', in Bundesministerium für Arbeit und Sozialordnung and Bundesarchiv (eds.), *Grundlagen der Sozialpolitik: Geschichte der Sozialpolitik in Deutschland seit 1945*, vol. i (Baden-Baden: Nomos Verlag), 689–798.

—— (2001c), 'Sozialpolitik in der Ära Kohl: Die Jahre von 1982–1989/90: Finanzielle Konsolidierung und institutionelle Reform' (Bremen, Heidelberg: unpublished book manuscript, to appear in Bundesministerium für Arbeit und Sozialordnung and Bundesarchiv (eds.), *Geschichte der Sozialpolitik in Deutschland seit 1945*, vol. vii, Baden-Baden: Nomos Verlag).

—— (2001d), 'Thesen zur Reform des Föderalismus der Bundesrepublik Deutschland', *Politische Vierteljahresschrift*, 42/3: 474–91.

—— (2002a), 'Warum Mittelmaß? Deutschlands Bildungsausgaben im internationalen Vergleich', *Politische Vierteljahresschrift*, 43/1: 3–19.

SCHMIDT, M. G. (2002*b*), 'Germany: The Grand Coalition State', in J. M. Colomer (ed.), *Political Institutions in Europe*, 2nd edn. (London: Routledge), 57–93.

——(2002*c*), 'The Impact of Political Parties, Constitutional Structures and Veto Players on Public Policy', in Keman 2002: 166–84.

——(2002*d*), 'The Consociational State: Hypothesis Regarding the Political Structure and the Potential for Democratization of the European Union,' in Steiner and Ertmann 2002: 213–27.

SCHMITT-BECK, R. (2000), *Politische Kommunikation und Wählerverhalten* (Wiesbaden: Westdeutscher Verlag).

——and WEICK, S. (2001), 'Die dauerhafte Parteiidentifikation—nur noch ein Mythos? Eine Längsschnittanalyse zur Identifikation mit politischen Parteien in West- und Ostdeutschland', *ISI (Informationsdienst Soziale Indikatoren)* (Mannheim: Zentrum für Umfragen, Methoden und Analysen), 26: 1–5.

SCHMITTER, P. C. (1996), 'Imagining the Future of the Euro-Polity with the Help of New Concepts', in G. Marks (ed.), *Governance in the European Union* (London: Sage), 121–50.

——and LEHMBRUCH, G. (eds.) (1979), *Trends toward Corporatist Intermediation* (Beverly Hills, Calif.: Sage Publications).

SCHNEIDER, H. (2001), *Ministerpräsidenten: Profil eines politischen Amtes im deutschen Föderalismus* (Opladen: Leske & Budrich).

SCHOENBAUM, D., and POND, E. (1996), *The German Question and other German Questions* (London: Macmillan).

SCHROEDER, K. (1998), *Der SED-Staat: Partei, Staat und Gesellschaft; 1949–1990* (Munich: Hanser).

SCHROEDER, M. (1987), 'Bildung, Bestand und parlamentarische Verantwortung der Bundesregierung', in Isensee and Kirchhof 1987: ii. 603–27.

SCHWARZ, H.-P. (1981), *Die Ära Adenauer: Gründerjahre der Republik. 1949 bis 1957* (Stuttgart: Deutsche Verlags-Anstalt and F. A. Brockhaus).

——(1983), *Die Ära Adenauer: Epochenwechsel. 1957 bis 1963* (Stuttgart: Deutsche Verlags-Anstalt and F. A. Brockhaus).

——(1986), *Adenauer: Der Aufstieg. 1876–1952* (Stuttgart: Deutsche Verlags-Anstalt).

——(1993), *Adenauer: Der Staatsmann* (Stuttgart: Deutsche Verlags-Anstalt).

——(2001), 'Der demokratische Verfassungsstaat im Deutschland des 20. Jahrhunderts: Gründe und Niedergang, Bewährung und Herausforderung', in K. Dicke (ed.), *Der demokratische Verfassungsstaat in Deutschland: 80 Jahre Weimarer Reichsverfassung, 50 Jahre Grundgesetz, 10 Jahre Fall der Mauer* (Baden Baden: Nomos): 11–26.

SEBALDT, M. (1997), *Organisierter Pluralismus: Kräftefeld, Selbstverständnis und Politische Arbeit deutscher Interessengruppen* (Opladen: Westdeutscher Verlag).

——(2000), 'Interest Groups: Continuity and Change of German Lobbyism Since 1974', in Helms 2000*a*: 188–203.

SIAROFF, A. (1999), 'Corporatism in 24 Industrial Democracies: Meaning and Measurement', *European Journal of Political Research*, 36/2: 175–205.

——(2000), 'Women's Representation in Legislatures and Cabinets in Industrial Democracies', *International Political Science Review*, 21/2: 197–215.

Siegel, Nico A. (2002), *Baustelle Sozialpolitik: Konsolidierung und Rückbau im internationalen Vergleich* (Frankfurt a. M.: Campus).

Sinn, G., and Sinn, H.-W. (1993), *Jumpstart: The Economic Unification of Germany* (Cambridge Mass.: MIT Press).

Smith, G. (1976), 'The Politics of Centrality in West Germany', *Government and Opposition*, 11/4: 387–407.

—— (1986), *Democracy in Western Germany: Parties & Politics in the Federal Republic*, 3rd edn. (Aldershot: Gower).

—— (1991), 'The Resources of a German Chancellor', in Jones 1991: 48–61.

—— Paterson, W. E., Merkl, P. H., and Padgett, S. (eds.) (1992), *Developments in German Politics* (Houndmills: Macmillan).

—— —— and Padgett S. (eds.) (1996), *Developments in German Politics 2* (Houndmills: Macmillan).

Smith-Owen, E. (1994), *The German Economy* (London: Routledge).

Soe, C. (1985), 'The Free Democratic Party', in H. G. P. Wallach and G. K. Rohrmoser (eds.), *West German Politics in the Mid-Eighties* (New York: Praeger), 112–86.

Sontheimer, K., and Bleek, W. (1999), *Grundzüge des politischen Systems der Bundesrepublik Deutschland* (Munich: Piper).

Soskice, D. (1999), 'Divergent Production Regimes: Coordinated and Uncoordinated Market Economies in the 1980s and 1990s', in H. Kitschelt, P. Lange, G. Marks, and J. D. Stephens (eds.), *Continuity and Change in Contemporary Capitalism* (Cambridge: Cambridge University Press), 101–34.

Staack, M. (2000), *Handelsstaat Deutschland: Deutsche Außenpolitik in einem neuen internationalen System* (Paderborn: Schöningh).

Staatsbürger Taschenbuch (2000), *Alles Wissenswerte über Europa, Staat, Verwaltung, Recht und Wirtschaft*, founded by O. Model, ed. by C. Creifelds and G. Lichtenberger, 30th edn. (Munich: C. H. Beck).

Statistisches Bundesamt (ed.) (2001), *Statistisches Jahrbuch 2001 für die Bundesrepublik Deutschland* (Stuttgart: Metzler-Poeschel).

—— (ed.) in cooperation with Wissenschaftszentrum Berlin and Zentrum für Umfragen, Methoden und Analysen, Mannheim (2002), *Datenreport 2002: Zahlen und Fakten über die Bundesrepublik Deutschland* (Bonn: Bundeszentrale für politische Bildung) (cited as Statistisches Bundesamt et al. 2002).

Steffani, W. (1983), 'Die Republik der Landesfürsten', in G. A. Ritter (ed.), *Regierung, Bürokratie und Parlament in Preußen und Deutschland von 1848 bis zur Gegenwart* (Düsseldorf: Droste Verlag), 181–213.

—— (1992), 'Parlamentarisches und präsidentielles Regierungssystem', in Schmidt 1992b: 288–95.

Steiner, J., and Ertmann, T. (eds.) (2002), *Consociationalism and Corporatism in Western Europe: Still the Politics of Accomodation?* (Acta Politica Special Issue) (Amsterdam: Uitgeverij Boom).

Stelzenmüller, C. (1994), *Direkte Demokratie in den Vereinigten Staaten von America* (Baden-Baden: Nomos).

Sternburg, W. von (ed.) (1998), *Die deutschen Kanzler: Von Bismarck zu Kohl*, 2nd edn. (Frankfurt a. M.: Fischer).

Stone Sweet, A. (2000), *Governing with*

Judges: Constitutional Politics in Europe (Oxford: Oxford University Press).

STÖSS, R. (ed.) (1984), *Parteienhandbuch*, 2 vols. (Opladen: Westdeutscher Verlag).

STREECK, W. (1981), *Gewerkschaftliche Organisationsprobleme in der sozialstaatlichen Demokratie* (Königstein, Ts.: Athenäum).

—— (1999), *Korporatismus in Deutschland: Zwischen Nationalstaat und Europäischer Union* (Frankfurt a. M.: Campus).

STURM, R. (1996), 'Continuity and Change in the Policy Making Process', in Smith et al. 1996: 117–32.

—— (2001), 'Divided Government in Germany: The Case of the Bundesrat', in R. Elgie (ed.), *Divided Government in Comparative Perspective* (Oxford: Oxford University Press), 167–81.

—— and PEHLE, H. (2001), *Das neue deutsche Regierungssystem: Die Europäisierung von Institutionen, Entscheidungsprozessen und Politikfeldern in der Bundesrepublik Deutschland* (Opladen: Leske & Budrich).

STÜWE, K. (1997), *Die Opposition im Bundestag und das Bundesverfassungsgericht: Das verfassungsgerichtliche Verfahren als Kontrollinstrument der parlamentarischen Minderheit* (Baden-Baden: Nomos).

—— (2001), 'Das Bundesesverfassungsgericht als verlängerter Arm der Opposition? Eine Bilanz seit 1951', *Aus Politik und Zeitgeschichte*, 37–8: 34–44.

SUNKIN, M. (1994), 'Judicialization of Politics in the United Kingdom', *International Political Science Review*, 15/2: 125–133.

SZABO, S. (ed.) (1983), *The Successor Generation* (London: Butterworth).

THAYSEN, U., DAVIDSON, R. H., and LIVINGSTONE, R. G. (eds.) (1989), *US-Kongreß und Deutscher Bundestag* (Opladen: Westdeutscher Verlag).

'The Berlin Republic: A Survey of Germany', *The Economist*, 6 Feb. 1999.

THOMAS, J. C. (1980), 'Policy Convergence among Political Parties and Societies in Developed Nations', *Western Political Quarterly*, 23/2: 233–46.

TOCQUEVILLE, A. de (1981 [1835/40]), *De la Démocratie en Amérique* (Paris: GF Flammarion).

TSEBELIS, G. (1995), 'Decision Making in Political Systems: Veto Players in Presidentialism, Parliamentarism, Multi-Cameralism and Multi-Partyism', *British Journal of Political Science*, 25/2: 289–325.

—— (2002), *Veto Players: How Political Institutions Work* (Princeton: Princeton University Press).

TURNER, L. (1998), *Fighting for Partnership: Labor and Politics in Unified Germany* (Ithaca NY: Cornell University Press).

VAN DETH, J. W. (ed.) (2000), *Private Groups and Public Life: Social Participation, Voluntary Associations and Political Involvement in Representative Democracies* (London: Routledge).

VAN SCHENDELEN, M. P. (ed.) (1993), *National and Private EC Lobbying* (Aldershot: Dartmouth).

VATTER, A. (2002), 'Politische Institutionen und ihre Leistungsfähigkeit: Der Fall des Bikameralismus im internationalen Vergleich', *Zeitschrift für Parlamentsfragen*, 33/1: 125–43.

VEEN, H.-J. (ed.) (1983), *Christlich-demokratische und konservative Parteien in Westeuropa 1: Bundesrepublik Deutschland, Österreich* (Paderborn: Schöningh).

VOLCANSEK, M. L. (ed.) (1992), *Judicial Politics and Policy Making in Western Europe West European Politics*, 15/3.

WACHENDORFER-SCHMIDT, U. (1999), 'Der Preis des Föderalismus in Deutschland', *Politische Vierteljahresschrift*, 40/1: 3–38.

—— (ed.) (2000), *Federalism and Political Performance* (London: Routledge).

—— (2002), *Politikverflechtung im vereinten Deutschland* (Wiesbaden: Westdeutscher Verlag).

WAGSCHAL, U. (2001a), 'Parteien, Wahlen und die Unabhängigkeit der Bundesbank', *Zeitschrift für Politikwissenschaft*, 11/2: 573–600.

—— (2001b), 'Der Parteienstaat der Bundesrepublik Deutschland: Parteipolitische Zusammensetzung seiner Schlüsselpositionen', *Zeitschrift für Parlamentsfragen*, 32/4: 861–86.

WAHL, R. (2001), 'Das Bundesverfassungsgericht in europäischem und internationalem Umfeld', *Aus Politik und Zeitgeschichte*, 37–8: 45–54.

WALLACE, H., and WALLACE, W. (eds.) (2000), *Policy Making in the European Union*, 4th edn. (Oxford: Oxford University Press).

WALTER, F. (2002), *Die SPD: Vom Proletariat zur Neuen Mitte* (Berlin: Alexander Fest Verlag).

WEBBER, D. (1992), 'Kohl's Wendepolitik after a Decade', *German Politics*, 1/2: 149–80.

—— (ed.) (2001a), 'New Europe, New Germany, Old Foreign Policy? German Foreign Policy since Unification', *German Politics*, 10/1, Special Issue (London: Frank Cass).

—— (ed.) (2001b), 'Introduction', in Webber 2001a: 1–18.

WEBER, J. (1976), *Interessengruppen im politischen System der Bundesrepublik Deutschland* (Munich: Landeszentrale für politische Bildung).

WEBER, M. (1976 [1922]), *Wirtschaft und Gesellschaft* (Tübingen: Mohr (Paul Siebeck)).

—— (1984 [1918]), 'Parlament und Regierung im neugeordneten Deutschland: Zur politischen Kritik des Beamtentums und Parteiwesens', in *Max Weber Gesamtausgabe Vol. I/15. Zur Politik im Weltkrieg: Schriften und Reden 1914–1918*, ed. by W. J. Mommsen in cooperation with G. Hübinger (Tübingen: Mohr (Paul Siebeck)), 421–596.

—— (1988a [1895]), 'Der Nationalstaat und die Volkswirtschaftspolitik', in *Max Weber—Gesammelte Politische Schriften*, ed. J. Winckelmann (Tübingen: Mohr (Paul Siebeck)), 1–25.

—— (1988b [1910]), 'Rede auf dem ersten Deutschen Soziologentage in Frankfurt', in *Max Weber—Gesammelte Aufsätze zur Soziologie und Sozialpolitik*, ed. M. Weber, 2nd edn. (Tübingen: Mohr (Paul Siebeck)), 431–49.

—— (1992 [1919]), 'Politik als Beruf', in *Max Weber Gesamtausgabe Vol. I/17. Max Weber—Wissenschaft als Beruf 1917/1919—Politik als Beruf*, ed. by W. J. Mommsen and W. Schluchter in cooperation with B. MORGENBROT (Tübingen: Mohr (Paul Siebeck)), 113–252.

WEFING, H. (2001a), 'Leuchtturm: Das Bundesverfassungsgericht wird fünfzig Jahre alt', *Frankfurter Allgemeine Zeitung*, 28 Sept.

—— (2001b), 'Jubeln Sie dem Grundgesetz doch einfach einmal zu!', *Frankfurter Allgemeine Zeitung*, 4 Oct.

WEHLER, H.-U. (1995), *Deutsche Gesellschaftsgeschichte, iii: Von der 'Deutschen Doppelrevolution' bis zum Beginn des Ersten Weltkrieges 1849–1914* (Munich: C. H. Beck).

WEILER, J. H. H. (1999), *The Constitution of Europe* (Cambridge: Cambridge University Press).

WEIZSÄCKER, R. VON (1992), *Richard von Weizsäcker im Gespräch mit Gunter Hofmann und Werner A. Perger* (Frankfurt a. M.: Eichborn).

——(2001), *Drei Mal Stunde Null? 1949–1969–1989: Deutschlands europäische Zukunft* (Berlin: Siedler).

WELZEL, C. (1997), *Demokratischer Elitenwandel: Die Erneuerung der ostdeutschen Elite aus demokratie-soziologischer Sicht* (Opladen: Leske & Budrich).

WEWER, G. (ed.) (1998), *Bilanz der Ära Kohl* (Opladen: Leske & Budrich).

WIESENTHAL, H. (2001), 'Interessenorganisation', in Schäfers and Zapf 2001: 335–49.

WILDENMANN, R. (1969), *Die Rolle des Bundesverfassungsgerichtes und der Deutschen Bundesbank in der politischen Willensbildung* (Stuttgart: Kohlhammer).

——(1982*a*), 'Unsere oberen Dreitausend: Woher kommen sie? Was prägt sie? Was wollen sie? Eine Eliten-Studie', *Die Zeit*, 5 Mar.

——(1982*b*), 'Die Elite wünscht den Wechsel: Unsere oberen Dreitausend (II): Mehr "rechts" als "links"', *Die Zeit*, 12 Mar.

——et al. (1982), *Führungsschicht in der Bundesrepublik Deutschland 1981* (Mannheim: University of Mannheim).

WINKLER, H. A. (1994), 'Das organisierte Vergessen: Die kalkulierte Unschärfe der PDS', *Frankfurter Allgemeine Zeitung*, 30 July.

——(2000), *Der lange Wege nach Westen*, 2 vols. (Munich: C. H. Beck).

WINTER, T. VON (1997), *Sozialpolitische Interessen: Konstituierung, politische Repräsentation und Beteiligung an Entscheidungsprozessen* (Baden-Baden: Nomos).

ZACHER, H. (2001), 'Grundlagen der Sozialpolitik in der Bundesrepublik Deutschland', in Bundesministerium für Arbeit und Sozialordnung und Bundesarchiv (eds.), *Grundlagen der Sozialpolitik: Geschichte der Sozialpolitik in Deutschland seit 1945*, vol. i (Baden-Baden: Nomos Verlag), 333–684.

ZAPF, W. (1965), *Wandlungen der deutschen Elite, 1919–1961* (Munich: Piper).

ZOHLNHÖFER, R. (2001), *Die Wirtschaftspolitik der Ära Kohl: Eine Analyse der Schlüsselentscheidungen in den Politikfeldern Finanzen, Arbeit und Entstaatlichung, 1982–1998* (Opladen: Leske & Budrich).

ZUCK, R. (1999), 'Der unkontrollierte Kontrolleur', *Frankfurter Allgemeine Zeitung*, 24 July.

INTERNET

www.bundestag.de/mdb14/mdbinfo/132/1322.
www.bundestag.de/mdb14/mdbinfo/132/1324.
www.bundestag.de/mdb14/mdbinfo/1322.
www.bundestag.de/mdb14/mdbinfo/1323.
www.bundestag.de/mdb15/bio.
www.bundesverfassungsgericht.de
Centre d'études et de documentation sur la démocratie directe (http://c2d.unige.ch/home-page-e.htm).

INDEX